John Koenig
G?S
Spring, 1979

The Way of the Word

THE WAY
OF THE WORD

*The Beginning and the
Establishing of Christian
Understanding*

JOHN C. MEAGHER

A Crossroad Book THE SEABURY PRESS · NEW YORK

Whatever you find most worthy in the pages that follow,
I ask you to think of as having been dedicated to these
teachers, colleagues, and friends, in gratitude not only
for what I learned from them in my journey toward this
book, but for the generosity by which they have memorably
graced for me, as for many others, the studies which they
so excellently profess:

> Charles Sheedy
> Roland Murphy
> André Feuillet
> Kurt Hruby
> Oscar Cullmann
> Edgar Bruns
> Gregory Baum
> Ed Sanders
> Ben Meyer

BT
60
.M4
c.2

The Seabury Press
815 Second Avenue
New York, N.Y. 10017

Copyright © 1975 by The Seabury Press, Inc.

LIBRARY OF CONGRESS CATALOGING IN PUBLICATION DATA

Meagher, John C
  The way of the word.

  "A Crossroad book."
  Includes index.
  1. Christianity—Essence, genius, nature. 2. Theology—Methodology.
I. Title.
BT60.M4   201'.1   75–4881
ISBN 0–8164–0270–1

Printed in the United States of America

Contents

Preface

*M*odern Christian theology has grown uneasy about its sense of its own foundations. Traditionally, it has normally been assumed that its validity depends upon its relationship to the historical beginnings of Christianity—to Jesus, to the apostles, to the creeds of the earliest believers. Yet modern scholarship has made it increasingly clear that it is impossible to achieve an exact and reliable critical reconstruction of those beginnings. Each attempt at such reconstruction must settle for being at best tentative and incomplete. Much must remain simply unclear and uncertain. On what critically responsible terrain can the historical dependency of Christian theology now be grounded?

Modern Christian history has grown uneasy about the character of its origins. The traditional assumption that the understanding of truth reflected in the early creeds represents the consistent teaching of the apostles and of Jesus himself has broken down under more careful critical examination. Where earlier Christian historians saw a reassuring uniformity, their modern counterparts tend to find in the beginning clear evidences of development, diversity, inconsistency. Not only are we unable to reconstruct the factual character of Christian beginnings: the indications are that even if we could, we would still be faced with troublesome variations in the ways in which earliest Christians interpreted them. How then can we hope to recover the content of an original orthodoxy if the very notion of an original orthodoxy is itself in question? And without an original orthodoxy, how is subsequent Christian theology to be validated?

History longs for an exact reconstruction; theology longs for an exact inventory of earliest beliefs. Both longings rest unsatisfied, and increasingly appear to be unsatisfiable. It is to that dilemma that this book is addressed.

The address is not directly to the dilemma itself. I shall not attempt to provide the exact reconstruction of which the historian despairs, nor the precise creed to which the theologian is apparently not historically entitled. The attempt is rather to pursue an issue that I believe to be

1

prior in the logic of history, and possibly more fundamental in the grounding of theology, and which I believe may mediate a way out of a dilemma that appears to me impossible to resolve on its own terms. My undertaking, in brief, is this: to find out from an examination of earliest Christian documentary evidence what we can learn concerning how earliest Christians thought they should go about making up their minds as to what belongs to Christian truth.

I have not even dreamed of approaching a definitive treatment of this problem. But I have tried to accomplish something soundly prelimi-nary. The informed reader will know—as I too know—that there are subtle qualifications that might legitimately be made to most of the observations and arguments that follow, even though these may stand as adequate summaries of their complex underpinnings. I am regret-fully aware that I have left many an interesting stone unturned, and even unremarked, in my effort to map with an appropriate degree of detail the over-all topography of the field. But the nature of the prob-lem is such that it appeared to me to be initially much more valuable to explore it broadly, in order to form a picture of the whole, than to aspire to the more rigorous and nuanced control that would be possible only by restricting the investigation to a much more limited scope, at the expense of achieving the very overview that alone can indicate the potential value of such an undertaking. For similar reasons, I have not attempted to show how I would situate my findings systematically within the present state of New Testament scholarship. Although it has been easy to find hundreds of books and articles that are germane to the question that guides this study, I find that little previous work has been done directly on any version of it. I have inevitably made exten-sive use of the available scholarly resources in the preparation and execution of this book; but since my essential dialogue is not with them but rather with the evidences that they have helped me understand more adequately, I have deliberately limited the footnote recording of my awarenesses, appreciations, and criticisms of secondary materials that may have some considerable bearing on, but are not indispensably explicit considerations in, the questions I pursue. Those questions are here pursued primarily through the most substantial bodies of early Christian documentary evidence: the Pauline, Lucan-synoptic, and Jo-hannine literature. Secondarily, I deal with the related literature of the Pauline and Johannine schools, and then with the other, mainly briefer, writings incorporated into the New Testament, touching also on some of the early non-canonical Christian texts.

The translations within are my own, unless otherwise credited. New Testament quotations are taken from the Nestle edition of the Greek text, and the translations of these passages attempt to be both close and idiomatic. I have tried to avoid tendentiousness, but anyone experienced in translation will realize that one must always settle for capturing some genuine nuances of the original at the expense of others. I have naturally attempted to bring out the ones that bear on the issues I treat: standard translations, which cannot afford such specialization of attention, are therefore less useful for the purposes of this study. My renderings of the texts aim at allowing a fresh and accurate glimpse of what may otherwise be hidden by familiarity or by the different priorities of other translators' purposes. They do not, and can not, aspire to disclose all that is meant in the Greek originals; but they do undertake to be faithful to meanings that are genuinely there.

I am glad to acknowledge my gratitude for the thoughtful criticism and encouragement given to earlier drafts of sections of this book by my colleagues J. Edgar Bruns and J. Terence Forestell—and above all, by E. P. Sanders and B. F. Meyer of McMaster University, who have worked with it from start to finish, and in doing so have in many instances helped me to bring both the accuracy and the adequacy of my findings closer to the standards of scholarship which they consistently exemplify. It is my good hope that their interventions have been successful enough to allow this exposition of my investigation to bring to its readers the ring of truth, and perhaps even the surprise of discovery, that I experienced in its execution.

Toronto
Epiphany, 1975

Introduction

*I*n the beginning, says the Book of Genesis, was a new-made heaven and earth, that must lie void and formless until the speaking of the word that could give them shape and order—a world whose face was drowned in darkness until the word was uttered that made light be. In the beginning, says the Fourth Gospel more succinctly, was the Word.

Goethe's Faust, pondering the opening verse of the Fourth Gospel, wondered whether it is quite accurate to see the Word as the ground of things. Might we not say rather that it was preceded by the Thought? or the Deed? or the Power? There are indeed times when the word has a certain priority, when the issuing of a command or the pronouncing of a name is itself the fundamental act by which chaos is tamed or shaped. But the word is often designed to be the adequate articulation of the thought it expresses, and may be revised or rejected if it is not quite what the thought had in mind. Or it is chosen as the adequate description of the deed that establishes or accomplishes, consolidating and defining that achievement by registering it in the understanding. Or it may be only the medium by which power is summoned and enacted. Usually, however, the lines of demarcation are not to be clearly drawn. Faust's various candidates for the beginning intermingle and blend.

Any of the ways in which life stirs may eventuate in a word that attempts to capture the meaning. Once it has emerged, that defining word can become a new beginning, even though it may be the end of a long process of self-discovery and self-articulation. The word itself, or the thought which it may imperfectly express, may be invested with an authority that establishes it as law—either the positive law of explicit definition, or the common law of deeply established and inviolable custom. The identity of persons and of societies is profoundly conditioned and regulated by the normative understandings that explicitly or implicitly structure what they take to be their proper consciousness. This complex of normative understandings constitutes the thought-law

4

by which the individual or the society governs itself as a self-regulating conscious reality.

Such thought-law may take the form either of positive law, the explicitly regulating word, or of the common law of authoritative habit and custom. The great virtue of positive law is its tidiness and clarity. It is this that induces artistic movements to develop their manifestoes alongside their characteristic styles, and contributes to the French national sense of the superiority of their legal organization over that of the sprawling common-law habits of the British Constitution. It is this that undoubtedly inspired (though one may wish to reserve the potential theological implications of the word) the Christian church to adopt a procedure for defining the laws of Christian thought so as to leave no uncertainty, and to that end imitated a procedure designed originally to effect a rigorous clarity in the proclamation of civil laws. The emergence of ecclesiastical dogma is a logical extension of the recognition that there are characteristic and customary Christian habits of thought, and that these matter. Dogma is not necessarily the inevitable extension, but it is the logical one according to one axis of development. Law is artificial custom—but custom itself tends to imitate that special artifice that makes law, and under certain conditions willingly transforms itself into law. In the conciliar movement, the most critically important customs of the Christian mind quite naturally (if not inevitably) became reformulated in accordance with the most absolute procedures of positive law.

Whatever one may think of this development theologically, it is clear that it has had unfortunate consequences for the study of the earliest Christian churches. Catholic scholarship, formed in the image and likeness of these later procedures, strained to find such a regulated belief reflected in the earliest records of the church's activities; Protestant scholarship, formed in the light of the Reformation's repudiation of Catholic thought-law, pressed through the tides of historical process to the firm shores of self-authenticating Faith. Conditions were not propitious for attempting to discover just how earliest Christians really went about the job of ordering their understanding properly within the new dispensation.[1]

It is probably not coincidental that the contemporary pursuit of the problem derives particularly from a study whose main thrust was precisely to undermine both the Catholic and the Protestant assumptions about normative Christianity: Walter Bauer's *Rechtgläubigkeit und Ketzerei im ältesten Christentum*, which appeared in 1934. That sort of undercutting was necessary if the discussion were to take place on a thoroughly responsible basis, and Bauer has accordingly been given the credit for being the initiator of a new era in the historical and theologi-

cal scholarship bearing on earliest Christianity, through his demonstration that what was eventually called "heresy" was not really a deviant
form of belief but only an originally legitimate alternative that was
ultimately unsuccessful in the historical-political competition by which
the Church consolidated and universalized its doctrinal understanding.
Bultmann's assessment of Bauer's achievement in this respect is typical
of modern scholarly opinion:

W. Bauer has shown that the doctrine which in the end won out in the ancient
Church as the "right" or "orthodox" doctrine stands at the end of a development or, rather, is the result of a conflict among various shades of doctrine, and
that heresy was not, as the ecclesiastical tradition holds, an apostasy, a degenera-
tion, but was already present at the beginning—or, rather, that by the triumph
of a certain teaching as the "right doctrine" divergent teachings were condemned as heresy.[2]

I say that Bauer has been given the credit, for virtually every contemporary scholar working on the problem of earliest Christian thought
acknowledges his foundational importance. But I do not say that he
deserves the credit. I believe, in fact, that he does not, and that this is
very easy to demonstrate.

I am not, in saying that, raising the question of the *quality* of Bauer's
achievement, although it is indeed my opinion that his book is far more
vulnerable to criticism than would seem to be implied by the unusual
reverence with which its recent republication[3] (and even more so, its
subsequent publication in English[4]) was surrounded.[5] I am simply
pointing to the nature of Bauer's real undertaking. The book is belied
by its title—not, as Goguel objected, that it is too vague and needs a
specifying subtitle,[6] or, as Bauer's new editor, Strecker, himself suggests, that its term *Rechtgläubigkeit* is unfortunately misleading[7]—but
that the title is simply inaccurate. Bauer does not deal with "oldest
Christianity." He studies second-century phenomena and retrojects his
conclusions. He himself, despite his title, is quite explicit about this: "the
New Testament," he writes in the final paragraph of his Introduction,
"seems to be both too unproductive and too much disputed to be able
to serve as a point of departure. . . . It is advisable, therefore, first of all
to interrogate other sources concerning the relationship of orthodoxy
and heresy, so that, with the insights that may be gained there, we may
try to determine the time and place of their origins."[8] But "try to
determine" turns out essentially to mean "guess at," and the curiously
glancing and desultory references to New Testament texts make it
quite impossible to justify calling this work a study of what obtained
im ältesten Christentum.

Why then did such a widespread misunderstanding of Bauer's accomplishment develop? My guess is that it was because Bauer's retrojected

conclusions coincided so conveniently with a powerful double movement associated with the work of Bultmann (and in part deriving from Bultmann, though its sweep of popularity obviously signals that it had at least as much to do with an over-all intellectual climate as with the convincing power of Bultmann's own remarkable scholarly production). The two complementary parts of this movement are the deconcretization of the foundations of Christian belief, achieved through a historical-critical methodology guided by a systematic skepticism of nearly Cartesian proportions; and an existentializing of Christian faith, achieved through a philosophical theology of a new kind. I suppose it no accident that this double movement was German in origin and in its most substantive accomplishments. I suspect that it is essentially the reactive offspring of a previous great wave of German scholarship which unsettled traditional assumptions about Holy Writ with a relentless and captivating swiftness that seemed to leave no middle ground between the intolerably domesticated Christianity of Harnack's *Das Wesen des Christentums* and the intolerably discredited Christianity left by the critical work of such as Schweitzer and Wrede. Caught in such a bind, the responsible agents of Christian scholarship might well be excused if they supposed that the only way to the survival of what still seemed somehow deeply important was to disqualify pre-kerygmatic historical reconstruction altogether and find a firmer refuge in the kerygma's capacity to awaken a felt existential truth that is invulnerable to the demythologizing insights that were dismantling what had been known as Christian truth. And thus comes the reception of Bauer, with an eager sigh of relief: if ultimate orthodoxy is really only an eventual *primus inter pares* whose primacy proves nothing theologically, then the new quasi-gnostic Christian existentialism is safe from the burden of critically vulnerable content.

To the extent that this sketchy reconstruction accurately maps the main outlines of a highly subtle and complex passage of intellectual history, there is a logic also to the present wave of reaction gathered around Bauer. The postulated condition is itself schizophrenic: on the one hand, its relativizing of orthodoxy insists intransigently on evidence of a decidedly historical kind; on the other, its kerygma cuts loose from all such limitations. It is, I opine, from this new implicit formulation of intolerable alternatives that the New Quest of the Historical Jesus was begotten, for it is really a New Quest of Theological Validation. And coordinate with this new quest comes another, its historical-critical complement: what was the character of earliest Christianity's own address to the problem of theological validation? Or in shorthand, what shall we say to Bauer? Helmut Koester, obviously with an eye on Bauer, poses the problem neatly:

In the beginning of the history of theology of earliest Christianity stands no "pure teaching," but the historical revelation in the word, deed, and fate of Jesus. This revelation is tied to the world-picture of a definite time and ambience. The belief of the community in the unique revelation of God in this historical form presented it with the task of explicating the content of the belief appropriately and intelligibly within the constantly changing assumptions of time and place, ambience and world-view—that is, simultaneously to construct a "teaching." The formation of this teaching is from the outset, in the absence of a prior endowment of a timeless pure teaching, exposed to a twofold danger of heresy: either the time-bound historical expression of the revelation might be absolutized, and thus lose the revelational quality of an evanescent form; or it might, in the consciousness of the timeless content of the revelation, surrender its linkage with the historical origin and thus perforce must be subjected to the new forces of alien religious powers. These heretical dangers befall Christology as well as ecclesiology and anthropology. From this fundamental problematic are produced the criteria for judging what, in the earliest Christianity, can be called "heresy."[9]

If this is a key problem for earliest Christianity, it is implicitly a still more radical problem for modern historical scholarship *and* for modern Christian theology. The former must contend with what now appears to have been a syncretism that had still more options and followed a yet less systematic developmental path than even Bultmann's critical assumptions made room for; and the latter must come to terms with the fact that there was indeed something there to begin with, and that its meaning is dependent not only on potentially translatable (if evanescent) categories but on facts, doings, real happenings that cannot be shrugged off merely on account of the insecurity of their critical reconstruction.

Thus the motivation and the opportunity for the New Quest. And thus also the linkage with the Bauer problem. Suddenly, the historical and theological questions merge. Something really happened, and the authenticity of its aftermath is conditioned by just what it really was. On the occasion of the German republication of Bauer's book, Hans Dieter Betz raised almost just the right question: "In the beginning there existed merely the 'heretical' Jew, Jesus of Nazareth. Which of the different interpretations of Jesus are to be called authentically Christian? And what are the criteria for making that decision? This seems to me the cardinal problem of New Testament studies today."[10]

The questions were already in the air. An answer had already been anticipated by Käsemann: 'My own questioning is aimed at finding out whether the earthly Jesus is to be taken as the criterion of the kerygma and, if so, to what extent. Whether the kerygma is historically verifiable is not important to me . . . We can now put our problem in a nutshell: does the New Testament kerygma count the historical Jesus among the criteria of its own validity?"[11] And almost immediately thereafter, Koester, with explicit reference to Käsemann and Bauer, posed his own formulation: "Accordingly, we are not confronted with the quest for a new image of Jesus to be used as a yardstick for true belief, but with the question, whether and in which way that which has happened historically, i.e., in the earthly Jesus of Nazareth, is present in each given case as the criterion—not necessarily as the content—of Christian proclamation and theology."[12] And yet once more, on the eve and occasion of the English edition of Bauer, G. Clarke Chapman Jr. raised the question of orthodoxy and provided his own answer: "it surely must be described as those streams of tradition which were relatively the most accurate and valid in their successive interpretations of the Christ event."[13]

Chapman's approach to the problem is obviously more critically naïve than Koester's and Käsemann's. All three relate directly to the issues posed by Betz, but Chapman only gives the ideal answer to Betz's first question and scamps his all-important second corollary question about criteria, which must be addressed if we are to move out of the realm of fantasy into sound procedure. The methodological wisdom of the German tradition knows better: both Käsemann and Koester demand a built-in criterion, and select the one which is most responsive to the history of the German conversation. If the Jesus of History is inaccessible to scholarly reconstruction, as the critical wing of the existentializing movement implies, then he must be approached some other way. The conviction that Christianity is radically conditioned by its historical ground permits no waffling on this point. The solution proposed by German scholarship reassesses the value of early witnesses, measuring them by how far they themselves seem to acknowledge the historical Jesus as their own norm.

This is a brilliant move. But its historical and theological value are both diminished by the fact that it begs the question, much as Luther's brilliant critical principles begged a similar question at the beginning of German New Testament scholarship. Criteriology is of the essence. But who is to determine the criteria? Not necessarily, I submit, either Luther or his successors. Nor their rivals. For if we are to go all the way with the logic of the inquiry, we may not presume *a priori* that any of us is in a position to impose *the* norm on earliest Christian understanding or on the modern theology that deliberately derives from it. We must let earliest Christianity speak for itself. Only then can the historical evaluative reconstruction have the proper measure of neutrality; only then can modern theology submit itself accurately to the discipline of its own conditioning origins.

Betz raised, I said, almost just the right questions. His failure, and the failure of others I have cited, is precisely his arbitrary delimitation of the cardinal problem. "Which of the different interpretations of Jesus are to be called authentically Christian?" Implicitly, the answer is Chapman's regrettably dreamy one: "the most accurate and valid." But it is the question itself that is at fault. The authentic interpretation of Jesus does not become the cardinal issue until it has justly been derived as the proper answer to a more fundamental question: How in fact did earliest Christianity interpret itself? I suggest that this, and no other, is the radical question in which the basic historical and theological issues converge. For it is no longer adequate to say, with Koester, that in the beginning stands the historical revelation in the word, deed, and fate of Jesus; or with Bultmann, that in the beginning was the kerygma; or, with Betz, that in the beginning there existed merely the "heretical" Jew, Jesus of Nazareth. We must allow earliest Christianity to speak for itself about where and how it perceived its beginning, without requiring it to answer to our sense of Christian history, and we must allow it to relate to its beginning in its own fashion, without requiring it to conform to later assumptions and others' criteria. The quest of theological validation becomes the quest not of Jesus but of earliest Christianity's sense of the ground of its own authenticity, the constitution governing its true understanding. It is not for us to prescribe what will do for an answer.

That principle is Bauer's real legacy to the students of earliest Christianity, even if his book hinted the problem only obliquely and at a significant degree of historical remove. If we are to take responsibility for it, we must go still further than Bauer did, and reject altogether his own assumption that "the New Testament seems to be both too unproductive and too much disputed to be able to serve as a point of departure." There is no other point of departure. Christianity as it was grasped *im ältesten Christentum* is now available to us only through the New Testament. Another relevant body of helpful evidence may be found in the so-called Apostolic Fathers, and there are supplementary insights to be gained from other still later literature, as Bauer himself has shown; but the basic problem of "Christian orthodoxy," the issue of how normative Christian understanding was constituted from the beginning, must be addressed primarily to the evidence of the New Testament.

The present study undertakes to pursue that problem. It is appropriate at the beginning, therefore, to acknowledge that it is in some respects an inquiry that is greatly handicapped from the start. That is, there is no chance of achieving a simple and universalizable conclusion. Common law does not have that sort of tidy rational consistency. I do not think it likely that there is *any* non-trivial generalization about earliest Christianity that can stand without qualification. It is not possible to make useful sense simultaneously about the whole spectrum of Christian affiliation that runs from St. Paul all the way to the seven sons of Sceva—and to draw a clear line of demarcation within that continuum is to act arbitrarily, as we are soberingly reminded in comparing the two quite different lines offered by Luke 11:23, where he who is not with Jesus is against him, and Luke 9:50, where he who is not against his followers is for them. Unqualified conclusions are out of reach. But it is enough to reach for central tendencies and characteristic patterns —and that is within the range of possibility.

I cannot deal with Luke's free-lance exorcist. But that is for two reasons, which are of different weight and instructive value. The obvious one is that we know far too little about him: and thus we must remember that there were many others about whom we know even less, who left us no traces whereby we might assess the whole—and one must remember that even if the surviving evidence can give a picture representative of the whole, that picture can only be a sketch, not a portrait. But the other reason is more enspiriting. Luke's exorcist is intrinsically marginal to this study, whatever his theology may have been. As a maverick, he may be said to be *for* the Christian movement, but he is not said, and perhaps should not be said, to be *with* it. Custom and law are *social* realities. The terms apply outside coherent societies only by imitative participation or by mere metaphorical extension. It is only within the group as such that norms of thought are fostered and formed and authoritatively applied; it is only within Christian society as such that the notion of Christian norms of thought can be fully meaningful, even though individuals may appropriate them for more solitary uses. Those who left no traces in the social fabric of self-understanding were thus perhaps not such as to give pause to either the historian or the theologian.

Admittedly, a group may comprise varying degrees of conformity to and concern about its own thought-norms. The evidence tends to get selected. Social relevance is a condition of its survival. When one interrogates the evidence to discover what it reveals or indicates about normative Christian understanding, therefore, one must remember that Luke's exorcist had no reason to try his hand at writing a gospel. If there were any who supposed that Christians might think anything they pleased, they are not likely to have invested much time in writing letters to churches in order to say so, nor are churches likely to have taken care to preserve such a record. In examining textual evidence, therefore, it is obviously important to stay alert not only for the author's convictions about thought-norms and about his sense of the common understanding he shares or should share with his addressees about such matters, but also his hints about those who are not within what he takes to be the social circle of consensus, and his sense of how this disparity ought to be resolved. This kind of attention is sufficient, I believe, to correct against the bias inevitably present in socially conditioned evidence. For socially generated documents are quite capable of absorbing adequate reflections of the pre-social or nonconformist dispositions of those who influence them: the social matrix can manifest its own secondariness, its incoherence, or even its own triviality, when that is the way in which it is composed or regarded by those who compose it.

Any society which, like earliest Christianity, is set apart within a larger society partly on the basis of beliefs, ideas, or behaviors that distinguish it from its surroundings is bound to be aware of its own peculiar manner of thinking as somehow characteristic of its life. The content of that thought becomes a way of identifying its own character. But when such a society becomes still more self-aware, it may begin to raise the question of *how* it thinks—that is, not what thoughts or understandings are in fact present within it, but by what means those thoughts or understandings entered their group mind, reached their present form, and may develop further. The participants will usually be ready to recognize that there are varying degrees of adequacy in the thought and understanding to be found within such a society, though they may differ about their importance and about just which are the more adequate. In earliest Christianity, were higher degrees of adequacy held to be of significantly greater value than lower degrees? and was there a minimum adequacy below which it was perilous to fall? The measure of adequacy is also a variable: did earliest Christians judge the adequacy of their thought by accuracy? by conviction? by comprehensiveness? by sophistication? And to what extent were they in agreement about how much it mattered, and in what way it mattered, to think adequately?

The present undertaking is concerned with these questions. But it is more immediately concerned with the matters that underlie them: the earliest Christian sense of the structure within which their thought was properly conditioned. If there are varying degrees of adequacy in Christian thought, how are the higher ones offered, indicated, achieved, authenticated, guaranteed? How does right understanding get revealed and discovered? And once revealed and discovered, how is right understanding to be recognized by the group for which it is normative, and accepted as the law that governs its thinking? How were they to tell what was normative Christian understanding and what was pioneering new discovery, or speculation of indifferent value, or illegitimate deviation from the Christian norm?

In short, the main question to be put to the surviving evidence is this: How did earliest Christians suppose their own authentic thought to be grounded, constituted, and regulated?

Early Christian churches were not theological institutes. If they attracted not many wise, not many powerful, they undoubtedly attracted still fewer intellectually prurient academicians. The members were not particularly busy about the advancement of religious science, and were probably for the most part content to suppose that they were somehow following the will of God more satisfactorily via the Christian way, and that they were to a certain extent privy to some of his previously hidden plans. The contract is effectual upon signing, whether one reads either the fine print or the bold; the medicine does not favor pharmacologists. But one need not suppose such a preoccupation even for it to be important to see how they presumed "right understanding" was to be arrived at. For, in the first place, the possibility of a right understanding is implicit in their act of Christian affiliation, even if they themselves were not particularly obsessed about possessing it; and in the second place, the development of early Christian self-understanding was ultimately less dependent upon what Christians at any given moment and place supposed God had told them than upon how they supposed he let men in on his will and knowledge. As implicit became explicit, as discovery and invention became custom and custom became law, the content of Christian understanding was less important in guiding its own trajectory than the sense of the constitution by which it was defined and governed. The main purpose of this study is therefore to discern not the norms of thought themselves, but the implicit theories of their genesis and development, and the ways in which they were understood to be made manifest.

That is where historical and theological issues properly join. The earliest Christian understanding of the modes of its own normatization substantially conditioned the development of its own authentic thought. Whatever we may prefer to have been the ground rules of such early Christian self-understanding, we are not justified as historians if we project our preferences on what may have been a significantly different sense of undertaking on their part. Nor are we theologically justified, if we have accepted the view that early Christian theology sets the pattern for theological validity in our time, and not vice versa. It is thus historically and theologically useful to discern the ways in which early Christian thinkers supposed, implicitly or explicitly, that authentic understanding was given to them and that its potential development, if such were permitted, might be critically refined. And if Christian theology accepts all that is implied in the traditional axiom of its historical conditioning, it must stand under the judgment of exactly the same issue: by what criteria is Christian thought to be interpreted? The earliest answers to this question are of the theological, as well as the historical, essence.

I am not speaking of particular content. It is inescapably true that in earliest evidence, as Bultmann remarks, "The diversity of theological interests and ideas is at first great." But if there is a discernible criteriology, *it*, rather than the provisionally entertained content, is the normative principle. Bultmann himself implicitly recognizes this in his subsequent statement: "A norm or an authoritative court of appeal for doctrine is still lacking, and the proponents of directions of thought which were later rejected as heretical consider themselves completely Christian—such as Christian Gnosticism."[14]

But Bultmann thus begs exactly the question I wish to raise. It may be true that proponents of eventually repudiated kinds of thought considered themselves completely Christian, but this establishes only that they did not invalidate their own thinking through their appeal to a normative procedure that transcended them, not that such a norm was non-existent. The question to be raised is precisely the one which Bultmann casually bypasses: to what extent was a normatizing procedure or an authoritative court of appeal present, explicitly or implicitly, in earliest Christian understanding?

In the hope of forestalling a possible misunderstanding, let me once more emphasize that this essential question, in all of the deliberately varied ways in which I have proposed it, is primarily historical in character. This book is nevertheless offered to the attention of the theologian—but as history, not theology. The theologies it articulates are meant to be those of the documents it scrutinizes, and the understandings it seeks are those of the earliest Christians. Its quest is for *their* ways—whatever our ways may be, or may come to be—of seeing the way of the Christian Word.

I

Paul

*T*he epistles of Paul provide a nearly ideal test case for the determination of a sample early Christian normative understanding. Not only are they many, substantial, and early: they are also highly various, addressing themselves to different problems, situations, and challenges in different parts of the world. Having made his way from Damascus to Jerusalem to Illyrica, Paul was perhaps the most widely travelled Christian of his day, and the most able to speak representatively for general Christian understanding, or to bear witness to its still not having come into being. And since his letters are not systematic treatises, they have the additional advantage of manifesting actual habits of mind rather than merely formal positions. Whatever may be learned from Paul about the sense of normative understandings in the early churches, and about the criteriology for validating norms of thought, will be something tempered by wide Christian experience, and addressed to a variety of Christian audiences. It is therefore a happy convenience that the letters of Paul must in this, as in most questions of early Christianity, be the starting point of any systematic investigation. What then has Paul to reveal about his—or others'—conceptions of the constitution of Christian thought?

To begin with, it is clear that being within the constitution of Christian thought is a matter of grave importance. At best, those who do not know God are delivered into subjection to the elements of this world (Gal 4:9); at worst, their failure to form their understanding in subjection to the true God means that they will be delivered over to an unfit mind (*adokimon noun*, Rom 1:28), whence all manner of impropriety will then proceed. Theoretically, there may be an escape from this pattern through the way in which God has revealed himself in creation (Rom 1:19–20); but practically, the religious "natural law"—including the law that governs the mind as well as that bearing on behavior—is as difficult to master without special grace as the revealed Law was to the Jews. Weak humanity may be blinded to the truth by the malevolent "god of this world" (2 Cor 4:3–4), or may simply fall victim to the

15

sheer inadequacy of the obsolete wisdom of this world, which counts no better than folly (1 Cor 1:19–21). Yet the helplessness that belongs to man of himself does not exonerate or protect him. If he does not somehow enter into a fit understanding, he has no appeal against the guilt of his consequent waywardness.

He must, of course, enter into proper *life* as well as proper understanding. But the global importance of the former does not render the special place of the latter inconsiderable. Understanding is not everything—but it is the proper governor of life. The unreconstructed man goes to seed in his life precisely because his mind is allowed to be unfit, undisciplined, unapproved. In the order of natural priority, first comes willfulness, and thence the *adokimos nous:* and if man is not rescued from his misguiding understanding, it takes him into a life-style that is unfit, undisciplined, unapproved. It is his whole life that needs to be rescued—but the rescue can take place only through the cooperation of his understanding.

Since the natural condition of willful man is that of the *adokimos nous,* the rescue must take place by intervention. His mind must be informed by the revelation of truth; and again, though theoretically the revelation that is implicit in creation might be enough (Rom 1:19–20), in practice a more forceful and explicit revelation seems to be required.[1] The final truth is not human but divine, and must be offered from its source. Thus it is that when Paul approaches the Jewish Law from this angle, rather than from that which compares it disadvantageously with Christ, he speaks of it in terms of the formation of understanding.

The Law is, to the pious Jew, not primarily a rule of conduct but "the form of knowledge and of the truth" (Rom 2:20). One who is instructed in the Law is in a position to be a guide to the blind, a light to those in darkness (Rom 2:18–19). Paul does not scoff at these claims, or belittle their suggestion of the priority of understanding. On the contrary, his two main critical representations of the vulnerability of the Jewish position both assume and reinforce this priority.

On the one hand, Paul argues that the problem is precisely that the formation of Jewish understanding falls unfortunately short. Israel pursued a Law of Righteousness, but did not attain it (Rom 9:31). Why? The subsequent verse offers what would ordinarily be taken to be the characteristic and definitive Pauline explanation: it is because they relied on works rather than on faith. Characteristic, indeed—but not necessarily definitive. For three verses later, Paul gives an alternative formula that clarifies his judgment, and shows that the issue is not simply pride versus humility, self-sufficiency as against submission to grace, the benighted ways of man contrasted with the unfathomably mysterious ways of God. The issue is understanding. The Jews, Paul avows, have indeed a zeal for God: "but not according to knowledge" (Rom 10:2). In their obtuseness, they have failed to understand rightly that form of knowledge and truth that was given to them, and thus they receive revelation impeded by a veil (2 Cor 3:13–16), not having grasped that this revelation itself points to the Christ who was to transcend and, by fulfilling it, abrogate the Law (Rom 3:21–22), even while reaffirming some of what belongs to it. Though their minds were not left as unfit as those of the Gentiles, in the end it was their misunderstanding that led them astray, not their perversity.

Perversity nevertheless has played its part. Yet here too, on the other hand, Paul insists on the governing place of understanding. The unruly flesh struggles on behalf of sin—but the mind may ascend to the spiritual Law, and be so informed by it that it actually becomes "law of my mind" (Rom 7:14–23). If one's entire life could be subjected to the Law of God, the Law might save.[2] The first step is being subjected to this through the mind's making God's Law its own law (Rom 7:25). Then, if the governing power of the mind were only sufficient to discipline the anarchical usurpations of the flesh, the prize would be won by the pious Jew. But alas, the regulation of mind by divine truth is a necessary condition, but unfortunately not a sufficient one. The mind may be willing, but the flesh is weak—and strong. The law of the flesh wars against "the law of my mind" (Rom 7:23), and wins. The Law does half the job of rescue, by freeing us from *adokimos nous.* On this count too, Paul's faulting of Judaism emphasizes the importance of the mind's right discipline, and does not despair of securing it. But Paul despairs of its natural capacity to impose itself effectually. The lusts of the flesh make us unable to follow its guidance, despite our will to do so—Gal 5:17 carries the same message as Rom 7. The Law is spiritual, but lacks the full power of the Spirit.

The Gospel overcomes the limitations that impede the Jews. It does so because, unlike the Law, which must rely on the inadequate power of law-formed mind to rule the fractious flesh, the Gospel itself has power. The wisdom of men is misled and misleading. The wisdom of the Law, which is spiritual (Rom 7:14), is true—but it is powerless. But what human capacity does not manage to do even when it possesses the form of knowledge and truth, Christ the wisdom of God and the power of God accomplishes through the Gospel (1 Cor 1:24, 2:4–5). Folly to the Greeks and to all those who are merely *psuchikos*, this is nevertheless the true and powerful wisdom of God—and therefore has the power to succeed in being our true wisdom, and righteousness, and sanctification, and redemption (1 Cor 1:30).

Let him who boasts, then, boast in the Lord (1 Cor 1:31), for his rescue is not credited to his own achievement. All the same, this characteristic Pauline emphasis on grace, on the divine initiative, on the private powerlessness of man, should not be allowed to obscure the indispensable place of human complicity in man's salvation. If he prefers to speak of our being known by God, that is nevertheless quite clearly, even for Paul, the reverent obverse of what we would more instinctively call our knowledge of God (Gal 4:9). Knowledge according to the flesh, even of Christ, may be of little account (2 Cor 5:16); but that may safely be said because we have knowledge in a higher key. The Gospel is not man's word but God's (1 Thess 2:13); but it is a word, not a mere infusion of power. It gives a wisdom not of this world, and makes us know (and permits us to speak about) what God has given us (1 Cor 2:7–16). It brings to us at once the power of God, and the knowledge of God.

The Gospel is a word of truth (2 Cor 6:7). Yet this truth is not readily evident to the *adokimos nous* of this world, to the Greek *philosophoi*, even to the zealous but obtuse-minded Jew. It is not connatural or even congenial to our clumsy and compromised minds. We may eventually come to see its truth plainly and easily, as we are transformed in Christ; but this recognition is not where disordered men may begin. We start estranged from truth. If it is to be appropriated by *our* minds—or, as Paul would probably prefer, if we are to be appropriated to it through our minds—it must be submitted to, obeyed.

The phrase by which Paul describes the purpose of his mission is "obedience of faith" (*hupakoē pisteōs*, Rom 1:5).[3] Fortunately this motif was central enough to his thought that we may piece together a sketch of its assumptions and implications. It is undoubtedly the same notion that he describes elsewhere as "the subjection of your confession to the Gospel" (2 Cor 9:13)—scarcely a pellucid phrase, but evidently pointing to the way in which the Corinthians' sense of the important truth has been disciplined by the Gospel, their understanding mapped in its image. Similarly, an alternative formula in Romans commends them in that they "obeyed from the heart that pattern of teaching to which you were delivered" (*hupēkousate de ek kardias eis hon paredothēte tupon didachēs*, Rom 6:17); and the same emphasis is sustained when Paul, in another epistle, speaks of his using his powers to lead every mind *(noēma)* captive to the obedience of Christ (2 Cor 10:5).[4]

The theme of obedience in Paul generates several equivalents. Obeying the Gospel is obeying Christ is obeying the truth is obeying the law. Not, to be sure, the law which governs detailed works, which is but the law of sin and death (Rom 8:2); but rather the law of spirit of life (Rom 8:2), the law of faith (Rom 3:27), Christ as the law of God (1 Cor 9:21). It is, in short, the conforming of oneself to that good news by which God calls us far beyond what we might otherwise become. For Paul, the root of Christian belonging lies in the gracious divine initiative, whence it is awakened and nourished. But the root itself is this conforming, this obedience, through which we put on a *dokimos nous* and receive the power to enact its dictates. If Jew and Gentile face an anthropological dilemma, the Christian dispensation eliminates the dilemma, not the anthropology.

The Christian norm is therefore a matter of *apprehension* and of *internalization*. Paul is obviously insistent on the latter. It is not the hearers of the Law who are justified, but the doers (Rom 2:13); it is possible to know God's will, and to be able to discriminate things that matter, and yet not be able to follow one's own teaching (Rom 2:18–21), and such is a sad condition. Paul was not, that is, a pure gnostic. The truth that really mattered to him was bound up with events and purposes and personalities and could not be metaphysically abstracted from such gritty stuff. To matter properly, it had to matter evidently. The Gospel should come not in Word only, but in Spirit and Power. Is it possible that the Gospel might be internalized by some short-cut that bypasses the understanding? I think not. Paul's "not in Word only" cannot mean "not in Word at all." Surely his complaint against the mere hearers of the Law means not that understanding does not matter but that some people may hear without *really* understanding the implications of what they have heard; and his mirror of self-confrontation for the Jew as would-be educator of the world in no way impugns the potential value of his *teaching* but only of his *conduct*. What doth it profit the teacher himself if he imparts wisdom but cannot live it? Nothing; but it may yet profit his hearers, if they obey what they have heard.

In fact, Paul on at least one occasion confronted the question of immediate internalization of spiritual power—that is, the relative values of spiritual transformation mediated by understanding, and the manifestation of spiritual power effected directly with the understanding not involved. He came down decisively on the side of understanding. The controversy in question is, of course, that with the Corinthians about the gift of tongues. The spirit may indeed pray without the understanding being involved (1 Cor 14:14). But that is simply undesirable: better five words mediated by *nous* than ten thousand without it, however spiritual they may be (1 Cor 14:19).[5] And then comes Paul's summary rebuke and admonition, which firmly establishes his conception of the mind's place in normative Christian life: do not be little children in understanding, but become mature in understanding (1 Cor 14:20).

Mature does not mean recherché or obscurantist. If Paul charges the Corinthians to become mature in understanding, he also warns them not to overrate gnosis (1 Cor 8:1), not to think above what is written

(1 Cor 4:6), not to deviate from their original simplicity in Christ (2 Cor 11:3) which was derived from Paul's own simplicity in speech (2 Cor 11:6). Essential understanding is indispensable, but it is not complicated.

All the same, Paul acknowledges that beyond the relatively uncomplicated formation of understanding that is a Christian essential, lies a range of further possibilities toward Christian perfection. He himself may be simple in speech—but he is not simple in knowledge (2 Cor 11:6). He does not wish anyone to credit him with any more than they can see and hear for themselves—but the truth is that he is in a position to boast much more, all the way to receiving indescribable messages which may not be expressed (2 Cor 12:6, 4). Thus are his addressees tantalized and put in their place. They are beginners, and need Paul's teaching to correct their ignorance (1 Thess 4:13) and supply deficiencies in their faith (1 Thess 3:10). They are still fleshly, and cannot be spoken to in the way that spiritual persons may be spoken to (1 Cor 3:1–3). They may know some things that others do not know—even, apparently, other Christians—which is in itself testimony of their growth in Christ (1 Cor 8:6–7): but if they should become too impressed with what they know, they should remember that they do not know as they ought (1 Cor 8:2). It is Paul who speaks: he who admits to his milk-fed children that there are some who partake of meat, that those who are perfect converse about a divine wisdom that this world would not recognize (1 Cor 3:2, 2:6–7). However simple the essentials of Christian understanding may be, there lies beyond them not only a maturing but a progress (Phil 1:25)—a progress, moreover, that leads not to more delicate speculations but to sturdier encompassing certainty. It is such that those who are perfect will recognize the truth of what Paul says —while those who are not will, if they continue to progress, ultimately have it revealed to them by God (Phil 3:15).

Hence a double standard emerges within Paul's teaching, as it relates to the state of normative Christian understanding and the operation of thought-law. There is one standard at the beginning of Christian life, and another for those who pursue the more perfected states to which that beginning is open. The understanding, and the coordinate law of thought, necessary for salvation (which is imperative) is evidently rather simple. But the understanding, and probably the coordinate law of thought, necessary for perfection (which is desirable) is not so easy a matter. Progress in knowledge is apparently a normal feature of Christian life; it is virtually a necessary concomitant of spiritual progress. Paul does not waver from the priority he consistently gives to God's initiative and to the Spirit by which his truth and power enter the lives of Christians. But neither does he forget that the Spirit's vehicle of entry is an intelligible word of truth, or that the Spirit is that which searches and knows the deep things of God and reveals them to the understanding of men (1 Cor 2:10–12). His communications to his converts are precisely the speaking of that which the Spirit has taught (1 Cor 2:13). Therefore, while he is aware that his own spirit, which knows his own depths most fully (1 Cor 2:11), may through its privileged liaison with the divine Spirit communicate with God in ways that transcend his own understanding (Rom 8:15–16, 26–27), he nevertheless also knows that just as his own spirit is especially manifest in his knowing mind, so the Spirit is especially characterizable as mind (Rom 8:27). To have the Spirit is to have the mind of Christ (1 Cor 2:16), and the correlative understanding is an indispensably characteristic component of Christian reality.

Sometimes elevated to states of spirit and achievements of insight beyond ordinary powers, the Christian community encounters a problem of discernment. If progress is one of the facts of Christian life, so are confusion, unwitting ignorance, false confidence, even deliberate fraud. How is one to tell the true currency from the counterfeit?

The initiate may in the first instance perceive the divine authentication of the word preached to him in the characteristic external signs and wonders and powers of the apostle, which Paul manifested not only to the Corinthians (2 Cor 12:12) but among all the Gentiles (Rom 15:18). At this stage, all the Christian needs to do, apparently, is notice what is happening. But not in the external order only, for the servants of the adversary may be endowed with specious powers; and the ultimate Satanic manifestation parodies the true apostle, perhaps even in signs and wonders and powers of falsehood (2 Cor 11:13–15; cf. 2 Thess 2:9). The greatest and most persuasive initial guarantee of the Gospel's truth is rather the internal sign of the Spirit (Gal 3:2), who comes with power (1 Thess 1:5) and illuminates the believer with knowledge of the glory of God in Christ (2 Cor 4:6). It is a knowledge that authenticates itself. In his appropriating act of obedient submission, the believer receives the mind of Christ, and participates in the wisdom and power of God. Evidently, Paul's converts *know* that they know.

The seal of the Spirit is, in fact, the fundamental category for both Christian belonging in general and Christian understanding in particular. Unless one possesses the Spirit of God (= the Spirit of Christ), one cannot belong to Christ (Rom 8:9); the man who still operates on the merely psychic level cannot understand the things of the Spirit of God, and thinks them foolish (1 Cor 2:14). But those who have received the Spirit are sons of God, heirs of the promise, free of the Law, members of Christ (Rom 8:14–15; Gal 4:6, 28; 5:18; 1 Cor 12:13, etc.); and those who have received the Spirit can know and understand the things of

God, the true wisdom, the saving divine righteousness (1 Cor 2:12–16, etc.). The Spirit is also the locus and medium of progressive understanding: for just as the simplest Christian insight into the Lordship of Jesus is given only through the Spirit, so also is it the Spirit who gives further words of wisdom and words of knowledge (1 Cor 12:3, 8).

Because of the gap between the unaided human mind and the mind of Christ, this canon of the Spirit is both absolute and circular. Those who are within the embrace of the Spirit cannot be readily understood by those outside. But within the circle of the Spirit, the Spirit's teachings may be readily unfolded to, and grasped by, spiritual persons (1 Cor 2:13–15). Paul is so confident of the reliability of this principle that he can assure the Philippians that the perfect should be of his mind, and that those who think otherwise will eventually come to the same position through divine revelation (Phil 3:15)—and he can tell the Corinthians that anyone truly spiritual will see things his way, and that anyone who fails to do so is simply self-disqualified (1 Cor 14:37–38).

If the understanding of all were fully transformed in the Spirit, this would presumably be all that needed to be said. The perfected understanding given to those who mature in the Spirit, and the new words of knowledge communicated in the Spirit, would register in the hearts of all spiritual persons with that vivid conviction by which they had rejoiced in their submission to the original word of truth in the Gospel. Paul would have it so, and would have his addressees perceive that it must be so. But he also sees that it is, alas, not yet so. The awkward and annoying fact of the matter is that not all those whom he has fathered in Christ perceive readily and unquestioningly the rightness of his teachings. Ironically, the Corinthian holdouts seem to have accepted Paul's fundamental assumptions concerning the circle of the Spirit, and have been thus led by their disagreements to the supposition that they are within that circle, while Paul is partially without: hence, in the absence of that immediate conviction that ought ideally to obtain when Spirit speaks to Spirit, they want some external proof that it is really Christ who speaks through Paul, rather than Paul's own partial ignorance or vain fancy (2 Cor 13:3). If, after all, there are degrees of perfected understanding, it is at least possible that Paul may speak from an inferior stratum and be properly contravened by one who is stronger in spiritual gifts. The Galatians, on the other hand, swayed by a plausible-sounding supplementary teaching, have come to suspect that the spiritually authentic in Paul's Gospel was unfortunately adulterated by doctrine that came not from the Spirit but from policy and man-pleasing compromise. Even the strangers in Rome seem to have heard that Paul preaches some highly suspicious notions that hardly recommend themselves as reflections of the mind of Christ or the purpose of God.

In situations like these, it is of little use for Paul to rest his case on his claim that he has the mind of Christ; for however true he may believe that to be, it is not an adequate answer when that is precisely the question. Where his usual criteriology is thus put to the test, he must adopt other tactics—and it is here, when he must address himself to alternative criteria, that he is most revealing about his over-all sense of the way in which Christian understanding is constituted.

From Paul's own point of view, of course, these other strategies of authentication are inferior. They are used only for those who are somehow too feeble in the Spirit to be able to discern by Spirit alone—babes in Christ who cannot yet handle solid food, beginners weak in conscience and knowledge, enthusiasts who overrate their spirituality and are unaware of how much the mind of the flesh still holds them in its power (1 Cor 3:1–3, 8:7–12, Gal 4:29ff.). Nevertheless, he approaches the argument with some conviction, as if there is sufficient connection among the elements of Christian reality to make it valid (however imperfect) to appeal to criteria that are not, like the Spirit itself, self-establishing. It ought to be enough for him to reiterate that what he has said is so, no matter who may attempt to controvert it—himself and angels included (Gal 1:8). But when that is not enough, to what criteria can he appeal in order to establish the truth of his teaching against misgivings that undermine both its content and his authority?

Consider first the challenge to his authority. The most efficient short-cut to its establishment was evidently to be known as an apostle. Paul and his Corinthian challengers seem clearly to share the general assumption that apostle is the highest title and the first role in the church (1 Cor 12:28–31), and that the authority of an authentic apostle is not to be questioned.[6] Hence in raising questions about the adequacy of his teaching or the authority of his commands, Paul's opponents must naturally express doubts about his apostolic commission. Paul is capable of asserting his right to the title by appealing to the will of God alone (1 Cor 1:1); but when he has been challenged, and polemical assertion is pointless, he turns readily to more particular criteria. If some of these, such as his claims to having seen the Lord (1 Cor 9:1), are not publicly verifiable, most of them are. His most effective appeal is once more to his addressees' own experience: even if others should be reluctant to recognize his claims, those whom his preaching has begotten in the Lord know that they are themselves living proof of his having executed the work of an apostle (1 Cor 9:1–2). Furthermore, Paul can appeal to a still more public criterion, referring to it as if it were a generally and internationally accepted canon: his early work with them was accompanied by "the signs of the apostle," signs and wonders and powers (2 Cor 12:12).

An apostle, then. But perhaps of a lower order. For it seems to be generally recognized that the chief apostles, the pre-eminent apostles, are those who were participants in the earliest origins of the Christian church. Surely no latecomer could hope to compete with their authority, or hope to be taken quite as seriously as they? Paul responds to this insinuation with the weary annoyance of one who has fought this specious argument far too many times. But the way he responds is instructive. In the first place, his calling and his qualifications as an apostle come not by human commission but by direct revelation and divine intervention (2 Cor 3:5, Gal 1:1) putting him on an equal footing with the most important apostles. He may claim this not only by positive assertion but by a solemn denial of the rumors that would have him historically subordinated to and dependent on the apostolic leadership of the Jerusalem pillars (Gal 1–2). Is it thought that he was commissioned by the Twelve and instructed by them? Then note that the historical fact is that he did not go to Jerusalem for a full three years after his conversion, and even then met only Peter and James. Is it supposed that he reported later to Jerusalem in answer to their summons, and that his companion had to submit to circumcision? Then be informed that he went in response to a revelation, and that Titus was *not* required to be circumcized. Is it thought that he had to have his Gospel authorized by the Jerusalem leaders, and that he accepted their superior position? Then be assured that they added nothing to his kerygma but rather acknowledged that Providence had itself given him the apostleship over the Gentiles—and that, in the spirit of this equality of office, he had personally faced down Peter when he had wavered from the truth in Antioch. The case for inferiority may be tried in the court of history, which will find for the Apostle Paul.

Far from being of an inferior order, then, he is—as he insists repeatedly to the Corinthians—in no way inferior to the most eminent apostles (2 Cor 11:5, 12:11). Some of his justification for this claim rests on matters of detailed historical record. Some of it rests on Paul's conviction that historical priority and early leadership amount to little in the divine scheme (Gal 2:6), and his bold assurance that to have known Jesus according to the flesh has little to do with the spiritual knowledge that now counts (2 Cor 5:16). These criteria, singly and together, are likely to have been generally acceptable in early Christian circles, even if the latter two were bracing challenges to common habits of thought. But there is a more ultimate criterion running beneath all these arguments, which is even more universally accepted and which really forms the basis for Paul's defense of his apostolic authority.

By their fruits you shall know them. If they look into their own history enough to see how they were reaped for the Lord, the Galatians and Corinthians must acknowledge that Paul has proved himself an apostle. It was by perceiving the effectiveness of his mission to the Gentiles that the Jerusalem group recognized that Paul was indeed the great Gentile apostle. It was his own steadfast fidelity to the truth of the Gospel that gave him the right and the duty to rebuke the bad fruit of the wavering and compromised Peter. If anyone doubts that Paul is in no way inferior to the most eminent apostles, let them look into recent history and they will see that his labors for the Gospel show him a greater servant of Christ than any (1 Cor 11:23), and that God's grace was not fruitless in him as he worked more abundantly than all the rest (1 Cor 15:10). God respects not persons, no matter what their reputation or standing, but good fruits (Gal 2:6). By these standards, Paul's apostolic authority is a matter not of arrogant self-promotion but of public record. Such a one may well speak belittlingly of those who must carry letters of recommendation (2 Cor 3:1).

Peter's performance in Antioch, however, must give one pause. If he, the great apostle of the circumcision, could play the Gospel false, then to establish that Paul is the apostle of the uncircumcision is not sufficient to guarantee his reliability unqualifiedly, no matter how abundant the fruit he has harvested for Christ. Paul too knows this. He sees and admits what an ironic scandal it would be—and could be—if, after proclaiming the Gospel to others, he himself should become unfit (1 Cor 9:27). It is for this reason, I believe, that he is so careful, so insistently jealous, of his reputation with respect to integrity and consistency. If his conduct suggests to the Corinthians that he is walking according to the flesh (2 Cor 10:1–2), this requires an answer that will explain away the false appearance. If, on the other hand, his conduct suggests that he cannot really claim the prerogatives of the apostle, he must both insist that he can and explain why it seems to him more fitting not to do so (1 Cor 9:3–19).[7] Do the Corinthians suspect that he is faking, being so bold in his letters and yet so self-effacing and meek among them? Then he must both reassert his right to boldness with a veiled threat about the power he has at his disposal, and explain why it is more appropriate and generous for him not to have employed it but rather to humble himself for the sake of their exaltation (2 Cor 10:1–11, 11:7–12). If his asceticism and abstinence raise suspicions about his real sense of freedom from the Law, and if his habit of adapting his behavior to his surroundings seems inconsistent, Paul must produce an account that shows the principle of honest consistency underlying these superficially doubtful practices (1 Cor 8:1–13, 9:20–27, 10:23–33; Rom 14:1–23). Good fruits must have good roots. Paul knows that he must contend with others whose impure or deceitful motives lead them to a certain degree of seductive success in Galatia, Corinth, Rome (Gal 4:17, 2 Cor

11:13–15, Rom 16:18). He himself aspires rather to be one of those whose work will survive the test of the final fires of judgment (1 Cor 3:12–15). For this reason, although he knows that the judgment of God is all that counts and not the clarity of his own conscience (let alone the assessment of other men, 1 Cor 4:3–4), he is nevertheless extremely sensitive to the slightest suggestion of suspected guile (2 Cor 12:16ff.) and repeatedly insistent that there is neither craft nor falsity in his dealings (2 Cor 4:1–2). His earnest concern for the Jews is not a put-on, but expressed with a clear conscience (Rom 9:1); he is not like the many, a mere peddler of God's word, but speaks from sincerity, as from God (2 Cor 2:17); in fact, his general boast is precisely the witness of his conscience to the divine simplicity and sincerity with which he has conducted himself in the world (2 Cor 2:12). But not even that is an entirely private criterion of reliability: for in this relentless integrity, he has commended himself also to the conscience of other men (1 Cor 10:28–32; 2 Cor 4:1–2, 5:11), thus establishing himself, by human as well as divine standards, as an entirely trustworthy guide in the things of the Lord, a clear channel for what the Spirit has disclosed.[8]

Or at least for what he thinks the Spirit has disclosed. But apostolic authority is not necessarily everything. It is not as if he is already perfect (Phil 3:12–13). Some admixture of the still-untransfigured carnal mind may yet remain, some confusion in what he makes out as he peers through a glass, darkly, at the divine mystery. If his authority stands respectable under public scrutiny, his doctrine is not, for all that, absolutely guaranteed. In a spiritually dynamic and gracious order, it is possible that a Corinthian prophet may be graced with a deeper and more authentic insight, or that a missionary to Galatia may carry a more balanced and ultimate teaching, than Paul was in a position to provide. And should it be suggested that this is indeed the case, to what criteria can Paul appeal to validate his version of the mind of Christ?

In a moment of earnest urgency, Paul can invoke his own authority to assure the Galatians that their adoption of circumcision would be a disaster, and that their inclination to do so does not come from God (Gal 5:2–8). But in calmer moments, he has alternative ways of establishing the soundness of his doctrine. The first step comes with remembering that it is, after all, not his doctrine but God's. To the charge that his Gospel is "according to men" and men-pleasing, he can answer that he received it not from men but from God, and that far from being ingratiatingly compromised, it is stern with the unadulterated scandal of a divine truth that shatters the wisdom of man (Gal 1:6–9, 1 Cor 1:17–24). It is an impressive move: if not checkmate, at least countercheck.

Paul's remembering, however, takes one further decisive step. Not only is it not his doctrine: it was not first revealed through him either. If it was to the advantage of his mission to emphasize that he received it from God rather than men, it was more deeply and ultimately to the advantage of the credibility of the Christian mission in general, although detracting from Paul's independent authority, to emphasize that what he received was essentially what others had received before him.

The rumor—later picked up by Luke for Acts—that he was well known to the churches is Judea was false. But the rumor which those churches themselves received, that Paul was now preaching as Gospel *the very faith* that he had persecuted (Gal 1:23), was true. However little communication there had been between them, they shared a common word of truth. Thus when Paul, fearing his mission threatened, laid out before the Jerusalem apostles the Gospel that he preached among the Gentiles, they did not find it necessary to add anything but the right hand of fellowship (Gal 2:6–9). Paul obviously did not feel that the authenticity of his Gospel was dependent upon their approval—but it is dramatically clear that their approval proved the coherence of Paul's Gospel with that preached by the first apostles, and therefore the inauthenticity of the critical interference Paul was suffering in his work among the Gentiles.[9] That coherence was strong and important enough to permit Paul to appeal against the first apostle to the Gospel they shared, convicting him on essentially the same point that Paul urged again years later to defend his Gospel as *the* Gospel to the wavering Galatians (Gal 2:11–16). The Gospel is one, consistent, and universal. Paul delivered to the Corinthians among the chief things what he himself had received, and later reined in their wandering understanding by reminding them of this, and assuring them that it does not matter which of Christ's ministering apostles is consulted: whether he or they, thus they preach, and thus the Corinthians first grasped the truth (1 Cor 15:1–11). To deviate from this doctrine is to deviate from the universal foundational teaching of Christianity. Whether or not they trust Paul in particular, an appeal to what all the apostles preach should help them tell the difference between an authentic spiritual revelation and a deviant pneumatic wind-egg. This compromise to his proud independence is Paul's decisive reassurance that the Gospel really is given intelligibly into the hands and minds of men.[10]

The Gospel is universally the same because it is the proclamation of the one Lord Jesus Christ in the one Spirit, according to the will of the one God. Its various ministers are simply servants through whom men come to believe in the one Christ (1 Cor 3:5). Not only do the apostles *happen* to be consistent with one another in what they preach: they *must* be. No one can lay another foundation besides the one Jesus Christ whom they preach (1 Cor 3:11). There is no such thing as a Gospel that deviates from what Galatia received from Paul; anyone who attempts to proclaim one is simply preaching subversive bad news and is accursed (Gal 1:6–9). This is not, I think, mere rhetorical hyperbole on Paul's part. It is a basic conviction. For what does it mean for him to say derisively to the Corinthians that they bear with it well if someone preaches another Jesus whom Paul did not preach, or they receive another Spirit which they had not received or another Gospel which they had not embraced (2 Cor 11:4)? What it means is that these are to Paul preposterous notions! There is no other Jesus; there is no other Spirit; there is no other Gospel. If there were, if there could be, one might well take them seriously; but there neither is nor can be any such thing. There can be other preachments, obviously, but they cannot possibly work the way the Gospel works, laying the one foundation, bringing the one Spirit, giving those who submit a participation in the wisdom and power of God. Another preachment can build flimsily, or can corrupt, but it cannot found.

When Paul reminds the Galatians that they had received the Spirit through a hearing of faith rather than through works of law (Gal 3:2), he is not pleading a special case. He is appealing to what he takes to be the universal experience of Christendom. In turning from their sound and vivid foundation in the Spirit to works of flesh, the Galatians are not being simply disloyal or inconsistent—they are being stupid (Gal 3:3).[11] Any Christian who reflects on what has happened to him should be able to know better than to confuse Gospel with ungospel, or to suppose that what worked as Gospel could possibly be one preacher's idiosyncratic views. Its local effectiveness is therefore a proof of its universal authenticity.

For basic Christian revelation, then, Paul sees an important correlation between authenticity and universality, as well as between both of these and sheer effectiveness. Because of the uniqueness and univocity of the genuine Gospel, the truth of its content is guaranteed by its intitial effectiveness and can be confirmed by its collation with the foundational Gospel as preached by other apostles, and Paul explicitly points to both these criteria in support of his claims. Again, it is clear that he does not suppose that the authenticity of his Gospel is *derived* from either its success or its correspondence to the Gospel as preached by Peter. It is derived rather from the truth and wisdom of God, as enacted by Christ and mediated to us by the one Spirit. It is ideally according to that scheme, rather than according to the sound but inferior evidence of the objective history of apostolic preaching, that the believer should realize that the one Christ is "not yes and no" but unequivocal yes to all the promises of God (2 Cor 1:19–20). But if he wavers, the other supporting evidence is there.

The last citation is also a reminder of another implication which Paul finds in the univocity of the Spirit. Supporting evidence for the truth of his basic Christian understanding is not only spread across the space of the entire Christian mission: it is spread across the time of the whole history of revelation. Just as Paul believes that the accuracy of his Gospel may and should be perceived in its comparison with the work of the other apostles, so he also believes that similar results will obtain in its comparison with the scriptures.

The unadjusted epistles of Paul must have been a terrible embarrassment for Marcion. Awkward enough that Paul seems to assert that the Torah is established by the faith rather than abolished (Rom 3:31), or that he appeals to the Law of Moses to prove that one of his teachings is clearly not merely "according to man" (1 Cor 9:8–9). But worse still for Marcion's case is Paul's testimony that he faithfully supports and perpetuates, in his teaching of the first things of the Gospel, the doctrine that the key Christian events took place "in accordance with the scriptures" (1 Cor 15:3–4).

The Law is our pedagogue to lead us to Christ (Gal 3:24)—not merely in its attempt to restrain our destructive lusts until the propitious moment arrives, but in its preview of the Gospel itself. The Gospel was previously announced in the prophetic scriptures (Rom 1:2, cf. Rom 16:25–26), not merely in the sense that the scriptures form the locus of those divine promises which the Gospel fulfills (2 Cor 1:20) but more explicitly: for Scripture not only records the all-important promises made to Abraham, but even foresaw the Gospel and foretold it to Abraham (Gal 3:8). The curious wording of this latter text, with its direct personification of Scripture, should not quite be taken to imply that the same Spirit who is at work revealing to us the fulfillment of the scriptures was the agent of their formation in the first place,[12] but does show at any rate that the coherence between Scripture and Gospel is total, and that the former is therefore another point of appeal for the verification of the latter.

The coherence is total not merely in the negative sense of non-inconsistency, but in a much more globally positive sense. The world of the Gospel is really what the scriptures are all about. What is reported in Scripture is there *typically*, designed for our admonition and instruction here, now, at this end of the ages (1 Cor 10:1–11, 1 Cor 9:8–9, Rom 15:4, Gal 4:21–31): a series of promissory notes that have now come due. Hence Paul's appeals to Scripture are not rhetorically decorative flourishes, but invocations of another dimension of the laws that govern Christian understanding. To the Galatians who incline to trust in the Law, Paul means to *prove* from the Law that his own Gospel is right in repudiating their position (Gal 4:21–31).

The law that governs normative Christian understanding is Christ, the law of God, as communicated in the Spirit, which mediates the mind of Christ. That is obviously where Paul believes he lives, and where all Christians ought to live. He betrays to us no anxious uncertainty about the adequacy of his own understanding, and it is certainly not for his own sake that he looks beyond what was revealed to him in the Spirit. But for the sake of the confusions, doubts, and misplaced confidences of others, he does appeal to more homely criteria; and in doing so, he sketches for us his conception of the way in which Providence has designed and constructed a coherent pattern of public correlatives to the transcendent mystery of salvation. Granted that the purest appropriation of the Gospel can afford to be disdainful of human ways; granted even that the communication of understanding within the Gospel repudiates words of human wisdom, and transmits spiritual things to spiritual persons by spiritual means (1 Cor 2:13). Nevertheless, God is not a God of confusion but of peace (1 Cor 14:33), and has not disdained to work in a way that establishes a visible human side to the constitution that governs Christian understanding, to which his spokesmen may confidently appeal whenever his more direct light may dazzle the weaker human eyes. God did not have Paul receive the Gospel from men or through human ways—but he did have Paul's converts do so. Paul knew both these truths.

I think that the evidence from Paul's epistles is sufficient to establish the claim that Paul believed that *the necessity of understanding the essential Christian Gospel in the way that he himself understood it can be demonstrated by evidence available to all Christians.* If the primary law of Christian understanding rests in the monarchial rule of Christ the Lord, it is nevertheless essentially replicated on a lower order by secondary common law based in Christian experience—a common law whose authority Paul evidently supposed all Christians would recognize.

How far does the jurisdiction of this secondary common law extend? For Christian understanding does not naturally limit itself to the essential Gospel; the spiritual dynamic of Christian life, on the contrary, is progressive in understanding as in other ways. The Spirit communicates an increment in words of wisdom, words of knowledge (1 Cor 12:8). The recipients strive to speak out so as to profit others, in a revelation or a prophecy or a knowledge or a teaching (1 Cor 14:6). When Christians assemble, it can happen that "each one has a psalm, a teaching, a tongue, a revelation, an interpretation" (1 Cor 14:26). And for all his cautionary emphasis on the importance of not going too far, not getting puffed up, not letting one's mind overreach, Paul is clearly aware of the value of these more removed and inessential levels of understanding—not only in the private life of the man caught up into

paradise to hear incommunicable things, but for the common edification of the community. It is not to appease the idle curiosity of the
Corinthians but to develop and stabilize their understanding that Paul,
having set them straight on the basic doctrine of resurrection, lets them
in on some of the details of the scenario of the final hour by disclosing
to them a mystery to which he was privy (1 Cor 15:51). He may already
have told them everything that is indispensable; but he evidently had
not told them everything that was worth knowing.

The normative constitution of things is not quite so clear at this level
of Christian experience. Once the irreformable true foundation is laid
in the Gospel of Jesus Christ, the builders who work further from there
will, one hopes, work as the agents of Christ under the direction of the
truth-giving Spirit. But while some will build with gold, silver, precious
stones, it can happen that others will contribute only wood, hay, straw
(1 Cor 3:11-12). This is not a matter of indifference, or only of relative
elegance. In the long run, the inferior work will be destroyed and those
responsible will suffer loss through the fire of judgment that definitively
discerns the truth (1 Cor 3:13-15). But that is future tense. Is there any
way of anticipating what will and what will not belong to this last Word?

The issue is not as crucial as that of the essential Gospel. To miss the
true foundation is a calamity, but to build upon it with what turns out
to be shabby stuff is, in the long run, only a grievous embarrassment.
Those who do so will be saved only as through fire, but they will nevertheless be saved (1 Cor 3:15). There is no suggestion that those who
follow them will be any worse off than themselves. Still, it matters. The
territory beyond the essential Gospel is not a mere blur of wonderment
in which we are free to poeticize indifferently and *ad lib.*, but a further
truth which we attempt to discern—the special province of prophecy,
which knows mysteries and knowledge (1 Cor 13:2)—and which will
eventually become manifest to the discredit of all false attempts. How
then shall we conform our present understanding to what *shall* be our
normative understanding of Christian truth?

Here again, Paul's personal solution, which he is ready enough to
recommend to his addressees, is relatively simple. Although he may not
yet be perfected (Phil 3:12-13), he is nevertheless one of those fully
advanced Christians who speak the wisdom of God (1 Cor 2:6-7). If he
and his Corinthian addressees are similarly of Christ, yet Paul is so with
more authority to minister to their edification (2 Cor 10:7-8). If there
are other apostles, Paul is yet the most tested and fruitful of the lot
(1 Cor 15:10, 2 Cor 11:23). He can back up his judgment with a telling
assurance that he has the Spirit of God (1 Cor 7:40). He has the mind
of Christ (1 Cor 2:16); it is no longer he that lives, but Christ lives in him
(Gal 2:20). On all counts, Paul stands ready to claim that he himself is

an incarnate—or rather inspired—norm of Christian understanding.[13]

This is why, although the way of Christian perfection is ultimately a process of putting on Christ (Rom 13:14), Paul can offer a more obviously concrete practical alternative: imitate me (1 Cor 4:16, Gal 4:12, Phil 3:17, 1 Thess 1:6; cf. 2 Thess 3:7). What validates this alternative is of course the principle expressed in another of his reiterations of this piece of advice: "become imitators of me just as I am of Christ" (1 Cor 11:1), but the implicit assumption is that Paul does it well enough to be representative, indeed well enough to be *normative*. Clearly, not many can be ready to make such a claim. But Paul obviously feels that his own right to do so is publicly apparent, even if it is not quite as apparent as he is in a position to make it. And if it remains obscure to some of the more fleshly minds, at least the more spiritual will recognize in him a facsimile of the Lord's presence and authority (1 Cor 14:37, Gal 4:14).

Paul evidently liked having his opinion asked. And although he distinguished at least sometimes, and perhaps always, between commandments of the Lord and his own judgment (1 Cor 7:10, 12, 25), he makes no bones about the authority of the latter (1 Cor 7:40, 14:37).[14] The same holds true for matters of doctrine in the less practical order: the facts of the Last Supper he "received from the Lord" and delivered in turn to his pupils in Christ (1 Cor 11:23), and his teaching on the Resurrection follows the same pattern (1 Cor 15:3). He obviously expects the Corinthians, in both instances, to reform their thinking in accordance with the implications of these definitive pieces of testimony. The historical source of authority is sometimes blurred. When he invokes another teaching "in a word of the Lord" with a formula that confidently explains that he does not wish the Thessalonians to be ignorant about these matters (1 Thess 4:13–15), he is evidently appealing to a tradition of Dominical pronouncement. But when he uses the same formula and the same confidence to share with the Corinthians insights on scriptural interpretation and on the relationship of spiritual persons to one another, the case is not so sure: these are not likely to have derived so directly from witnessed public teachings of the Lord (1 Cor 10:1, 12:1; cf. 15:51). Paul could afford a degree of insouciance on such matters. If he thought with the mind of Christ, it was not necessary to keep track of just how that mind was formed in him in every particular. His disciples were obviously supposed to conform their minds to his in important matters, and that was about all that needed to be established, until someone made an issue of distinguishing the various ways of receiving from the Lord.

Paul liked having his opinion asked, and understood himself to be communicating something rather more authoritative than mere opinion. Accordingly, he bristled with annoyance when his correspondents manifested some hesitation about the adequacy of his teachings. In most cases, those who hesitated had small claim to authority, and could be disciplined as babes, ignoramuses, or upstarts puffed with pride. In other cases, Paul had to contend with those who had some legitimate pretensions to both status and charismatic gifts; and it is significant that Paul does not put them down in the same way, but fences with them more cautiously, appealing to considerations other than his own successful internalization of the mind of Christ. The most interesting case is, of course, Paul's indirect competition with Apollos.

Apollos has obviously deeply impressed some of the Corinthians with the profundity of his Christian wisdom, and some of them have registered this to the disadvantage of Paul, whose simple Gospel and unprepossessing manner are rather disappointing by comparison. Paul is quite prepared to be forthright about competitors who seem to him to be frauds, but Apollos is none of these. Paul will not fault him as a minister to the Christian mind. Apollos evidently had built on the foundation that Paul had laid; and if he built where Paul had not built, or more elegantly than Paul had done, at least he does not seem to have built at cross-purposes to Paul. Therefore, however hurt and defensive he may be about the invidious comparisons, Paul's appreciation of Apollos gets no more critical than the dark warning that those who build on foundations laid by others must be circumspect about how and what they build, knowing that it will meet a severe trial (1 Cor 3:10–15). For the rest, he simply appeals beyond their dissimilarities to that theological point at which he can claim that they are both mere servants of the Lord's gift, only God's co-workers, indifferent agents of God's grace and the one Christ—that, in fact, from the proper unfleshly perspective, Paul and Apollos are one (1 Cor 1:11–13, 3:4–9).

Superficially, it may seem that Paul backs off from competing with Apollos because he finds himself at a disadvantage. Such a judgment would be unfair to Paul, and it would be inconsistent not only with his demonstrated willingness to stand up to the most renowned apostle when need be, but also his willingness to respect the spiritual integrity of his own children in Christ. For he readily allows that they may indeed have many pedagogues in Christ (1 Cor 4:15), and that the Spirit who works powerfully among them will make them agents of their own edifying instruction. He will not abide their disrespect, for good reasons which I shall touch on shortly; but he will acknowledge the dignity of their claim to understanding when it is well founded, assuring them that he will not lord it over them in faith: like Apollos, they become his fellow-workers through their constancy in the Gospel (2 Cor 1:24).

For Christ is the norm, the law of Christian minds; and whoever succeeds in putting on Christ, to that extent internalizes the norm. Paul is not the only venerable exemplar. He is the most spectacular case he knows, but he points to analogues on a smaller scale: no one is to despise Timothy, who does the work of the Lord like Paul; he will remind you of Paul's ways (1 Cor 16:10–11, 1 Cor 4:17). The family of Stephanas, long devoted to the service, are worthy of your submission (1 Cor 16:15–16). In fact, all who are distinguished for their work in the Lord are to be especially revered (1 Cor 16:16, 1 Thess 5:12–13). But Paul is cautious. He does not say that they are to be imitated, or that their knowledge is especially to be trusted. Conservative that he is, he says such things about no individual but himself.

But that requires two qualifications. The first is the usual and by now probably anticipated one: he says such things about Christ, and that is the reason that he can say them about himself. The second qualification is less obvious, but scarcely less important in Paul's sense of the discernment of Christian understanding: because he says such things about Christ, he also says very similar things about the ekklēsia.

Paul seems doubtful about whether any member of the Christian polity has been as richly and representatively endowed with the Spirit as himself. But the polity itself is another matter. What he is somewhat hesitant to accord to individuals, he freely acknowledges in churches. What he seems distinctly disinclined to say to any one person—perhaps above all to any Corinthian—he will say to the church at Corinth: "you were enriched in him in everything, in every word and every knowledge . . . so that you are not inferior in a single charisma" (1 Cor 1:5, 7).[15] Together, they form a body of Christ (1 Cor 12:27) with many members (1 Cor 12:12); to this body, the one Spirit gives the various spiritual gifts (1 Cor 12:4). The gifts are not, however, collected together in one recipient, but are distributed to various persons in order that the composite fellowship may participate in them all (1 Cor 12:7). Thus not all are apostles, not all prophets, not all teachers, and so on (1 Cor 12:29–30); but God has, through the Spirit, placed all of these in the ekklēsia so that it may be self-edifying—or, more accurately, so that the body of Christ may be the more effectively joined to the head, more amply and dynamically vivified and edified by the one Spirit.

It is not clear in the writings of Paul why the Spirit works in this radically communal way with the individual churches. He himself appears to be endowed with all the charisms he lists, with the possible exception of the interpretation of tongues; yet he expects that these gifts will be normally separated in the normal Christian community. Since he does recognize a hierarchy of charisms (1 Cor 12:31) and recommends that one pray for the more edifying in preference to the less (1 Cor 14:1ff.), we may suspect that it has something to do with maturing in the Christian life: for instance, we may suppose that the

Spirit mercifully supplies to the community, in the name of Christ's wholeness, gifts which individuals would ordinarily not expect to attain to until later in their development.

For whatever reason, that is in fact the way in which the Spirit works. And that being the case, it is notable that Paul's sense of the hierarchy of these gifts puts a strong premium on the formation and development of Christian understanding: the three top-ranking contributions of the Spirit to the community are apostles, prophets, and teachers (1 Cor 12:28);[16] and he prays that the love of the Philippians may abound increasingly in knowledge and perception, so that they may examine the things that make a difference (Phil 1:9–10).

This latter remark suggests what Paul took to be the characteristic way of determining and regulating Christian understanding, aside from a special appeal to one who, like Paul, is himself a pattern to be followed (Phil 3:17). Having in a collective way the Spirit who searches and knows the things of God, having the mind of Christ, the community is equipped to sift out what is offered to its collective consciousness and separate the true from the false. These are, of course, spiritual things, and can be examined only by spiritual persons (1 Cor 2:13–16), but the Lord has provided. Even the saying of a prophet can and should be subjected to a spiritual discernment (1 Cor 14:29, 32).[17] It is, of course, according to precisely this principle of charismatic economy that the Corinthians presumed to raise a question as to whether Paul himself was really speaking the mind of Christ (2 Cor 13:3). They knew that not everyone who seemed to be, or claimed to be, authentically inspired really was so. But it was in accordance with his trust in the same principle that Paul answers: if any one take himself to be a prophet or a spiritual person, let him acknowledge the things I write, that they are the commandments of the Lord (1 Cor 14:37; cf. 1 Cor 10:15).

For the process was not cosy. Apparently it was not always entirely obvious phenomenologically that "God is not a God of confusion but of peace," as Paul puts it in urging the Corinthians to be more orderly (1 Cor 14:33). The growth of understanding was not a simple evolutionary process, but more a dialectic. The gift of discernment was indispensable; and even then we have Paul's sobering warning: there must be party-factions *(haireseis)* among you, so that the approved may become manifest among you (1 Cor 11:19).[18]

If there must be such disputes, how—without invoking the prestige of Paul—were they to be resolved? In fact, even if Paul's prestige does enter the lists, there remains a chance that someone may set that of Apollos or his equivalent against it; and the problem accordingly remains. But despite the difficulties that arose for Paul personally, and despite his tendency to insist on his paternal rights over his converts, he evidently believed that his churches were equipped to deal adequately with such problems of discernment even apart from him.

The fundamental part of the necessary equipment is of course adherence to the Gospel, with the concomitant life in the Spirit. The essential question for the discernment of understanding is: What is in accordance with Christ? And unless those who undertake the discernment are themselves founded on the one true foundation, they cannot proceed. If they are well founded, however, they are in a position to discern independently of even Paul, as co-workers rather than subordinates (2 Cor 1:24). This is not a matter of the mind alone. To be accorded with Christ is to be given over into a great deal more than accurate thinking. The communities to which Paul wrote were not primarily academies, prepared to pan patiently through moraines of speculative opinions in search of nuggets of pure truth; they were living churches, bodies of Christ infused with the Spirit that guides life and illuminates the understanding. The discipline by which they are raised and matured in Christ therefore includes guidelines and regulations for behavior as well as for thinking and understanding; and their arriving at some Christian maturity requires a fidelity to the Gospel's way of life as well as its truth, conscience confirming consciousness.

Paul had no doubt that he was thus accorded with Christ, and believed that his converts could not go wrong if they imitated him and followed his instructions, just as he imitates and is submissive to Christ. Having provided his churches with his personal example and with "those ways which I teach everywhere, in every church" (1 Cor 4:17), he left them in a position to make the first steps toward authentic discernment.

First, they must remember. Their constitutional state is not one of isolated independence, but of coordinated inter-connectedness with the larger Christian world: "was it from you that the word of God went out? or was it to you alone that it came?" (1 Cor 14:36)—"for who distinguishes you? and what do you have that you didn't receive? and if you received, why do you boast as if you hadn't received?" (1 Cor 4:7). They may be organically Christian and in possession of all necessary faculties, but they were cloned into Christ through a movement of the Gospel which antedated them and which, taken globally, is more definitive of the lineaments of Christianity than they, at least until they reach maturity. The first act of Christian understanding is therefore to remember the Gospel into which they were reborn.

The second is to be faithful to it and to its ways. The Thessalonians are admonished to walk in accordance with what they received so that they may abound the more (1 Thess 4:1; cf. 2 Thess 2:15); the Philippians are told to recall what they learned and received, and what they saw and heard, and to act accordingly (Phil 4:9). Timothy is sent to Corinth as one faithful in the Lord "who will remind you about my ways in Christ, as I teach them everywhere and in every church" (1 Cor 4:17); and the Corinthians are commended "because you have remembered all the things from me and hold fast to the traditions as I delivered them to you" (1 Cor 11:2). The universality of this basic stratum that is to be remembered and obeyed is not confined to the Pauline churches alone: when Paul writes to the Romans, whom he himself has not taught and has not seen, he still writes "partly as reminding you" (Rom 15:15) of that one Gospel of Christ in which they, like Paul's own converts, were born into Christian life. This act of remembering is not a trivial exercise of piety but an important protection. It is apparently easier to lose track of oneself, in Paul's opinion, than his general air of optimistic confidence might suggest. There are some who are servants not of Christ but of their own belly, who by beguiling words deceive the hearts of simple people into things contrary to the teaching which they have received (Rom 16:17–18). A clear recollection can form the basis of a discernment that would discredit them. You are saved through the Gospel, says Paul to Corinth, "if you retain a certain word *(tini logō)* which I evangelized to you" (1 Cor 15:2)—whereupon he reminds them of the tradition which he had received and in turn passed on to them, and accordingly corrects their serious mistakes about the Christian understanding of resurrection.

To remember well is to recover with one's understanding that foundation in Christ on which all sound development depends, and also to embody it as far as possible in one's life. The habit of *doing* the truth is a way of remembering that is superior to mere recollection. Paul represents his principle not as a private idea of his own but as a basic assumption common to all churches. In this respect, the earliest Christianity to which Paul bears witness was radically "conservative," in the sense of cumulative preservation of its ways as well as the resulting restraint against novelty. What was inconsistent with that one Gospel that was the universal foundation of Christian life was *ipso facto* disqualified. But *progressive* conservative. What was consistent with the Gospel might eventually be revealed as flimsy hay or straw, but it also had a chance of being the genuine work of the Spirit—and for all his prudence and caution, Paul does not ask the churches to be timid but to grow, to abound, to become mature in thought.

How then to discern the more advanced communications of the Spirit? There is in fact the possibility of appealing beyond the potentially dangerous closed circle of those who claim the special gift of discernment. And here, once again, we return to Paul's understanding of the Spirit and to his principle of knowing them by their fruits. The

Spirit searches all the depths of God and knows his thoughts; it touches our spirits and fills them, and makes those thoughts partially accessible to our minds, transforming them in part to the mind of Christ. But Spirit is not simply mind any more than it is simply power. It is the source of the truest life. It is that which forms groups of men into bodies of Christ. Its characteristic manifestation is therefore not understanding, not prophecy, not exotic tongues, not even faith—but love.

Paul said some things about the freedom and power of the Spirit, and about the impossibility of subjecting it to human judgment, that could if taken in isolation completely undermine all the principles of stability within a Christian community eager to participate in spiritual gifts. What most decisively protects Paul's doctrine from such a result is his insistence that love is the key sign of the Spirit's work and presence. Though it may be theoretically possible to know all mysteries and all knowledge without love, it is an empty condition (1 Cor 13:2). Complementing and completing the other aspects of the Christian constitution as Paul understood it, this understanding of the Spirit gives in the direct experiential order the kind of stable coherence within and among Christian communities that is given in another order by Paul's understanding of the publicly coherent and orderly way in which God moves the Gospel through human history.

Repeatedly, Paul reminds his addressees of the importance of this principle as a canon of discernment.[19] Envy and strife are signs of a fleshly mind (1 Cor 3:3), and the party-promoters for both Paul and Apollos are therefore self-incriminating. Factions and sects are themselves among the works of the flesh, and are opposed to the work of the Spirit (Gal 5:17–21). Knowledge is valuable, but tends to puff up where not under the discipline of the love that builds—and the conviction that one has knowledge is misleading all by itself, whereas love *is* a sign of knowledge (1 Cor 8:1–3), and apparently tends to beget knowledge: writing to the Philippians, Paul prays that their love may abound in knowledge and discrimination so that they may examine the things that make a difference, in order to be sincere and inoffensive for the day of Christ (Phil 1:9–10). There could hardly be a clearer testimony to the supposition that love is the root of true Christian discernment.

The fact that Paul's letters abound with exhortations to unity and mutuality ought not to be discounted as a platitudinous touch of good will or a request not to rock the boat. The kind of mutual concern and unifying love which Paul promoted touches the very life of the Christian design. This is the sign of, and the way to, the deepest good health in the vivifying Spirit. And that too is the final justifying reason that Paul must demand loving respect from his children in Christ: anything less than this would be a betrayal of their own origins and their own unity.

For however free and powerful the Spirit may be to wrench the unbeliever into receptivity to the Christian good News, there is no
wrenching once his unbelief has been healed into "faith operating
through love," which is all that matters (Gal 5:6). From that point on,
the movement is gradual, tentative, a salvation not conquered or raided
but worked out with fear and trembling (Phil 2:12). Quarrels, factions,
disputings are suspect, symptomatic of an unreconstructed fleshly
mind. The burden of argument is evidently placed heavily on the dis-
senter to show cause that any alteration of understanding is in order;
and until the community in Christ perceives that such a change is for
the better, it is a message in an uninterpreted tongue. But the approved
will be made manifest through such divisions, and the manifestation is
undoubtedly through their comportment. What belongs to Christ can
be expected to show itself outwardly as worthy of the Gospel. Some
disagreement is therefore allowed, since it may lead to growth and
deepening, a progressive development of understanding about what
belongs to Christ; but no violence, no purges, no divisive reforms. The
proper Christian community strives to have the same disposition toward one another (Rom 15:5), to speak the same thing without divisions
(1 Cor 1:10), to think the same thing (2 Cor 13:11), indeed to be of one
spirit and one soul (Phil 1:27). That is the way that the mind of Christ,
already invested in the community through the Spirit, can come increasingly to be experienced and articulated in the minds of the members. If the community really lives in Christ, its mind will be capacious
enough to entertain and resolve inconsistencies in a manner that im-
proves its conformity with the mind of Christ.[20]

The discernment of the basic Gospel, I concluded some pages back,
was for Paul a grave necessity and methodologically a public possibility.
For the mind to be rightly accorded with the essential truths of the
Christian foundation was a matter of life and death; and although one
who is thoroughly alive in Christ may experience its revelation more
perfectly, its external groundings are adequate to demonstrate it to the
more imperfect or skeptical. The way of demonstration is inferior to the
immediacy of the Spirit, but sufficient. The concrete manifestations are
several and are mutually supportive: what Paul claimed to be the Gospel is consistent back through sound historical memory, it is consistent
across present universal preaching, it is consistent with (and shadowed
by) the scriptures, it is consistent with (and productive of) gracious
comportment when faithfully obeyed and lived. Just as the invisible
things of God may be adequately and bindingly inferred from visible
creation, so the essential law of Christian understanding is indelibly
imprinted in the world, and may be seen in the marks left by the
Gospel.

The discernment of what belongs to normative Christian understanding when one passes beyond the essential Gospel is neither so important nor so clear. But I believe that there is a way of translating his ultimate theological criterion of what truly belongs to Christ into a more practical one. The full content of Christian understanding cannot be determined in this world, but to a considerable and important extent it can be settled; and the means by which it is settled is *the sense of appropriateness generated in the cumulative self-consciousness of the community living out in loving mutuality its life in Christ.* It was not a logic, although logic clearly plays a part in the sorting-out of issues; it was not an ethic, although ethical criteria were clearly important in qualifying and disqualifying; it was not a technique of scriptural interpretation, or a conservative sense of history, or a loyalty to tradition, though all of these are involved. It was an art of discernment, which relied on a sense of appropriateness that was grounded in and disciplined by a way of life and a mutuality that valued all the considerations I have been discussing. To the Thessalonians Paul concludes: do not quench the Spirit; do not disregard prophecies; but test all things, and hold fast to the good (1 Thess 5:19–21). And that, I think, is it in a nutshell. Let the Spirit abound in its characteristic gifts, above all its gifts of love; be always ready for new direction, new understanding; but be very careful to discern with all the stabilizing equipment you have—and then, when you have come upon something that survives as worthy, appropriate, belonging to Christ, make it your own. This is the law of the mind of Christ.

2

Luke and the Synoptic Gospels

Matthew begins at once where the Promise began, and Mark plunges boldly *in medias res*. Luke might well have done similarly, and that he elected to do otherwise is a great and undeserved blessing for anyone who would inquire into early Christian understanding. The historian would have been grateful for any editorial aside whatsoever, no matter how unrepresentative—or even whimsical or idiosyncratic—its author may have shown his attitude to Christian knowledge to be. But Luke gives us a prologue that offers far more. He tells us what he is about; he anticipates explicitly the needs and interests of his reader; and he sets his efforts against the backdrop of similar undertakings that had gone before, even going so far as to indicate the ultimate sources of his material and the ultimate guarantee of its accuracy. One could hardly ask for more.

The bulk of chapters 2 and 3 will be dedicated to the pursuit of two lines of investigation. The first will examine the introductory remarks of Luke's Gospel in order to discover to what degree they imply some kind of theory of normative Christian understanding, either on the part of Luke himself or on the part of those others to whom he makes reference, and then will examine the Gospel itself, and the two other Gospels which stand in the same immediate tradition, in order to see the extent to which the theory or theories thus adumbrated are reflected within them, or refined, or qualified.[1] The second investigation will be of the Acts of the Apostles, to see whether Luke's reports of the early Church correspond in these respects to the foundations implied by the synoptic traditions and the Gospels formed from them.

Luke's prologue invites us to test his ideas thus, for it claims that his act of Gospel-writing is a *typical* response to the material gathered and transmitted by the earliest witnesses and ministers. He is doing what many have tried to do before him; and what he and they were attempting was a way of carrying on the work of the earliest agents of the word.

41

If Luke has done his intended job as well and accurately as he alleges, one might fairly expect that the content of his Gospel would reveal traces of just such an understanding of the ministry of the word and of proper responses to it as Luke himself professes—not due to any sort of editorial projection, but quite the reverse. Luke presents himself precisely as a typical (if editorially distinguished) representative of a tradition that variously includes apostles, early gospellers, and Theophilos' catechist. If his notions of normative understanding were well formed, they ought to have been learned from the very tradition that shaped and preserved the accurately transmitted material from which he now composes his Gospel. And if these notions are important, they can be expected to have been so firmly embedded in the synoptic material, before the writing of the Gospels, that they would necessarily be reflected in Matthew and Mark as well, in confirmation of Luke, witnessing to the earliest implicit or explicit sense of the constitution by which Christian thought is governed.

How seriously does Luke take the efforts of his "many predecessors" as narrators of significant deeds? He does not say whether he supposes that he is improving significantly on an often attempted task, or whether he is merely doing for himself what others have succeeded in doing before him—although it is at least clear that he takes his own effort to be worthy of the best of them. But it is especially important that Luke distinguishes his anonymous Gospel-writing predecessors from the fundamental material on which they were working. The many who tried their hands at narration addressed themselves to data which antedated and transcended their own witness and their own authority. They were making narratives *about* something, and that something consisted in fulfilled actions to which they had access only because they were handed down from those who were witnesses from the beginning and the earliest ministers of the word.

Luke's phraseology is greatly suggestive. In the first place, it suggests an important evaluative difference between those who compose narratives and those who are responsible for providing the indispensable material from which those narratives are built. The gospellers are left casually anonymous, with Luke standing, it seems, at least as their peer in authority and competence. But the witnesses, although unnamed in the prologue, are presumably those whose identity is to be disclosed in the course of the ensuing narration, which records who were in a position to be witnesses and earliest ministers of the word. It would follow that anyone who can appeal directly to their testimony can safely bypass the mediation of the other narrators whom Luke follows (and, presumably, exceeds) in careful accuracy—for Luke implies that the essential Gospel in some sense originated with these earliest ministers. He does not say that they were witnesses and reporters of deeds which became Gospel-stuff only at the hands of others' prophetic interpretation. He says that they were the original witnesses and ministers of the *word*—that is, that they are the founding fathers of true Christian understanding.

Luke's Gospel-writing predecessors seem to have thought it important to report the "fulfilled deeds" accurately. All have aspired to report the deeds just as *(kathōs)* they were transmitted by authoritative witnesses. This is one of Luke's more significant implications. In order to enhance the standing of his own composition, he might have concentrated on the relative inadequacy or inaccuracy of earlier attempts; but he does no such thing. Nor is there any need to read his emphasis on his own accuracy as an indirect invidious slight against his predecessors. He does not fault them or even claim that they are either less accurate or less complete. Indeed, what is especially striking about his introductory remarks in this regard is precisely their easy assumption that no such problem exists. The early witnesses and ministers are grouped together as an undifferentiated unit; the early narrators are grouped together as their faithful followers. Luke suggests that the basic material of Christian understanding has received wide publicity and is uniformly consistent: he leaves not the slightest ground for doubting that it is entirely uncontroversial within the Christian fold.

What are these "fulfilled deeds," this "word," and the "words" with which Theophilos was "catechized"? One implicit answer, more detailed than any other, may presumably be found in the Gospel of Luke itself. The introduction to Acts characterizes the Gospel in a capsulized way as "what Jesus did and taught" up to the time he was "taken up." This may be what Luke intends by "fulfilled deeds" and "the word," but it is not clear either that these two phrases are identical, or that the former has its scope restricted to the Gospel of Luke—for the introduction to the Gospel more probably had an eye on the "fulfilled deeds" of Acts as well as those of Jesus' pre-ascension career:[2] but more of this later.

What one may glean from Luke's introductory remarks, then, is essentially this: the word which Theophilos has heard about may be shown to be the more certain by the presentation of a narrative, consisting essentially in reported doings and teachings. The guarantee of the accuracy of this narrative resides in the fact that the earliest reporters and transmitters of it were themselves witnesses of that which they turned into message. Their testimony is then, perforce, the norm. And although they themselves are no longer directly accessible, their testimony is. Luke implies that it has had wide publicity, and that there has been no internal controversy about its content; for while the attempts at narrative may have been various, there is no hint of variation in the essential materials from which the narratives were composed, which is apparently the geological stratum in which the word as such is embedded. Therefore, the loss of the earliest authoritative witnesses is not a serious problem for determining normative Christian understanding. Their witness itself has been distilled and preserved and is evidently readily accessible.

As for the truth and importance of the authoritative word, Luke does not bother to point out what was apparently obvious to both author and audience. This word is the Christian specific difference. Christians are those who think it true and important; those who find it neither, may possibly be *for* Christians (if not against them), but are surely not *with* them. How the truth of this word might possibly be tested, for the sake of those who are not prepared simply to trust in its truth, is left somewhat obscure. To be sure, Luke assumes that Theophilos either will or should trust in his assiduous scholarship: herewith, the definitive edition, so that you may be fully satisfied. But although Luke thus commends his own work, his satisfaction with his accomplishment is not the key to his achievement with respect to Theophilos. He does not claim to have undertaken this task so that Theophilos may know "the most accurate version" of the things he has heard about, or "the most ample account" of them, but rather the *certainty*. The New Testament contains an exasperating number of words with slippery semantic ambiguities, but *asphaleia* is not one of them: firmness, reliability, certainty is what Luke's Gospel is to give to the objects of Theophilos' earlier reflection.[3]

It is significant, if unsurprising, that Luke shows a confidence in the truth of what the Christian tradition has passed down. It is both more surprising and more significant that he evidently believes that under proper and manageable circumstances, it can also be shown to be certain. How *certain?* Evidently, Luke believes that there will be something inherently convincing, something immediately persuasive, about a narrative of the deeds and teachings themselves, and the more accurately told the better. This supposition is not altogether unprecedented. It is a literary analogue of Paul's notions about the convincing power of the proclaimed word. For Paul, the word heard trustingly is its own proof of truth: it begets conviction far beyond the trust with which it is initially entertained. It is possible that for Luke, the Gospel story, when written out accurately and gracefully, likewise proves itself somehow upon the heart and inspires conviction. Once Theophilos has faced the written word fully, he will know that what it says is certainly so. The difference from Paul is that Luke supposes that the whole story itself —the matrix of wonders and fulfillments and achievements far beyond the bounds of probability, as well as the Word that was nurtured in and emanated from that matrix—will simply be too resonant with the ring of truth to be doubted, and too redolent of an assisting divine power not to induce in Theophilos the same theological conclusions as Luke himself draws. Luke's suppositions are tamer than Paul's: straight history, he implies, is quite adequate as a court of appeal to establish not only the true content but the true soundness of the words of *katēchēsis*.

For Luke even more than for Paul, then, there seems to be a convenient coincidence between the ways of inspiration and those of ordinary investigation: we may find out the truth by taking the testimony of witnesses, and this will turn out to be the most inspiring and revealing story as well as the best attested one. So far, Luke says nothing about the Holy Spirit or about Faith. If such agencies are involved, Providence has apparently synchronized them with responsible historical scholarship. If we do not yet know whether Theophilos was with us or merely not against us, I suggest that it is because it does not matter according to Luke's implicit sense of the constitution of Christian understanding. It merely determines whether Theophilos was to find the Gospel of Luke a deepening reminiscence or an important breakthrough. The believer and the unbeliever alike may have access to what the earliest witnesses handed down. Luke appears to suppose that an accurate recounting of it also gives them equal access to certainty.

It is not so easy to determine what its importance is to the standing of men before the presence of God. Luke does not claim that the words he is about to pen are salvation and life, or that the ignorant are doomed. Though stylistically solemn, his introduction does not make great claims for the intrinsic importance of conforming one's mind to the accurate representation he is about to impart. Yet it is clear that Luke takes for granted that at the heart of Christianity lies the word—not ritual piety, or special customs, or institutional order (though any or all of these may participate), but essentially a *logos* of which the earliest witnesses of Jesus' deeds were ministers. It is now necessary to confront more directly a problem which I have been skirting up to now: what does Luke take "the Word" to be, and what is its relationship to the "fulfilled deeds" that are to form the main fabric of his narration?

For it will not do to presume that what Luke means by "Gospel" is identical with his twenty-four chapters thus subsequently entitled. The title is ours, not his: he tells us not that he is going to write a Gospel, or even that he is going to record the Word, but only that he will narrate the fulfilled deeds as they were handed down by those first witnesses and ministers of the Word. That is, the deeds in question may, rather than being the substance of the Word, be only ancillary and supportive to a Word of another kind. The problem, then, is to determine what Luke means by the Word of the Gospel.

What does he seem to mean by it elsewhere in his writings? One key piece of evidence is to be found in what might be called the Second Gospel of Luke—the miniature synoptic Gospel preached by Peter in chapter 10 of Acts. Here Luke has represented for us an almost ideal test situation. One of the original witnesses and ministers of the Word is seen in the act of witnessing and ministering, with reference back to his experience of the things that Jesus did and taught from the beginning. Peter's performance in Caesarea should help considerably in defining what Luke supposed the earliest witnesses and ministers to believe about the relationship of the essential Gospel to the deeds they had witnessed, and the place of each in essential Christian understanding.

"You know the thing that happened throughout Judea," says Peter to his audience—just as Luke was later to address a Theophilos who had heard some words about such matters, and to try, as Peter is now trying, to take him a few steps further along its Way. "Jesus from Nazareth, how God anointed him with holy spirit and power—who went about doing good and healing all those suffering oppression under the devil, because God was with him" (10:38). The deeds of healing, the manifestations of power, are signs of anointing and divine favor. As such, they are important pieces of public evidence, which Peter implicitly acknowledges in establishing Luke's next link: "and we are witnesses of all the things he did in the region of Judah and Jerusalem" (39). The crucifixion and resurrection of Jesus, and the subsequent fellowship of the foreordained witnesses with him, are duly recorded. We have now come to the end of that story of fulfilled deeds that Luke has written out more fully in his first work for Theophilos, and we have virtually all the ingredients remarked in the prologue to it.

Having introduced the fulfilled deeds, the witnesses, and the missionary situation, Luke is now in a position to offer the clarification we need. What is the Word of which this Peter is a minister? How much of these fulfilled deeds belong to the message itself and how much merely constitute the credentials that support confidence in its authenticity? Luke leaves us rather in the dark about the Word as preached by Jesus, or even *whether* the Word as such was preached by Jesus; but with respect to those characterized elsewhere as "ministers of the word and witnesses from the beginning," Peter is fairly explicit. It is Jesus himself who instructs them about the content of their preaching, and in doing so he presumably defines for them the Word of which they are witnesses and ministers: "and he commanded us to proclaim to the people and to testify emphatically that he is the one chosen by God as judge of living and dead." The proclamation and witness enjoined on them contain not a word about the healings and miracles, not even about the crucifixion. They are to preach Jesus' election as judge. Is it possible that this election (which undoubtedly includes the resurrection as its mode and sign of occurrence—cf. Acts 2:32–36) constitutes the quintessential

Word? Not only possible, but probable, since the same conclusion is further strengthened by the corroboration of another major body of testimony. For what have the prophets been saying all along? "All the prophets bear witness to him, that every believer in him receives forgiveness of sins through his name" (43). The convergence of the prophetic tradition thus defined with the express briefing by the post-resurrection Jesus seems clearly to isolate the quintessential word, as Luke understands it from his knowledge of the earliest tradition, as the proclamation of God's having endowed Jesus with the power of determining whether we are to be saved or lost in the judgment.

Notice, however, that this already assumes an awareness of the judgment; and notice that Peter begins his background account with "you know the thing that happened . . ." (or perhaps, "you know the word that came about"—*humeis oidate to genomenon rhēma*, 10:37). He is not addressing beginners. He evidently assumes that they know about Jesus already. Except perhaps they are not aware of the last things there are to know: that after the presumably notorious curcifixion there was a less publicized resurrection, and that there has been an appointment to a foreordained judgeship, along with a power to secure forgiveness of sins for believers. This is the quintessential Word. It is not necessarily all of the essential word. Both *logos* in 36 and *rhēma* in 37 are vexingly ambiguous. Both might, but neither need, point to the Gospel that Jesus himself preached publicly, and whose previously undisclosed capstone Peter is about to deliver to his God-fearing audience. At any rate, in answer to Cornelius' announcement that they are all gathered "to hear all the things that have been commissioned to you by God" (10:33), Peter gives a sketch of the whole story, from John the Baptist onward.

Here it would not be wrong, I believe, to remember that Peter had at least two stages of this commission. He is now acting especially on the one he received after the resurrection, to preach the forgiveness and judgment that are to come through Jesus the Messiah. But this does not necessarily abrogate—and is obviously compatible with—the commission he had received earlier, to preach to others the news of the kingdom that Jesus had been preaching and teaching in the synagogues and among the crowds of Galilee.

Those who were witnesses and ministers of the Word from the first: we are left with three interlocking possibilities. The same cast of characters can be described as ministering witnesses of the resurrection-ascension and of the teaching that took place in between; or as early witnesses of Jesus' preaching and among the first to share in its ministration; or as witnesses of his career from the beginning, and the first to grasp and proclaim its revelational significance. Which sense of "word" divides the indispensable from the dispensable?

Luke reports some fulfilled deeds that are part of the quintessential Gospel itself: Jesus is now entered into his glory, and forgiveness of sins is now available through his name (24:26, 47–51). But most of what he records has to do with one of the other orders: either pertaining to the preaching before the crucifixion, or pertaining to the career of Jesus as either agent or object of a "word." In the former two cases, the term "Word" may obviously be readily applied, though in different senses of perfection. But even in the latter case, "Word" is not entirely inapt, although in a curious sense. For these deeds are in part mere context, and in part the fruits by which we know and come to have confidence in Jesus: but they are also the seeds from which the ultimate Word must grow, since the full Gospel is dependent on Jesus' election to a position for which only a certain career can make him eligible. That career itself reveals God's plan, as well as making its fulfillment possible. In short, it is artificial to impose rigorous lines of demarcation: the deeds participate variously in the value and meaning of the ultimate Word, and Luke's proper response is to tell the whole story. Although he might have been hesitant to entitle the work he is introducing "the Gospel According to Luke," he evidently understands it to be at least the unfolding of the Word up to the emergence of the ultimate Gospel.

Luke's sense of the way the Word unfolded comes through in the historical schema that underpins his narrative. It manifests his sense of the historical structuring of Christian thought, and concomitantly his sense of the constitution of authentic Christian understanding. It runs essentially like this:

1. A projected fulfillment of the promise to Abraham has been consistently reaffirmed by the prophets all along. Zacharias' capsule version is representative of Luke's view: "just as he said through the mouth of the holy ones, his prophets from the age," God offers "a salvation from our enemies and from the hand of all those hating us, to perform mercy with our fathers and to remember his holy covenant and oath which he swore to Abraham our father—to allow us, without fear, rescued from the hand of our enemies, to worship him in holiness and righteousness in his presence all our days" (1:69–75). Those who have rightly grasped the prophets' assurance that it would be fulfilled may not know all that the scriptures really meant about God's plan, but they are generally expectant of some such deliverance. Simeon is not only "just and pious" but also "waiting expectantly *(prosdechomenos)* for the consolation of Israel" (2:25); Anna has a ready audience for her observations, in the form of "all those waiting expectantly *(prosdechomenois)* for deliverance *(lutrōsin)* in Jerusalem" (2:38). It is probable that a similar general anticipation of a happy ending is what is intended in describing those around John the Baptist with the phrase "and the people being in expectation" *(prosdokōntes de tou laou,* 3:15). For convenience, I shall

call this first level of the Word the Expectation.

2. The major breakthrough that makes this expectation more urgent and specific is the News of the imminent consummation, and its first agent is John the Baptist. "The Law and the Prophets were until John: from then on, the kingdom of God is proclaimed" (16:16).[4] "Proclaimed" here is of course the same verb *(euaggelizetai)* that Luke uses to sum up the over-all preaching of John the Baptist: "and so, exhorting also many other things, he preached the good news [*euēggelizeto*] to the people" (3:18).[5] The basic content is the news of the imminent end and the possibility of rescue, and those who accepted it moved from general expectation to a specific hope. John's preaching is double-pronged: he proclaims the imminent judgment, and exhorts the need for repentance (especially in conjunction with his baptism of water) to make one ready for it. It is in these ways that he is said to "prepare for the Lord a ready people" (1:17), to "go before the Lord to prepare his ways," and to "give his people knowledge of salvation in forgiveness of their sins" (1:76–77). With John, the Expectation is revivified and particularized in specific News.

3. In the public ministry of the unfolding Word, the next stage of further specification is the preaching of Jesus, and its specific difference from John's message turns on the technical phrase "the kingdom of God." To be sure, Luke has left us the one hint in 16:16 that this phrase may also be used to characterize John's proclamation, as is done by Matthew; but for the most part (as I shall further particularize presently), he arranges things so as to emphasize Jesus' independence of John and the new dimension present in his preaching. Unlike Matthew, Luke (except in 16:16, and there probably inadvertently) does not use the term "kingdom of God" in conjunction with John, but makes it persistently the keynote of the proclamation of Jesus. Jesus has been sent "to proclaim the good news [*euaggelisasthai*] . . . of the kingdom of God" (4:43), and travels through every city and village "announcing and proclaiming the good news [*kērussōn kai euaggelizomenos*] of the kingdom of God" (8:1); he sends the Twelve "to announce [*kērussein*] the kingdom of God," and they accordingly "travelled through the villages, proclaiming the good news [*euaggelizomenoi*]" (9:2, 6). The seventy are likewise instructed simply to say "the kingdom of God has come upon you" (10:9). This good news of the kingdom which Jesus was sent to proclaim, and in turn sent his followers to proclaim, may also be called "the word of God," which is the way it is put when the crowd comes to hear him at Lake Gennesaret (5:1). Accordingly, when Jesus explicates the parable of the sower, he explains that "the seed is the word of God," and that the seed by the roadside describes the fate of those from whose hearts the devil takes the word away "so that they may not, as believers, be saved"; while the seed on the rock represents

those who receive the word with joy but only "for a time believe," then fall away (8:11–13). That is, the key issue is not in *doing* the word of God (as might be the case if it were applied to commandments and other practical matters), but in *believing* it—viz., believing in the good news of the kingdom, in the reliability of the now specific Expectation whose resolution is imminent. This is more than John's News, although the specific difference is hidden behind the mysterious term "kingdom." Those who respond have a still more particular trust and expectation: thus Joseph of Arimathea is one "who waited expectantly [*prosedecheto*] for the kingdom of God" (23:51). This gospel is not yet the Gospel, the final and full version of the Word; but it can be called gospel—especially since the unbelievers in it are in serious jeopardy.

4. The next great public breakthrough in consolidating and specifying the good news of the kingdom does not come until after the resurrection of Jesus. To be sure, there have been suspicions that he was to have a prominent place in its realization, as there had been in the case of John the Baptist. Cleopas and his companion, evidently members of a relatively inner circle of disciples (for they heard the report of "our women" and identify the tomb-visitors as "some of those with us"— 24:22, 24), hoped that Jesus was the one who was going to redeem Israel (24:21). But despite the demonic confessions, the Petrine insights, and the veiled hints that were not grasped until much later, this part of the news remained secret. Less publicly, a few were let in on it. The angel Gabriel tells Mary that Jesus is to reign eternally on David's throne (1:32–33); and Mary's belief is confirmed by Elizabeth, who proclaims her blessed for believing that there will be fulfillment to the things told her from the Lord (1:45)—adding her own recognition that Mary may be called "the mother of my Lord" (1:43). The shepherds are given the good news *(euaggelizomai)* that the child born in Bethlehem is saviour and Messiah, and apparently pass the news on to those around the manger (2:10–11, 17–18). Simeon, assured by the Holy Spirit that he would see the Messiah before he died, recognizes and acknowledges that the child Jesus is he, the salvation of Israel and the light of revelation of the Gentiles (2:26–32). But despite his prophetic response, Simeon's understanding apparently went to the grave with him; and despite Mary's belief, she kept these things in her heart (2:19, 51). All the rest wondered at such claims, and had no effect on the development of public understanding of Jesus' personal relationship to the gospel of the kingdom—nor even any discernible effect on private understandings, to judge from Mary's puzzlement after the young Jesus explained his truancy in the temple (2:40–50). The disappointment of Cleopas and his colleagues was not to be relieved until the proper exposition of the scriptures demonstrated that the recent events were not frustrations but genuine and necessary fulfillments (24:25–27, 44–46). And with that

good news came the definitive Gospel, the news of the next, still un-fulfilled, stage: in the name of the Messiah, Jesus, repentance and for-giveness of sins are available and are to be preached in all the nations, beginning from Jerusalem (24:47). This is the most advanced stage of the Word, and what Luke seems to mean by the Gospel.

Luke offers, therefore, four basic strata in the disclosure of the Word.[6] The first, already realized before the mission of John, is the eschatologi-cal understanding of the promise to Abraham. Luke implies that it was a rather exceptional one—but he does not offer any explanation con-cerning how some came to accept it and others did not. Given his over-all scheme, he need not linger on this point. The expectant are privileged, but there is no indication that the others are seriously disad-vantaged; and things are about to be equalized anyway, by the new phenomenon of John, whose general invitation to believe in the good News of forgiveness of sins in preparation for imminent judgment will render obsolete the vaguer state of Expectation which it is intended to perfect and replace.

John's preaching, the vehicle of Luke's second stratum of the Word, was according to a directive from heaven (3:2). It is evident that the tradition from which Luke learned, believed unhesitatingly that this was so, even to the extent of treating John's prophetic doings and teachings as virtually equivalent to Scripture. Hence John's mysterious utterance about the one who will come after him, baptizing with the Holy Spirit (3:16), is echoed repeatedly as a revelational landmark: we find reference to it in a Baptist enquiry about where Jesus might fit into this established scheme of things (7:19-20); in Luke's version of Paul's words, first in Pisidian Antioch (Acts 13:24-25) and subsequently in Ephesus (Acts 19:4); and even in Jesus' last instructions before the ascen-sion (Acts 1:5, cf. 11:16). And as for the central phenomenon of John's public ministry, the baptism of repentance which he preached and administered along with the rest of his News, Luke records not only that Jesus' hearers had received John's baptism (7:29) but that "the Pharisees and the lawyers rejected the purposes of God for themselves, having not been baptized by him" (7:30). These are strong words, importantly definitive of one article of orthodoxy in early Christian circles, and they are echoed again, almost as explicitly, in the small catechism which Jesus later puts to the high priests, scribes, and elders: Was John's bap-tism from heaven or from men? (20:4). They obviously did not believe it was from heaven, for, as they rightly observe, it would then be impos-sible to account for their not having received it. But here it is not merely a question of getting them to admit that they had not perceived its heavenly origin, and had therefore not done heaven's will and submit-ted to it: they perceive now that its heavenly origin is an article of faith so important to the sons of the kingdom that they will endanger their lives if they deny it (20:6). They beg off with the prudent strategy of agnosticism. That may save them from being stoned, but it saves them in no other way. Their failure to believe in John (or possibly in the baptism) in itself marks them as outsiders, as not with us even if not necessarily against us—and as rejecters of God's purposes.

Here is a test case of potentially vast importance for divining the early Christian notion of normative understanding. What criterion of discernment operates here to distinguish the right-minded orthodoxy of the Baptist believers from the reprobate unbelief of the religious elite? Alas, John was too strong a presence in the earliest Christian sense of God's plans, and Luke does not bother—as very likely the tradition which he received did not bother—to preach this axiomatic point to the converted. Apparently, it is the sheer impact of John, experienced as self-evidently prophetic. There are no claims of signs and wonders, no attesting voice from heaven, no transfiguration. His place was axiomatic, but not quite central enough for the tradition to dwell on his role sufficiently to reveal how one actually became convinced. We are probably to conclude (and practically, we have no option but to conclude) that he, like other prophets before him, presented the sign of Jonah only; and that those who had ears to hear, heard. Either one recognizes the expression of the will of heaven, or one remains outside. And it is of course quite pointed that in chapter 20 the same formula can be immediately applied to the case of belief in Jesus. Those who were uncertain or doubtful about the authority invested in John must remain just as uninformed about the authority of Jesus—and evidently, for the same reason. If they had been unable to grasp the meaning of John, they were self-revealed and self-condemned among the hard-hearted and unreachable. As Abraham points out in the parable a few chapters earlier, if they do not hear Moses and the prophets, they will not be persuaded even if one should rise from the dead (16:31). The Son of Man will be to this generation, just as John was, as Jonah to the Ninevites (11:30).

Authority is not quite the same as authorization. The inquirers were apparently asking about the latter, unable to bypass it by a more direct insight. Jesus' point, which could be grasped by his followers because they had already responded to John himself, was that authority transcends authorization and obviates the need for credentials. Some perceived that John spoke with authority, and some were scandalized. If you have to ask, you have already missed the point.

This is, I think, the basic lesson of the relatively stark confrontation of chapter 20. Elsewhere in the Third Gospel, it is supplemented by other criteria for validating John and his baptism. The infancy material contains the signs and wonders that are missing later, and indeed even the voice from heaven making John the object of a gospel—for Gabriel's heavenly assurance of the greatness that John will have before the Lord, his fullness of holy spirit, his success in turning Israel to the Lord, are all described in summary with "I was sent to speak with you and proclaim to you this good news [*euaggelisasthai*]" (1:19).[7] For those who were not in on this early heavenly attestation, there is still the independent confirmation given John by the way in which he can be seen as a fulfillment of prophecy—the voice crying in the wilderness (3:4), the messenger sent to prepare the way (7:27), one whose baptism of forgiveness and announcement of the coming rescue advance the completion of the promises made to Abraham (1:70ff.).

There is one other criterion implicit in the witness borne to John by Gabriel, by Zacharias, even by the soldiers and tax-collectors who came to his baptism. "He will turn many of the sons of Israel to the Lord God," Gabriel assured his father, ". . . and disobedient ones in the wisdom of the righteous, to prepare for the Lord a ready people" (1:16–17). Zacharias subsequently echoes the prediction in a sudden burst of holy spirit: "you shall go before the Lord to prepare his ways, to give a knowledge of salvation to his people in forgiveness of their sins" (1:76–77). Whatever the secret workings of the invisible order or the reserved plans of God, there was no question about the visible results: whores and collaborators and members of the occupation forces were turning to God, thirsting after righteousness, and getting a sweet taste of experienced forgiveness by which they might know something real about salvation. When they turned to John for comfort, he demanded from them behavioral fruit worthy of genuine repentance; when they asked what they should do, justice and charity were demanded of them (3:8–14). Every tree not bearing good fruit was to be destroyed. John's influence visibly multiplied the crop of good fruit in some of the most unlikely soil.

Luke does not follow the fortunes of John's disciples independently of Jesus far enough to tell us any more than that they were accustomed to frequent fasting and prayer, that they had learned from John to pray, and that they may have had some difficulty seeing where Jesus fit into the scenario of the final days as given by their master (5:33, 11:1, 7:18–20). That is enough to suggest what we learn also from other indications, viz., that John's word was allowed to rule not only forms of religious observance and ethics, but also thoughts about God's way of dealing with the future. In the episode of the Baptist's question (7:18ff.), the figure of the Coming One, *ho erchomenos*, is apparently taken for granted as a given in adequate eschatological thinking, an implicit item in Baptist orthodoxy. But it is not tested by controversy or explored by curiosity, and we are accordingly left unable to guess more than that what John proclaimed was probably taken for gospel, literally. We are not let in on how John's followers resolved disagreements about his words, or new questions, or deeper versions of the old ones. Except, of course, in the case of one particular species of Baptist disciples: those who were absorbed into the movement surrounding Jesus. And this brings us into Luke's third revelational stratum, whither we must proceed if we are to find any further insight into the rules that must have obtained in the second one.

For Luke is rather cagy about measuring Jesus against John. He includes more Baptist material than the other evangelists, and is clearer than they are about establishing that the good News begins with John. But he writes as if guided by a corrective or guarded intention, as if at pains to leave it clear that Jesus is not to be thought of as an agent of John's work. Matthew and Mark place the vision of the Holy Spirit as dove and the voice from heaven in immediate connection with Jesus' baptism by John; Luke reports that these occurred after Jesus' baptism, while he was praying—John, unmentioned, seems to be quietly left out of the entire scene, which is placed just after Luke records his imprisonment. Matthew and Mark explicitly connect the beginning of Jesus' public ministry with the imprisonment of John, and characterize his message in ways that make it clearly reminiscent of John's—Matthew even going so far as to have Jesus repeat *verbatim* what he has already quoted as the essential message of John. Luke, by contrast, introduces the ministry of Jesus without reference to John, and characterizes it in terms not of the proclamation of the eschatological judgment but through a more elusive general reference to his teaching in the synagogues, thus sidestepping all reminiscence of John. Matthew and Mark record that John identified the eschatological *ho erchomenos* as both mightier than himself, *ischuroteros mou,* but also as "following me," *opisō mou:* when Luke accepts the former epithet but does not mention the potentially awkward *opisō mou,* which could suggest that Jesus was John's disciple, we may fairly suspect that this is not an instance of a Lucan non-interpolation but an editorially purposeful omission. It is probably significant in a similar way that Luke's introduction to the Lord's Prayer makes it Jesus' independent alternative to the way in which the Baptist had taught his disciples to pray, while Matthew recognizes no such occasion for this event and therefore does not confer a similar emphasis upon the independence of Jesus and his group.

Because of this tendency in Luke, we should not expect to find as clear an indication of Baptist orthodoxy within his work as we might have done had he been motivated only by his recognition that John was the beginning of the final phase of the Word's disclosure. There is strong reason for believing that the original followers of Jesus and the original post-resurrection converts were substantially, and perhaps almost exclusively, drawn from the ranks of Baptist followers and fellow-travell-ers. Aside from the curious case of the Ebionites, it appears that the Christian movement uniformly appropriated John as the initiator of the last great revival, and the forerunner of Jesus: Christian theology could be accommodated within the basic framework, and even the specific categories, of Baptist expectation. There was no need to waver on points of Baptist thought-law such as the forgiveness of sins, the coming terror, the eschatological harvest of the just, the need for righteousness. It appears that the Christians simply assumed Baptist doctrine, and subsumed it within their own. The latter was more complete and more interesting to them, and the early writers do not bother to discriminate between what was new within the Christian dispensation and what was Baptist inheritance (and, unfortunately, there survives no early record of a clash between Christians and unconvinced Baptists that might establish the line of demarcation). This is true of Luke above all: for despite allowing John the credit—which seems to have been universally granted anyway—of initiating the Gospel movement, Luke would be the last of the synoptic evangelists to want to emphasize that this truth or that one is unoriginal with Jesus and a precious inheritance from John.

Thus it seems probable that in spite of Luke's deliberate, if not stud-ied, attempt to represent the beginnings of Jesus' ministry as an original and perhaps new departure in the development of the Word and its revelation, the bulk of his evidence is best read as suggesting that the main outlines of the gospel Jesus preached were probably anticipated by, and certainly consonant with, that of John. For many in Israel, that conformity to John would have been the first foundation of Jesus' credi-bility. But it is also clear that there would have been many for whom consonance with John was not an important consideration, for whom Jesus gave the first introduction to the gospel of the kingdom. Not all Galileans had made the pilgrimage to John's baptism. There is no sub-stantial indication that the prophetic authority of John was any part of Jesus' message to the synagogue and crowds of his early evangelizing, although it is imaginable that if it had been, it might have been diplo-matically suppressed in Luke's reporting. The general impression is rather that he proclaimed his gospel directly, as an agent of the Word itself rather than of John. He came into Galilee, says Luke, in the power of the spirit, and in his teaching was glorified by all (4:14–15): "they were astonished at his teaching, for his word was authoritative" (4:32).

The pattern by which Jesus' authority made its impression seems to have been like that of John, with just enough difference to secure that distance between them upon which Luke insists. The more dramatic testimonies of angels and prophets surrounding Jesus' birth had appar-ently disappeared, like John's, into thickly veiled memory. He does not seem to have been readily recognizable from scriptural prophecy; the identifiable correspondences are no more, and no more specific, than the little that was claimed for John. Even the transfiguration was left both private and confusing to its three witnesses. Luke thus manifests a strong thematic tendency to have Jesus offer to the public—and even to the main body of his closest followers—only the sign of Jonah, which was presumably enough for those who had ears to hear (11:29–32). John himself might well have been able to understand and accept this, and even without the cures of the blind, the lame, the lepers, the deaf, and the dead, might have thought it sufficient evidence to be reminded that "the poor are given the good news, and blessed is he who is not scandalized in me" (7:18–23).[8] That some were indeed scandalized was not in itself a scandal to those who were not, but merely one of the facts of revelational life which John himself demonstrated by being a sign of contradiction who finished the way all prophets do. The Pharisees and scribes murmured when "all the tax-collectors and sinners drew near to hear him" (15:1–2), but those who had learned the lesson of good fruits from either John or Jesus knew that this disapproval was only further evidence of his authenticity, however deviant from traditional scribal norms. There is thus a firm ring of plausibility when Jesus pauses at prayer to inquire through his followers about the character of the impact he is making, and is told that some take him to be John the Baptist, others Elijah, others one of the prophets of old come back (9:18–19). This much was said of John as well, and so was the conclusion reached by those closest to Jesus, that he was the Messiah (9:20; cf. 3:15). At this third level of the Word's disclosure, this is sufficient. The Word still has precedence over its bearers.

Nevertheless, there *were* the cures of the blind, the lame, the lepers, the deaf, the dead, and these were something new on the evangelical scene, without precedent in the work of John. Even if some could attribute these to the power of Beelzebub, and others could not regard them as a real sign but required a clearer indication of heaven's approval (11:15–16), the less skeptical saw in them clear support to Jesus' implicit and explicit claims to authority, a practical manifestation of the power that guaranteed his teaching (4:36; cf. 4:32). Furthermore, there were the miracles of the loaves, and the stilling of the tempest, and (for all its short-term inefficacy) the transfiguration. The Sign of Jonah is enough, Luke seems to imply, but it is not all there was. Jesus is, at this third stage of the Word's unfolding, manifested like John, but significantly advanced beyond him. The way is prepared for a later stage, where Jesus will be part of the *content* of the Word.

Luke implies that there were original twists in Jesus' gospel in which he differed from John, as his less abstemious life-style and his non-baptizing and healing mission did—the *erchomenos* of John was, to

Jesus, "the Son of Man," *ho huios tou anthrōpou,* and it is possible that "the kingdom of God" was (as Luke seems to try to imply) not a term used by John. The difference in their recorded relationship to the practice of fasting and prayer suggests also that some of Jesus' ancillary teaching about the preparation for the kingdom might well have been unanticipated by John. But the main lines of the gospel were undoubtedly congruent between them, if not identical; and while the followers of Jesus did not need to appeal to John to validate the authority of Jesus' Jonah-sign, and undoubtedly took Jesus' version of the gospel as the more definitive, the basic means for determining the proper norms of sound gospel-thought are very much the same in Luke's second and third strata of revelation: conform your understanding to what the evidently authoritative prophet teaches.

For all of Luke's attention to the celestial spectacular surrounding the conception and birth of Jesus, he is obviously much taken with that quieter and more profound form of revelation that occurs when the bearer of the Truth meets the right-minded heart. This is for him not only the characteristic (even if not altogether exclusive) mode of discovery at the second and third stages of the Word, but even a real possibility for the fourth and highest stage. For that, I take it, is the essential meaning of the event, which he alone reports, in which the Good Thief was able to acknowledge not merely the righteousness or prophetic authenticity of Jesus but even his title to the kingdom with which he was being mocked, in spite of the most discouragingly disconvincing circumstances and the absence of any affirmative claim on Jesus' part (23:42). Nevertheless, the highest and most complete realization is not, for Luke, characteristically a function of spiritual discernment alone. It might well have been. The scandal of the cross need not necessarily have been more disruptive to the confidence of Jesus' followers than it was to the Good Thief: after all, John and the prophets before him had likewise been unjustly killed, and yet popular rumor was ready enough to stand by their authenticity and postulate for them a resumed career post-mortem in the form of Jesus' ministry (9:7–8, 18–19). Once the followers of Jesus had recovered from their initial disappointment, it was not out of the question for them to argue that the crucified Jesus would soon be raised to come in glory and judgment as the Son of Man, and that those who were properly tuned in to the right spiritual wavelengths would see that this was so, while the others are, alas, judged already. Once they were themselves sure that he had already been raised, they might have insisted that his present lordship communicates instant intuitive conviction to all those who think about it, if they are really fit to be sons of God. With the stages of the Word's revelation (or at least the last three stages) apparently reaching progressively smaller groups of responsive hearts, some such quasi-gnostic refuge must have seemed not only convenient but fairly logical.[9] But the fact is that Luke's representation of the actual behavior of those guiding the constitution of Christian understanding at this, its highest reach, shows just the opposite tendency: there is a deliberate effort to define the truth by reference to grounding evidences that are less esoteric than ever.

In the first place, Luke establishes Jesus' eligibility for such lordship via the most literal sort of resurrection, reserves the grasp of his lordship by even his most devoted and trusting followers until they accepted this literal resurrection, and endows them with the thickest incredulity until they are provided with the most incontestably palpable evidence. When Peter heard that the women found the tomb empty, and were encountered by two in shining garments who not only told them that Jesus was risen but also reminded them that he himself had told them that this was the way it was to be, it might have inspired some confidence, or at least a vigorous hope; "but their words appeared to them like an idle tale, and they disbelieved them" (24:11). Even after Peter had confirmed with his own eyes the empty tomb and discarded cerements, he went no farther than to wonder what has happened (24:12). The initial post-resurrection appearance that convinced him is not described; but even after he has managed to persuade his fellows that the reported resurrection has indeed occurred, the next appearance frightens them as the apparition of a ghost, until their own hands and eyes and the sharing of a meal resolve their doubtful hearts (24:36–43). No hint of spiritual intuition here: one of the most unreasonably skeptical juries ever assembled is simply overwhelmed by the weight of vulgar proof. Short of repeating such demonstrations endlessly to each new candidate for belief, this establishment of the fact of Jesus' resurrection against the grain of disposition might well be taken as definitive of a new law of Christian thought, proved beyond reasonable doubt at the basest level of *l'homme moyen sensuel*, requiring no special equipment or illuminated discernment but only a circumstantial occasion which the brethern ought not to have required and did not deserve and which need not be repeated to others.

Resurrection itself does not establish lordship, and need not even be considered technically necessary as a condition. Given the way that the earlier form of the Word had been established at the second and third stages of its disclosure, it might now have been enough for the witnesses to claim that Jesus, obviously all the more to be credited in his present resurrected condition, merely assured them that he was ascending the messianic throne and ordered the proclamation of forgiveness through his name. But although such a procedure might have been quite sufficient for the formation of early Christian understanding, the appeal to assent is instead once more grounded on more public testimony. This is no special mystery revealed for the first time. In a way, it is not really news at all. A proper understanding of the scriptures shows that this has been God's revealed plan all along for the career of the Messiah: "thus it is written, that the Messiah had to suffer thus and rise from the dead in the third day, and have repentance and forgiveness of sins proclaimed in his name to all the nations" (24:46–47). The fullness of the good News, the outlines of the fourth and final stage of the Word, could theoretically have been found in Moses and the prophets and the psalms long ago, even in the days of stage one. What Jesus has been doing, far from causing consternation, should have been seen as a systematic fulfillment of the plan God had laid out publicly long before.

To recognize this, of course, it was now necessary for Jesus to "open their mind to understand the scriptures" (24:45). It would be possible to suspect that this expression constitutes a revelational wild card, and represents some gift of mystical intuition by which the now-fulfilled events and the future mission might be seen shadowed in material that yields no such thing to the unilluminated eye. But that Luke is not taking refuge in this gnostic loophole any more than in the other, is evidenced by the parallel story of the conversation en route to Emmaus. There Jesus meets the discouragement of Cleopas and his companion not with an invitation to initiation into mysterious ways of reading, but with a flat scolding for being dimwits and slow to believe in their hearts what the prophets have said (24:25). Not "understandably unable to see what the prophets were *really* saying," but reluctant to believe what was there, and unintelligent about it too. The initial apostolic response to public scriptural evidence is put on the same plane as the initial apostolic response to the evidences of the resurrection. Only the most outrageous reluctance could continue to cherish doubts about the latter with all that had happened; only the most insensitive and unbelieving reader/hearer could fail to see that, according to scripture, "it was required that the Messiah suffer, and enter into his glory" (24:26).[10] According to Luke's report, Jesus does not leave even that rebuke to be taken on faith (and indeed he could scarcely do so on his own authority, since he was still an unrecognized stranger to them) but demonstrates the validity of what might have seemed a gratuitous and unjustified insult by explaining "in all the scriptures the things about himself" (24:27)—evidently to their satisfaction, for their hearts burned as he did so, presumably with the excitement of insightful realization.

The argument based on the explicit claim of the risen Jesus, independently supported in its plausibility by an intelligent and trusting exposition of all the scriptures from Moses to David to the last of the prophets, does not need further support from coordinate teachings of John. Those, one may fairly suspect, were by this time already recognized to be supported by the scriptures, at least in their general outlines, and the present revelation undoubtedly appeared to confirm them independently as well as particularize and advance them. But in addition to the palpable proof of the resurrection itself, further ancillary confirmation is offered through appeal to the disciples' own memories. The angels at the tomb remind the women that Jesus had already pointed out that the crucifixion and resurrection of the Son of Man was part of the heavenly agenda, whereupon "they remembered his words" (24:8); and Jesus himself tells the assembled disciples that the lessons he is now opening their minds to understand from Scripture "are the words which I spoke to you when I was still with you" (24:44). Evidently, the publicity of these advance predictions and explanations was not restricted to the Twelve: those who ought to remember them include the women, Cleopas and his companion, and not only the Eleven in Jerusalem but an unspecified group of "those with them" (24:33). Luke, who does not restrict the earlier explication of the parable of the sower to the Twelve aside but seems to have it addressed to a whole crowd of disciples (8:1–21), apparently suggests that the fuller version of the Word was substantially implied and predicted not only in the scriptures but in the open teaching of Jesus' public ministry. Despite the dull inability of the disciples to see it at the time, the fourth flowering of the Word may now retrospectively be perceived to have been virtually contained within the third: and the third was the fulfillment of the second, just as the second was the realization of the first—and all of them stood prophetically anticipated in the scriptures, simply waiting to be discerned, or at least to be recognized as they were duly enacted in the fullness of time.[11]

I am not proposing this tidy view as a critically authenticated exposition of the way it really happened, for that is not to my purpose even if it were demonstrable. I am interested only in manifesting Luke's version of how, and with what connections, and with what possibilities of verification, the truth was made available and came to light.[12] His story, told so that Theophilos might know the certitude of the words he had heard, has implications concerning the constitution of Christian understanding, implications that are all the more important for discerning the nature and trajectory of earliest Christian normative thought insofar as Luke claims that his is a normative version of that widely distributed story. He will, of course, have more to say about the constituting of post-ascension Christian understanding when he writes Acts: but it is useful to pause here, at the emergence of the full flowering of the basic Gospel, to see what Luke's instruction suggests about how one may come to know—indeed, to know with certitude—God's deeds and plans, and what kind of difference it may make.

In the first place, although Luke occasionally manifests a fairly tolerant attitude toward sturdy forms of pre-gospel piety, it nevertheless is clear that acceptance of the Word makes the difference between life and death. He hints this for even John's level of the Word's disclosure (7:30), and makes it quite explicit at the next stage. In the parable of the sower, the seed that falls by the roadside represents those who hear, but subsequently suffer the misfortune of having the devil take the word out of their hearts. So say all three synoptic versions. Luke alone adds "so that they may not believe and be saved" (8:12). The emphasis on belief is significant; its linkage with salvation is even more so.[13] It is also Luke alone who has Jesus send forth the Seventy to preach the gospel of the kingdom, with the comment: "he who hears you, hears me; and he who rejects you rejects me—but he who rejects me rejects the one who sends me" (10:16). Rejection of the gospel, even when preached by an apostolic missionary rather than by Jesus himself, is a rejection of God. With that once said, it is scarcely necessary to suggest the consequences: "whoever is ashamed of me and of my words, of him will the Son of Man be ashamed when he comes in his glory, and in that of the Father and of the holy angels" (9:26). His words are more enduring than heaven and earth (21:33), and those who do not keep them in their hearts, believing, might as well have been citizens of Sodom. Mere opacity is no excuse: Jerusalem will be shattered simply for not knowing the day of its visitation (19:44). Cumulatively, then, it is clear that those whose understandings are not ruled by the gospel of Jesus are doomed. The converse shows the gospel just as decisive: "whoever has confidence in me before men, the Son of Man will also have confidence in him before the angels of God" (12:8). If the word is heard and kept faithfully in a good heart, it will bring forth the fruit by which men are saved; but accepting the gospel of Jesus and his kingdom may even be enough itself, for the Good Thief is saved on the basis of that fruit alone (23:39–43).[14] A confident right understanding is not Luke's only preoccupation, of course. He warns us repeatedly about repentance, about works of righteousness, about love of God and neighbor. But he also issues a clear warning about the decisive importance of conforming one's mind to the true understanding of God's plan as revealed in the gospel of Jesus.

The plan is more completely and perfectly disclosed in the next and culminating revelation, which shows Jesus' true role in the kingdom he had preached. It is here that God's wisdom is made fully manifest to men; it is here that the scripturally anticipated arrangements are completed; it is here that the hidden secrets of Jesus' preaching are brought to light and the scandals of his career justly resolved. Whatever the salvific importance of earlier stages of the Word's unfolding, it is the understanding available at this final stage that finally determines the norm of thought for the way of salvation. It may therefore be said for

Luke, as for Paul, without an especially drastic shift of meanings, that the norm is the wisdom of God expressed in the career of Christ. And to determine what belongs to the Christ-wisdom, one may turn to public evidence. True, the most experienced and most carefully instructed expounders of it are those who had both the privilege of close association with the teaching of Jesus before the crucifixion and the rarer privilege of direct association with his more explicit teaching after the resurrection. They are therefore in the best position to define its content once Jesus himself will no longer intervene directly. But their privilege does not include exclusive access to the wisdom of Christ, because this is independently available in two converging ways.

One is Jesus' public preaching and teaching: for in addition to the clear and widely experienced main lines of the gospel of the kingdom delivered by him to congregations and throngs throughout the land, appreciable numbers of his followers heard also anticipated touches of the ultimate Word—those basic details of his personal role that were yet to be acted out. To rediscover their access to the then partly hidden purposes of God, they had only to search their own memories carefully and intelligently.

On the other hand, yet more publicly accessible, there were the scriptures, from first to last filled with news of the Messiah's scandalous and glorious career—themselves the wisdom of Christ writ large by ancient prophecy under divine inspiration, albeit in a hand which the dull-minded, not looking consistently for the Messiah, might not readily decipher.

Christ himself, his specially instructed apostles, his public utterances, the scriptures, all coincided as alternative manifestations of the ultimate Word of God, the Word of Christ. That large convergence is what guarantees Theophilos' access to certitude about the words he had heard. That, with one addition: those who have undertaken to narrate the deeds fulfilled among us offer one more manifestation of the ultimate Word by recording the fulfillments themselves, the ways in which the penultimate stage of God's plan was concretized and completed, thus making the Messiah ready for his final role. Such a work, rightly understood, reveals the divine Christ-wisdom more directly to the newcomer, and makes it unnecessary for him to have further confirmation from hearing Jesus' preaching, exploring the memories of his hearers, interviewing the special witnesses, working out the right exposition of Scripture. It renders these supererogatory because it honors them all faithfully in presenting, via the reliable testimony of those who best represented them all, the fulfilled deeds which were the locus of their convergence, the events in which the mind of Christ both enacted and became coincidental with the mind of God.[15]

Such is the theory of providentially guided thought-law underlying and reflected in Luke's Gospel. It is consistent with the claims of his prefatory remarks. Those who witnessed the publication of the Word in its second stage by Jesus, and who witnessed in Jesus the fulfillment of events in the messianic career that made the fourth stage possible, were also ministers of the last two stages of the Word, first under the direction of the pre-crucifixion Jesus and then under the instruction of the risen messiah.[16] The testimony which, as the risen Lord had reminded them, they were in a position to give (24:48) virtually or explicitly manifested a revelation of God's mind in some four different ways. Conforming one's mind to this revelation makes salvation possible; conforming one's life perseveringly to such an understanding rooted in a good and virtuous heart brings forth the fruit that makes salvation assured (8:15). It may therefore be thought profitable to examine the received tradition carefully, knowing that the testimony of the most complete and privileged witnesses will bear confirming comparison with the prophetic intent of Scripture and with the recollections of the many less privileged witnesses, and thus to establish both its true content and its reliability. And this once done, it is most appropriate to present that potentially fruitful testimony to one who has heard some distilled version of the Word, and most appropriate that he should find in such a presentation grounds for conviction of its certain truth.

One may wish that Luke had been even more thorough. If only he had supposed his audience much more deeply skeptical, he might have supported his theory more satisfyingly by reproducing the content of the exegesis given on the road to Emmaus and in the room in Jerusalem, rather than merely reporting that a thorough explication was given and that it was quite enough to satisfy the skepticism of those hearers. Or he might have detailed the remarks made by the pre-crucifixion Jesus to the effect that he was to fulfill prophecies concerning him in the Law, the Prophets, and the Psalms, rather than settling for the report that Jesus subsequently reminded the assembled witnesses that he had said such things. But then, Luke never claimed to be writing an exhaustive treatment of the subject. He claimed only to be writing enough to establish the conviction of his dedicatee, Theophilos. And if it seems that Theophilos' standards of scientific skepticism were not up to modern snuff, there is one thing that one should remember in addition to the inappropriate anachronism of using such a standard of judgment. That is that Luke did not postulate that his work was all that Theophilos had. He writes only as a sound and accomplished representative of a tradition that transcends both his authority and his account. He consistently points beyond himself, implicitly offering his reader other courts of appeal if his curiosity or dull-heartedness should induce him to ask for more ample demonstrations. Luke does not claim to present everything that the Christian movement has remembered from the first foundation of the Word, but only that that memory is his source, and that the things it has especially cherished are his object. And in defining his procedure in that way, he has given a court of appeal not only to Theophilos but to us: for we have access to at least two other independent efforts to record that memory's heritage, drawing from the same general stock of tradition and thus permitting a test of Luke's implicit claim that his theory of the constitution governing Christian understanding is indeed none of his invention but part of the bequest of earliest Christian conviction.

There are, among the synoptists, some differences in the revelational scheme; but I believe them to be essentially reconcilable with the one which Luke proposes. Mark, for instance, begins abruptly with John the Baptist, and does not bother to glance back to observe a state of Expectation before him. But since John is seen as a fulfillment of prophecy (1:2–3), it is virtually certain that Mark would acknowledge the reality and functional importance of Luke's first stage, the eschatological understanding of the promise to Israel. Luke's second stage, John's News, is somewhat muted in Mark but there is no question about either its importance or its novelty. Neither is there any doubt about its command over understanding. John not only baptizes but also *proclaims* a baptism of repentance (1:4), to which is added news about the coming one who will baptize in holy spirit (1:7–8). Mark's witness to the popular belief that John was a prophet (11:32) is also further amplified by the curious vignette in which John not only reproves Herod but subsequently makes him his pupil (6:18–20). Thus although Mark's treatment tends to diminish notice of John and heighten the representation of Jesus, he nevertheless offers us enough to allow a reconstruction, even from his material alone, of a stage of mind-formative News. No essential feature of Luke's picture at this stratum is without its corresponding Marcan evidence.

The softer treatment of John permits Mark to give a greater emphasis to the novelty of Jesus' gospel. But the significant difference from Luke lies in the degree to which the final stage of the Word is anticipated during the preliminary preaching of the gospel of the kingdom. Symptomatically, Luke's reservation of *euaggelion* to the fourth level of revelation is not followed by Mark, who uses the term for the title of his own work, for the characterization of the first preaching of Jesus (1:14–15), and for the characterization of the future preaching of the apostles (13:10). But of what is this symptomatic? Not, I submit, of Mark's having conceived his work as a sort of visualization of the basic kerygma, but of a confusion and inconsistency in Mark's handling of traditional terms and ideas. One may, indeed, read *euaggelion* in 1:15 as if it referred to the ultimate kerygma—but that is quite against the grain. Nothing in the text invites such a projection; everything points to Luke's third stage, Jesus' gospel of the kingdom. On the other hand, the instance in 13:10 is just as clearly pointing to Luke's fourth and final version of the Word. And as for Mark's title verse, I think that—especially in view of 14:9, particularly with an eye to those MSS. which read *touto*—by far the most plausible interpretation is that the word here carries essentially its eventual *Gattung* freight: the account of the teachings and doings of Jesus Christ, Son of God.

Mark is less careful than Luke about observing boundaries. But he acknowledges them all the same, even though somewhat inconsistently. Luke allows for partial news leaks of the final Gospel even during the third stage of the Word, but reserves all effectual understanding (and the fullest disclosure) until after the resurrection. Mark shows that he too acknowledges that the Gospel was, and was not, disclosed during the period of the gospel of the kingdom, but he (rather more implausibly) handles this more strictly according to a division between exoteric and esoteric teaching, with the latter sometimes characterized as the gospel of the kingdom (which for Luke is consistently public) and sometimes as the fuller Gospel message, and with the disciples sometimes understanding (which Luke does not grant to the hints of the ultimate Word) and sometimes being quite obtuse. In short, Mark witnesses to a tradition that included all the basic elements of Luke's sense of stages, but presents them in a more disorderly form that would invite Luke's reconstruction even on the basis of Mark's text alone, simply as a way of making more coherent and plausible sense of the Marcan tradition than Mark himself manages to accomplish. Once this is recognized, and the necessary allowances made, it is possible to see that the tradition which Mark bears is fully coherent with the Lucan interpretation, even if Mark's own management of it presses it in different interpretative directions. But does this then mean that Mark's editorial work manifests an importantly different understanding of how it was, such as to undermine any generalization about a common understanding among those involved in the synoptic tradition? I think not. Mark's re-organization is in fact to be explained precisely on the basis of his emphatic application of one of the four complementary principles in the constitution of Christian understanding: the full Gospel was somehow present in the pre-crucifixion teachings of Jesus. Luke's own handling of the predictions of the passion and resurrection (to which I shall turn shortly) shows that he knew this principle but had no comfortably intelligible way of representing its historical manifestation. Mark has a similar problem and tries to resolve it differently. His resolution has the disadvantages of being inconsistently applied, and of making the obscurity of the final Gospel's prolepsis depend in part on a rather arbitrary and unfair exclusion on the part of Jesus; but these disadvantages do not remove him from what I take to be the tradition's sense of the basic constitution, but merely permit us to wonder temporarily about the justice of Jesus' implementation of it (and then, when we have got past presuming that Mark has not tampered with the Jesus he received, to wonder permanently about Mark's own sense of justice). His handling of the tradition is theologically unpleasant, but it does not obscure either the basic suppositions of the tradition itself nor his acceptance of them.

Matthew offers little more than Mark by way of an elaboration on the time of the Expectation, even though he treats of the birth and infancy of Jesus; but like Mark, he witnesses to the reception of John as the fulfiller of eschatological expectation (3:3). If his failure to link the child Jesus with any promise but the conventional messianic one indicates that Luke may have elaborated on a more perfunctory early Christian sense of stage one, it matters little: Luke too sees that the appearance of John renders the first stage obsolete, however it may have shadowed the second.

If Mark's John falls somewhat short of the revelational significance accorded to him by Luke, Matthew's John goes well beyond. John proclaims the news of the approach of the kingdom (3:2), so explicitly that the first preaching of Jesus, though formulated by Matthew as "the gospel of the kingdom" (4:23), is given an abbreviated representation that echoes *verbatim* the preaching of John (4:17). Matthew, in short, emphatically reinforces the impression given by Luke that John preached a News that at least bordered on and may have anticipated the explicit gospel of the kingdom.

Luke's tendency is to suggest that Jesus originated the gospel of the kingdom; Matthew does not follow this (and of course there are hints in Luke that Matthew is here more accurate), but shares with Luke, and with Mark, the assumption that whether or not he was the first to mention it, Jesus was nevertheless *the* prophet of the kingdom par excellence. Despite the bold notice given to John at the beginning, Matthew neglects him almost altogether once Jesus' ministry begins. And if the initial preaching formula of Jesus had been fully anticipated by John, nothing in John's ministry remotely approaches the bolder claims made by Matthew's Jesus concerning his own fulfilling work (5:17–18). And that is, of course, more important than the simple question of John's anticipation.

Matthew does not differ significantly from Luke in his representation of the proper type and grounds of response at the second and third levels of the Word. He does share with Mark, however, a tendency to anticipate the final Gospel more explicitly within the pre-crucifixion teachings of Jesus—though without imposing on this anticipation so much of either Mark's arbitrary esotericism or his occasional failure to distinguish the gospel of the kingdom from the Gospel of Jesus Christ.

In general, I find that even after the differences have been appreciated, the schema which I have induced from Luke remains fully coherent with the material presented by Mark and Matthew, and with their independent management of it. The differences between them are not substantive, and can be accounted for as differently weighted applications of the same body of assumptions about the unfolding of the Word and about the corresponding formation of normative understanding.

Luke's synoptic colleagues, in short, offer some solid support for what he claims he learned from the tradition. I do not mean merely that they share with him descriptions of many of the same fulfilled deeds and offer similar versions of the other events and teachings, or even that they show similar assumptions about the unfolding of true understanding. I am pointing rather to ways in which they illustrate more clearly than he himself does some of the important aspects of his implicit theory.

Luke, for instance, alleges but does not adequately exemplify the scriptural anticipation of Jesus' career—let alone Jesus' pre-crucifixion application of scriptural prophesy to the events of his own life. Matthew is of course notorious for the number of instances in which he correlates Scripture with incidents in the life of Jesus, and clearly confirms Luke's suggestion that general tradition is likely to manifest this as a typical assumption and procedure in earliest Christian thinking. Both Matthew and Mark likewise have Jesus say explicitly that his arrest is taking place "so that the scriptures may be fulfilled" (Mt 26:56; Mk 14:49), thus bearing witness more overtly to a significant feature of tradition's recollection which Luke claims but does not so clearly support. Even Jesus' general unconventional uses of Scripture in support of his teachings, an implicit prerequisite to Luke's theories, comes clearer in Matthew and Mark: they, unlike Luke, supply Jesus' scripturally based criticism of the Pharisaic teachings (Mt 15:1–19; Mk 7:1–13). Even more dramatically, it is they, and not Luke, who report Jesus' bold claim that the Sadducees have not merely reasoned wrongly but simply "do not know the scriptures" (Mt 22:29; Mk 12:24)—not to mention the even more audacious claim that Moses only compromised with hard-heartedness in allowing divorce, and should be corrected in practice by a return to more ancient ways (Mt 19:3–9; Mk 10:2–12). On the whole, Luke's allegation that earliest Christianity followed Jesus in supporting even the more scandalous features of the Gospel in detail by appealing to a sometimes unconventional but sounder reading of Scripture, is not only echoed by the other synoptic evangelists but better evidenced by them than by Luke himself. If Theophilos, or Luke's other readers, had suspected that Luke was fudging in what he had said about the availability of scriptural support, or its employment by Jesus before the crucifixion, Matthew and Mark make it seem probable that they would have been reassured by a more direct appeal to the tradition of the eyewitnesses and first ministers of the Word. Which is, of course, just what Luke himself implies.

The case is similar with Jesus' pre-crucifixion predictions of the events to come. Luke's women remember retrospectively the predictions of the passion and resurrection (24:6–8), and his other witnesses are reminded of them later by Jesus himself (24:44). Still, the earlier representations of the predictions themselves do not establish confidence. There is no indication that the first prediction was heard at all, for there is, rather implausibly, no reaction or response (9:22). The second prediction meets the grossest incomprehension: "but they did not understand this remark, and it was concealed from them so that they might not perceive it; and they were afraid to ask him about this statement" (9:45), while the third prediction is no more successful in illuminating their minds: "and they understood none of these things; and this matter was concealed from them, and they did not know what was being said" (18:34). By contrast, the other synoptic accounts more unambiguously give the auditors something to remember later: Mark assures us in the first instance that "this statement was made quite plainly" (8:32), and both he and Matthew substantiate its clarity by reporting Peter's vigorous objection to the inappropriateness of such a fate (Mt 16:22; Mk 8:32). Mark represents that they did not understand the second prediction and were afraid to ask about it (9:32), but does not suggest quite so deep an uncomprehension as Luke—while Matthew, who reports their grief upon hearing it, obviously credits them with understanding. And as for the third prediction, far from concluding in Lucan inarticulate bafflement, the Matthean and Marcan versions have it occasion the dispute about whether the sons of Zebedee may have privileged positions in Jesus' subsequent place of Glory! (Mt 20:18–21; Mk 10:33–37). Thus the disciples have indeed grasped something of the Gospel's future in the other two synoptists, far more than Luke explicitly endows them with for their later recollections; and shortly thereafter, Matthew and Mark (again, unlike Luke) have Jesus also provide his followers with the further piece of information that before the end, the Gospel must first be preached to all the nations (Mt 24:14; Mk 13:10). Thus once again, Luke reports post-resurrection claims by Jesus that seem to be belied by an appeal to his antecedent evidence; but if some Lucan Theophilos should turn suspiciously to the tradition, he would apparently discover that according to it, these claims were much more justly earned than Luke himself establishes. Evidently Luke had understood tradition rather more satisfactorily than he had reported it.

Matthew and Mark are not less supportive of Luke in the other main vectors of his implicit theory. Jesus' post-resurrection claim to Lordship is yet more explicit in Matthew than in Luke: "all authority in heaven and on earth has been given to me" (28:18). Mark's final placement of Jesus at the right hand of God is in the narrator's voice rather than said by Jesus, but its easy confidence makes it obvious that this is a foregone conclusion that does not need reiteration by Jesus: as I have already observed, it is not a new realization here in Mark's scheme of things but had been unquestioningly assumed by the sons of Zebedee well before (10:37), and thus has no less post-resurrection reconfirmation in Mark's Gospel for not being expressly announced by Jesus.[17] The supplied ending of Mark handles similarly the reconfirmation of the mission to evangelize the world in the discipleship of Jesus. The text could scarcely be firmer: "having gone forth into the entire world, proclaim the good news to all creation" (16:15), and Matthew's parallel formula is equivalent: "having gone forth, proselytize all the nations" (28:19). In fact, all of the elements of the basic structure given by Luke to the constitution governing Christian understanding are replicated in each of the other synoptic redactions of the traditional "fulfilled deeds" material passed down from the early witnesses.[18]

Just as they confirm Luke's theory concerning where the true Word has been made available to human understanding, so the other synoptists confirm his sense of the importance of conforming one's understanding to it. Mark's John the Baptist preaches only a baptism of repentance for the forgiveness of sins (1:4), but the first preaching of his Jesus commands not only repentance but that one also "believe in the good news" (1:15)—and Jesus' last remarks reveal starkly what is at stake: "proclaim the good news to all creation: he who believes and is baptized shall be saved, but he who does not believe shall be condemned" (16:16).[19] His version of Jesus' explanation of the reason for parabolic teaching implies that those who do not understand the mystery of the kingdom will not have their sins forgiven (4:11–12).[20] The indispensably prerequisite understanding is, at least that stage of the Word's unfolding, given only by election and explanation; but it is the fulcrum on which the difference is made between salvation and damnation.

Matthew's parallel account likewise draws a line between those who have, to whom are given the secrets of the kingdom, and those from whom this privilege is withheld, who do not have, and from whom all will be taken away (13:11–12; cf. 25:29–30). If the latter should understand, they would repent and be healed (13:13–15); but since they do not, they are lost. Though more oblique than Mark, Matthew attests to the ominous consequences of failing to confess a faith in Jesus: whoever acknowledges him before men will be acknowledged by him before the Father (10:32). On the occasion of the centurion's expression of faith, Jesus admits that Israel has not responded so well, and warns that others will take the place of the sons of the kingdom, who will go to perdition (8:10–12). "Understanding" is admittedly not Matthew's primary theological category. His visions of judgment (7:22–23, 25:31–46) concentrate on the division not between believers and unbelievers or between those who have grasped the Word and those who have not, but between two species of believers and understanders: those who have lived out the Word according to Jesus' precepts and those who have failed to do so. Those whose opacity or hard-heartedness kept them from knowing the truth in the first place are simply ignored. But it nevertheless appears that Matthew presumes a grasp of the Word as prerequisite to salvation. In his version of the parable of the sower, unlike the explanations given in Mark and Luke, the key disqualification of these imaged in the seed by the roadside is that they hear the Word of the kingdom but do not understand, and therefore the Word is easily rendered ineffectual; the key difference in the seed on good ground is that the Word is not only heard, but understood: this is what makes it possible to bear the fruit by which salvation comes (13:19, 23). By their fruits you shall know them, and by their fruits they will be judged; but for Matthew, no less than for Mark and Luke, the fruits in question are those that grow from the seed of the Word rightly understood.

The future orientation of this last metaphor is of the essence, and deserves extra stress in the light of Luke's apparent past-orientedness in his key reference to "fulfilled deeds." I say *apparent* past-orientedness, because a more systematic look at his Gospel suggests that Luke is fully aware that the dynamic of the Word is forward, not backward.

For Luke is interested in the problem of revelation, and in what may be called the basic pattern of gospel—viz., the process of proclamation and acceptance of a wonderful, if implausible, good News. He explores this pattern briefly in several instances of its appearance within the over-all fulfilled deeds of his main story, and the implications are instructive.

The first full instance is that of the gospel of Gabriel, which, although part of the story of John the Baptist, is really concentrated on a point that is quite independent of the significance of John himself. The point resides rather in the conflict between Zacharias' own hope and doubt. Not that he has any reason to hope that Elizabeth's shame will be removed by the birth of a child: we are assured both that she is sterile and that they are both advanced in years. The situation seems clearly beyond hope. Yet when Gabriel appears, he sets his gospel (he was delegated, he says *euaggelisasthai soi tauta*) in the context of the answer to Zacharias' prayer. Evidently, despite the apparent closure of the question, Zacharias has not given up on the possibility of appealing his case. Yet when he is told that his sustained hope is to be rewarded, he fails to transform it into belief. And so, as a combination of confirming sign and rebuking punishment for his doubt, his tongue is sealed.

Zacharias' fault is specific. He is not in general a man to be punished: on the contrary, he is just and has walked in all the commandments and regulations of the Lord. But he has not believed in the gospel proclaimed by the apostle Gabriel *(apestalēn . . .)*. The angel has spoken words which shall be fulfilled in their due season. Zacharias is evidently obliged to recognize that this is the case, and to see that his speculative hope has more truth than his practical incredulity. Gabriel's message defines an orthodoxy to which Zacharias is expected to conform his understanding, and his failure to do so is a significant and punishable blunder.

How, in this case, should Zacharias have known what to believe? Luke seems to take it for granted that we will know that the angel has spoken the truth, and that Zacharias therefore ought not to have been hesitant to accept it. This is, after all, a piece of literary craft, not a psychological study. But to the extent that Luke works with Zacharias' response, he is presumably conditioning his treatment by his non-literary sense of moral truth. Luke seems to suppose that the circumstances of this announcement are sufficient to guarantee its reliability: Gabriel does not identify himself until after Zacharias has expressed his disbelief, but the latter's fear has disclosed that he saw more than mere impudence in the appearance of this stranger by the altar. Abraham was indulged when he greeted a similar announcement with a laugh, even though it was made by the Lord himself. But in these more severe times, such assurances are not to be trifled with. Evidently, it was Zacharias' responsibility to recognize that this was an authoritative message, and that the only appropriate response was assent.

The lesson is reinforced by the succeeding *exemplum*, where Mary humbly accepts the angelic announcement (although it is not easy to see a moral reason why her momentary confusion and puzzlement are received so much more accommodatingly than Zacharias' doubt). Elizabeth subsequently drives the point home: Mary is blessed because she has believed that what the Lord has told her would be fulfilled. To accept and believe in an authoritatively promised deed is blessed, while even to waver substantially is a fault. The key is apparently in the recognition of authority. And that authority is ultimately God's. As in the case of John's baptism, the fundamental issue is whether this is from heaven or not. If so, the only proper response is belief. And how is one to tell whether it is from heaven? Angelic authority is evidently the external clue in these cases, but not the only one. In both instances, it is apparently accompanied by a corresponding internal sign—the fear to which the angel responds reassuringly. Similarly, the angel inspires a holy fear in the shepherds to whom he proclaims the gospel *(euaggelizomai)* of Jesus' birth—although this time the more spectacular mode of appearance makes the fear more inevitable—and reassures them. Once again, the gospel in question comes with clear authority and is evidently believed—the interest of the shepherds in confirming the sign promised by the angel is apparently inspired not by skepticism but by a cooperative acceptance of heaven's implicit will that they should become witnesses as well as believers. When the shepherds have paid the visit hinted at by the angel, they praise God because everything they saw and heard was just as they had been told it would be. Their gospel, like the Gospel of Luke, is based on deeds that have been accomplished among us, themselves being now enlisted among the original witnesses and ministers of the word.

Although they were not, in a sense, surprised to find the angels' words accomplished in Bethlehem, the shepherds were nevertheless amazed, smitten with the wonder that appropriately rises to the beholding of great deeds. A similar response can be found in Simon on the occasion of one of Luke's most interesting gospel-patterns, at the beginning of chapter 5. Here almost everything has changed but the pattern itself. The good news is not the birth of a saviour, but a catch of fish. Its proclaimer is not an angel who immediately inspires fear, but a man who has been teaching a crowd from a boat. The fear comes after the promise is fulfilled, when it has become evident that this is a man of God, with whom it might be dangerous to mix. But the bare gospel-structure remains. An improbable event is asserted by someone, with the kind of authority that permits the assertion to be accepted despite its apparent doubtfulness. The fishermen's night's toil is ample evidence that there is no point in throwing their net in again—but on his word, they will do it. This is not mere obedience to command, but acceptance of authoritative assurance: if you say so, then there must be a catch there to be netted after all. It is perhaps significant that they had not, even in their belief, anticipated that it would be an extraordinarily large catch—that is, the literary devices may stand for their discovery that the recognized authority turns out to be itself of extraordinary dimensions. But their realization had to wait for the realized event, the accomplished deed. The initial act of faith had far less to go on. What criteria did Peter have to appeal to in order to found his acceptance of this implausible gospel? Apparently, it was neither more nor less than the personal experience of this man teaching the crowds. Evidently, he had spoken with authority, and not as the fishermen.

The pattern appears once more in the case of the blind man along the Jericho road, though this time the proclamation in question is not an explicit test of assent but an implicit capacity—an inverted proclamation, in effect, in which it is the blind man rather than Jesus who proposes the good News. He has already not only recognized Jesus' authority to make such a bold claim as that his sight will be restored, but has believed in advance that if the promise should be made, it will be honored. The pattern of the little gospel has here shifted one more step: the good News is neither to induce nor to confirm faith, but to reward a faith that anticipated it. This story is shared with the other synoptic Gospels; Luke echoes it in another key with his unique representation of the Good Thief, who perceives not only Jesus' innocence but—despite his silence—the rightness of the claim thrust upon him: this is the king of the Jews, *ho basileus tōn Ioudaiōn houtos.* Although it is not explicitly said that it is his faith that renders him eligible to share in Jesus' kingdom, there can hardly be any question that this is the point. The Gospel preached out of spite by the mockers becomes the occasion for the thief to see and believe its implausible truth, evidently through the authoritative, however scandalously vulnerable, presence of Jesus. This is (and probably deliberately) the most extreme example of Luke's little gospels. Even though proposed as a joke by the incredulous, the good News rings true enough in the presence of Jesus to awaken a faith that was not even asked for—but saves just as surely.

Luke's "little gospels" presumably came, at least for the most part, from the general tradition from which he ostensibly formed his understanding of the rules governing Christian thought. Their coherence with the larger lessons of that tradition is substantial. The little gospels consistently imply that there are indeed understandings that make a crucial difference, and that they are communicated to us in such a way that those who are rightly tuned in will recognize the authority of the persons who proclaim them. Those who have ears to hear will recognize their authority, and those who recognize their authority will accept what they give in assurance, and those who so accept will be rewarded —while those who fail will be punished. Gospel is characteristically the news of intent rather than of accomplishment, and to respond is to grasp the future, not the past.

Luke's little gospels are not only illustrations of pattern: they are credentials for the larger Gospel. Each moves far enough into the realm of accomplishment to awaken further confidence in the greater and still unaccomplished reaches of the associated promises. And that is how, finally, one must understand Luke's sense of fulfilled deeds. Enough has been accomplished to permit us to accept the larger form, the greater promise, and the reliability of the future it presents. The Gospel of Luke is itself a little gospel offered in support of the fuller Gospel whose lineaments are to be found not merely in Acts, but all round. Theophilos is, after all, being finally invited to return to the words of his *katēchē-sis,* and to the Way and greater expectation to which they pointed. If he can discern promises with a proper spiritual eye, he will know the importance of this one. And if he takes Luke at his word, what may he know of the content of this promise?

If Theophilos should go rooting about in the tradition from which the synoptic evangelists drew up their narratives, I conclude that there are some important lines of consensus that would emerge with respect to the question of normative Christian understanding. He would discover that it is consistently urged that God's plans for men are to be perfected in a heavenly kingdom, and that the main object of God's Word to man is to prepare him for eligibility to enter that kingdom. The conditions of eligibility include that one conform one's understanding to what God's Word announces, for otherwise one has implicitly rejected God and failed in required obedience. The fullest form of God's announcement has now been revealed through Jesus the Messiah and through those appointed by him to spread the News, and from now on it is necessary to found one's understanding, and through it one's life, on that fullest form, the Gospel. Where can the understanding appeal, so that it might be rightly formed in the way of salvation? *The pattern of right understanding that is the ultimate wisdom of God for men may be found in the scriptures, properly read; or or in the pre-crucifixion teachings of Jesus of Nazareth, properly grasped; or in the post-resurrection teachings of Jesus the Messiah; or in a discerning appreciation of the career of Jesus up through the time of his taking-up; and these four manifest one and the same messianic saving plan and the Word of God, with respect to which we can either submit in trust and be saved, or withhold ourselves and die.* And further *all of these are immediately accessible, or accessible through reliable witness, to ordinary human capacities.*

Such is the early Christian theory of how right understanding is constituted and sanctioned, as it is embedded in the tradition from which the synoptic evangelists wrote.

Ideally, the complementarity and relative independence of these manifestations of the Gospel might be able to establish a clear and stable common denominator that could stand as the basic law of Christian understanding. But to raise the question of ideal coherence is to confront one important remaining theoretical inadequacy in that way of formulating the normative courts of appeal. There are too many wild cards: Scripture "properly" read, Jesus' teachings "properly" grasped, "discerning appreciation." Unless there is a norm within the norm, also accessible to human capacities, these providential arrangements are hollow and useless. And there is such an ultimate norm, which can be readily perceived if one backs up enough to see the whole arrangement within the over-all theological frame which the synoptists generally take for granted.

It was universally recognized among the earliest Christians, and among the groups to which they had belonged before the Gospel, that the ultimate locus of the norm of understanding is the mind of God, who —despite his finally impenetrable ineffability—graciously makes available to men as much as they really need to know. He has ordained a plan of salvation from before the ages, revealed it in inspired Scripture, unfolded it in human history, and now wills that men understand and accept and cooperate with his way of going about it. It was also generally granted that his way of communicating his intentions to men, and thus establishing norms of understanding, was through his Spirit— hence the unanswerable clincher which Jesus gives to his argument about the Messiah's origins: listen to what David says "in the [holy] spirit" (Mt 22:43; Mk 12:36: "holy" in Mk only). The descent of the spirit upon Jesus at the brink of his public ministry (Mt 3:16; Mk 1:10; Lk 3:22) is thus, among other things, the transaction that theologically establishes his authority and validates his subsequent pronouncements as authentic revelation. The inspired proclaimer makes manifest the mind of God. The most perfect realization on earth of this manifestation now becomes the mind of Christ—the mind that could unfold in post-resurrection appearances the veiled meanings of God's mind as expressed in Scripture, the mind that instructed men about God's will both before the crucifixion and after the resurrection, the mind that accepted and enacted the most scandalous part of the divine plan when no other could perceive its appropriateness. *The mind of Christ is the locus of coincidence of the components that make up the constitutional theory behind the synoptic Gospels,* and the entire thrust of the synoptic tradition may be characterized as the record of attempts *to bring the minds of men into conformity with the mind of Christ, so that they might obediently echo the mind of God and be wise with the highest wisdom available to men, and thus be able to live the life of well-rooted and fruitful seed.*

The synoptic tradition seems to imply that this was achieved, at least for a limited circle of believers, after the resurrection. Finally learning not to think merely humanly but rather to submit to thinking in the ways of God as revealed through the mind of Christ (Mt 16:23; Mk 8:33), the early witnesses were in a position not only to report significant matters but to understand more or less with the mind of Christ, and thus to act as effective surrogates for his understanding once he had been taken up. Now, if they might perdure in this condition, *caeteris paribus,* there would be a lifetime guarantee for a virtually perfect Christian understanding; and if they could communicate effectively to others the transformation into the mind of Christ which they themselves had undergone, there need be no waffling or uncertainty in the laws of Christian thought all the way to the parousia, whenever it might arrive. Thus if Theophilos should note that the Gospel of Luke only records a tantalizing sample of the deeds, the teaching, the scriptural interpretation, and the post-resurrection disclosures through which the Christ-wisdom was manifested to men, he need not feel anxious about its not being an omnicapable repository of all the riches of Christian understanding. It points to the stabilizing principles that transcend it.

If he has followed Luke's hint, and gone to the other records of the tradition, Theophilos will be reassured about the basic reliability of Luke's version of the constitution of Christian thought-law; but he will also have discovered something demoralizing. From the synoptic tradition itself, he can perceive that the received state of the tradition does not appear to be symptomatic of unqualified success in the transmission of the exact mind of Christ. The other two texts are as inadequate as Luke's to deliver the decisive and unequivocal Christ-wise answer to any question that may need asking. All three offer the general principles clearly enough, but when one presses closer toward a particular, they begin to look a little like the pillars on which Seth—or was it Shem? —had engraved the priceless knowledge infused in Adam before the Fall, unable to surrender their secrets.

Unless Theophilos himself possesses the mind of Christ, he cannot make it alone. If he were to set about attempting to master the proper reading of Scripture, for instance, how shall he proceed? Is every interpretation that is inflected toward a foreshadowing of Jesus of Nazareth, crucified, risen, and glorified, quite sound? As he turns the scrolls of the Law and the Prophets, he might well decide that this is a tricky business. Just where are the right texts to demonstrate that it was required that the Messiah be raised from the dead? And what shall he do if, when casting about for the proof that he had to be crucified, he stumbles upon Moses' solemn assurance that "cursed by God is everyone hanged upon a tree" (Deut 21:23)? This is not an undertaking for amateurs, he might conclude as he then turns to the most probable source of help, the accumulated tradition which presumably preserves the insights gleaned through Jesus' own instructions and refines scriptural understanding in the most authentic way. And as he probes the tradition for guidance, he may find other sources of unsettlement. All three synoptic Gospels witness to the firm tradition, this time based on obvious meanings of obvious scriptural texts, that Jesus as Messiah was of the lineage of David; yet all three also record a striking piece of exegesis by Jesus himself, which appears to lead inexorably to the conclusion that the Messiah cannot be the descendent of David (Mt 22:41–46; Mk 12:35–37; Lk 20:41–44).[21] This does not disqualify the theoretical axiom, but it does make it rather difficult to employ it for rigorous calculation. Evidently, the tradition did not integrate its understandings as well as it might have done.

If Theophilos moves on to the teaching of Jesus, he meets a similar difficulty. Presumably, the Word is there in the parables. But how are they to be interpreted? Is Matthew's sense of them right when he brings Scripture to bear on them to show them open revelations, "I will open my mouth in parables; I will proclaim things hidden from the foundations" (Mt 13:35; Ps 78:2), and shows Jesus' hearers impressed and edified? Or when he applies another scriptural text that makes the parables instruments of concealment (13:13–15), and shows the closest disciples mystified until they have a private explication? Where in the pre-crucifixion Gospel did Jesus teach the necessity of baptism in his name? Theophilos would also meet new confusions, born this time not from lack of integration but from overzealousness about it. Mark has Jesus deny flatly that this generation shall be given a sign (8:12); Luke says they will have only the sign of Jonah, viz., the authoritative preaching of repentance (11:29–32); Matthew repeats this in an abbreviated version (16:1–4), but offers another edition which interprets the sign of Jonah as the resurrection (12:38–42). No sign, or dramatic and definitive sign? The gospel of saving repentance or the Gospel of the risen Messiah? It may well be that the pre-crucifixion teaching virtually contained the whole of the post-resurrection understanding, but it appears that the traditional retellings of the former were too convinced of this to avoid being over-enthusiastic about making it plain.[22]

Post-resurrection teaching, then? Aside from puzzling inconsistencies about where and how and to whom the appearances occurred, the tradition seems to have weakened its own capacity for disclosure here by relying too much on its own riches. The apostles are to proselytize, to preach the Gospel, to make known the things that Jesus now tells them. But that instruction is only reported, not repeated; and just what is meant by the Gospel is assumed rather than stated, as are the criteria for "making disciples" of the nations. Theophilos is driven back to the problematic territory he has just covered, unless he can make his own assessment of the revelation implicit in the career of Jesus as an acting-out and fulfillment of God's saving plan. But this requires that he see it in the light of what God has said about its meaning in the scriptures, and so . . . back to the beginning of the hermeneutical circle.

Theophilos' problems would not invalidate the theory he could have gleaned from the Gospel of Luke. The body of synoptic tradition suggests that, however difficult the Christian constitution might have been to a latecomer apprentice like Theophilos, its theoretical neatness corresponded to an existential reality, at least for a while after the ascension. Peter and his colleagues were not in Theophilos' position. They knew what they had witnessed, what they had been told and shown, what they had discovered and understood. Their memories were capable of mediating the mind of Christ. To that extent, the synoptic tradition is right in manifesting in them at the end, and the new beginning, none of the anxiety that might belong to Theophilos, and in leaving the constitution of Christian thought a theory implicit in a common law.

Furthermore, the common law was still being applied. If Theophilos should get no satisfaction from an appeal to Matthew and Mark, he had the option of appealing beyond them to the living memories from which they too had drawn. The understanding at the convergence of norms, which had been transmitted to the original eyewitnesses, had presumably been handed on by them in turn as they ministered the Word. Synoptic omissions could theoretically be supplied; synoptic inconsistencies could be resolved, even if only at the tolerable expense of faulting one or another of the ministers of tradition.

Such an optimism may indeed have been justified in Theophilos' day. Luke claims an analogous optimism, although applying particularly to the tradition's historical memory rather than to its sustained Christ-wisdom. But the indications are not clear that Luke was quite right about the former, or that a great deal could be properly claimed about the latter. The synoptic Gospels themselves suggest that the tradition had already absorbed enough misunderstanding, error, uncertainty, and confusion to be, if not exactly sandy, yet softer than the rock upon which one may build with total confidence. The main outlines of Christian thought are there, but with enough blurring to make detail uncertain, and enough unsettlement and incompleteness to make it unlikely that the tradition is any longer capable of applying its sense of Scripture or of Jesus' teaching or of any other constituting court of appeal, either singly or in mutually corrective combination, with enough control to achieve such detail reliably. The human element has made its mark. The wine was new; but the bottles, however thoroughly cleansed, were of the same old stuff. It had been gracious of the Lord to make such treasures available to the ordinary capacities of men; but ordinary capacities inevitably take their toll. However well the eyewitnesses and first ministers of the Word may have put on the mind of Christ, they apparently did not succeed in imposing it thoroughly on the tradition that devolved from their teachings. And now the procedure for discerning the true norms of Christian understanding is far from being entirely clear.

This too had been foreseen: Matthew's Jesus remarks that "every scribe instructed in the kingdom of heaven is like a householder, who brings out of his storehouse new things and old things" (Mt 13:52). *Pistos ho logos!* But when it is not obvious which of the available new and old things are authentic to the true Word and which are false or obsolete, how shall our scribe proceed to make sound use of the materials so tantalizingly within his reach in order to achieve a way of thinking that is worthy of, and eligible for, the kingdom of heaven? The problem is all the more troublesome when the situation is unstable, *caeteris non paribus.* The new things brought forward are not entirely the option of the instructed scribe. Experience—especially the multiform and unforeseeable experience of an outgoing missionary activity—has its own storehouse, from which new things and old may be produced at a dazzling rate. Even the instructed scribe may be taxed in his efforts to apply the common law to what it had not clearly foreseen. The synoptic Gospels, by prudently terminating at the ascension, are not necessarily required to offer the missing factor in the Christian constitution, the procedure for resolving matters which are not plainly met by the Gospel itself, or rigorously determinable by the Gospel's interface with Scripture and Christian memory. But, to their credit, they are honest enough to raise the problem implicitly, by glancing forward to an alarmingly demanding future that will try the Christian participation in the mind of Christ as in the fire: there will be false Christs and false prophets, armed with signs and wonders, ready to lead astray, if possible, even the chosen ones (Mt 24:24; Mk 13:22). Forewarned, unfortunately, is not forearmed. Unless the faithful have a sturdier point of reference than their tradition, built in part on just such convincing evidences as are to be pitted against it, how shall they be able to tell the damaging innovations of the false prophet from the legitimate novelties of the instructed scribe?

The saving grace is that the mind of Christ has not retreated to their memories' length, but abides. Matthew's account closes with his enspiriting assurance, "and listen, I am with you all the days up to the end of the age" (28:20),[23] and Mark looks into the early mission to see that "they proclaimed everywhere, the Lord working with them and confirming the Word through accompanying signs" (16:20).[24] Luke has Jesus add a similar assurance just before his final departure: "and look, I am sending the promise of my Father upon you, but stay in the city until you are invested with power from on high" (24:49). But in the meantime, what practical and procedural face does this synoptic assurance of the abiding aid of Jesus the Messiah turn toward the struggling Christians?

None of the synoptic evangelists confronts this problem very directly. Luke has the excuse of being able to save that side of the story for its proper place in Acts. Matthew hardly presents as ample a projection as one could wish, but does have a variety of interesting suggestions, some of which are shared by Mark. All in all, the tradition manages to point to a few specific ways of receiving post-ascension guidance from on high.

In the collected versions of the tradition, there is one curious common denominator. It appears in general from the first three Gospels

that the great missionary undertaking of giving Christian witness to the
nations is assumed to be able to run under whatever information has
come under its own power, relying on the understanding acquired by
the time of the ascension. Evidently, this is to work by rather ordinary
human means, albeit effectually monitored by Christ. But there is also
a less deliberate witness, no less a part of God's plan for getting the
Word to important places, which seems to merit a special intervention.
All three synoptic accounts predict that the followers of Jesus will be
found offensive, and will accordingly be hauled up before sanhedrins
and synagogues and magistrates and kings and will therefore have privileged opportunities for proclaiming the Word. Where one might expect
advice to prepare an apologetical brief carefully in advance, assisted by
the best of instructed scribes, just the opposite occurs. All three accounts unanimously record Jesus' admonition not to be concerned
about it beforehand and his assurance that the Holy Spirit will take care
of providing them with the right things to say (Mt 10:19–20; Mk 13:11;
Lk 12:11–12). Luke even repeats the assurance, in a variant of the same
advice that reminds us that the Holy Spirit, being the way in which the
mind of God communicates with men, is, after all, the functional
equivalent of the mind of Christ: says Jesus, "*I* will give you speech and
wisdom, which all your opponents will be unable to oppose or resist"
(21:15). And there rests the consensus of the synoptic evangelists on the
heavenly intervention into post-ascension Christian understanding.
The indicted will have a special privilege of inspiration. In the dock and
on the carpet, the mind of the Lord will rise up and speak directly
through men.

There is unfortunately little anticipation of what might occur in connection with this interesting supposition. The logical result would be
that the testimony of witnesses in such circumstances of prosecution
would be especially cherished as prophetic utterances. The trials of
Stephen, of Peter, of Paul—even of Jesus himself—may have been
remembered with just such a pointedness. It is possible that such privileged moments of prophecy were to be used as ways of settling questions for the earliest communities. But there is too little to go on, and
this point of synoptic consensus must therefore pass without yielding up
the secrets of its eventual implications.[25]

In addition to this special quasi-prophesy, there was to be a more
standard variety. Although Mark has nothing to say about any other
mode of authoritative guidance in the post-ascension Christian groups,
his projection of future false prophets (13:22) may imply that he believed the true prophets whom they would imitate to be a part of the
early Christian scene. At any rate, Christian prophets are clearly projected in Matthew. In fact, Matthew has an interesting trio of offices, all

of them represented as being sent not by God or by the Holy Spirit but by Jesus, who says, "Look, I am sending to you prophets and sages and scribes" (23:34). "Scribes" here are undoubtedly identical with the "scribe instructed in the kingdom of heaven" (Mt 13:52), that is, a scholar who turns his learning to Christian uses. Such would surely have been an important figure in the formation of early Christian under-standing, correlative with the constitutional principle that Scripture rightly understood is normative for Christian thought.[26] "Sages," *sophoi*, is a difficult term, appearing elsewhere in the synoptic Gospels only in the so-called Johannine logion, where Jesus rejoices that revela-tion has been hidden from the sages and given to the simple ones (Mt 11:25; Lk 10:21). Matthew's Christian *sophoi* are presumably the Chris-tian equivalents of the *hakamim* cited frequently in the *Mishnah,* where the term has the approximate weight of "the experts," "the authoritative theologians."[27] The *Mishnah* appeals to the "sages" as a way of settling questions of subtle halakic law, but also to deal with matters of more speculative theology, as when the sages are said to have opined that the purpose of Elijah's return will be "Neither to remove afar nor to bring nigh, but to make peace in the world, as it is writ-ten . . ." (Eduyoth 8:7). If this suggested equivalence is fundamentally correct, the Christian "sages" must also have been important points of reference in determining points of thought-law in early Christian com-munities, correlative with the teaching of Jesus and of his apostlic successors.[28] Matthew's other category, that of prophets, is much better known and more fully attested in early Christianity, and would cer-tainly have been most important in providing new inspired input for the accumulating materials of early Christian thought. But the nature and office of prophecy is visionary and exhortational, the former tend-ing to reach into territory too untamed yet to be ruled by law, and the latter tending to assume the law already established. Despite the high place of honor properly accorded prophets in earliest Christianity, and despite the more spectacular and dramatic character of their activities, it is not unlikely that those whom Matthew designates as scribes and sages were procedurally as important in the formation and stabilization of normative Christian understanding. Still, the inspired prophet seems to have remained for some time the most obvious vehicle for the mind of Christ to communicate with Christians; and even though the quieter modes of the scribes and sages may have been more steadily influential, the prophet always has a clear place of privilege.

To be sure, Matthew does not have Jesus peer forward into Christian history in enough detail to permit us to check out these speculations. We hear no more of the Christian scribes or the Christian sages—or indeed, even of the Christian prophets, except that to receive them as such earns the reward of a prophet (10:41), and that some who prophesy in the name of Christ will nevertheless be rejected by him in the end (7:21–22). But Matthew does have a few words pertaining to the settling of questions within the Christian fold, and they deserve a careful look.

The most celebrated passage is, of course, that in which Peter, on the occasion of his manifesting an insight into Jesus' true role and nature, is told that he shall be given "the keys of the kingdom of heaven; and whatever you bind upon the earth shall be bound in the heavens; and whatever you loose upon the earth shall be loosed in the heavens" (16:19). I have no interest in entering the endless controversy which has been stimulated by sectarian uses of this text, and wish to make only a couple of rather simple observations about it. One is that it establishes a clear principle of earthly authority, either accepted by or synchronized with the will of God. That is, while Peter's recognition of Jesus as the Messiah is said to be a function of a special revelation of an antecedent truth, the promise about binding and loosing is not that adequate additional inspiration will be provided but that actions taken will be recognized and validated in heaven. Whether the binding and loosing pertains to matters of thought as well as of behavior, we simply are not told; but there is no evident restriction to the latter. The second observation I would like to make is that while the singling out of Peter here is a significant datum, it is not required by the text, nor in keeping with the rest of the Gospel of Matthew, to suppose that Peter's position is one of exclusive authority. That sort of position is occupied permanently and exclusively by Christ alone: his followers should not be called rabbi, or leader, because he himself and he alone continues to keep those titles (23:8–10). They are all brethren, and the greatest of them should become the servant of the rest (23:8, 11). The former of these principles establishes the theoretical basic equality that pervades the Gospel of Matthew and makes it difficult to find a basis for a Petrine monarchy; the latter solves the problem of acknowledging the fact of leadership (and even its origin in the one true leader, Christ, who will send scribes and prophets and sages) without violating the egalitarian theory. It is imaginable that, as *diakonos diakonōn theou*, Peter could bind and loose, to the approving nods of heaven *and* his brethren. But otherwise, there is another passage in Matthew which is a bit more characteristic of the over-all Matthean habits of mind.

This time it is in the plural: "I say to you solemnly, whatever you bind upon earth shall be bound in heaven, and whatever you loose on earth, shall be loosed in heaven" (18:18). The addressees are ostensibly "the disciples," which is plausible enough. The immediate context suggests that a slightly more refined reading may be put on it. The verses immediately following underline the general principle that two or three

Christians in agreement can make themselves definitely heard in heaven, because of the abiding presence of Christ: "If two of you should agree on earth concerning any matter at all which they may be asking about, it will come about for them from my Father in heaven: for where there are two or three assembled in my name, there I am in their midst" (18:19–20). It is not clear whether the theological implication is that two or three can bind the acts of providence because Christ will mediate on behalf of Christian mutuality, or because those who are initiated into his name will automatically speak with his authority when they coincide with one another; but it is at least clear that the power of binding and loosing has something to do with participation in the authority of Christ. The previous verses are not less instructive. If your brother offend against you, try to correct him privately. If that fails, bring one or two others with you and try again. If that should fail, "tell the assembly; and if he should disregard the assembly, let him be to you just like a Gentile and a tax-collector" (18:15–17). Here two or three in agreement have some weight for binding and loosing, but the ultimate appeal is the full body—not the apostles, or the disciples, but the *ecclēsia* itself. And this appeal is so ultimate that to disregard what it binds is apparently to be lost to the way of salvation, effectually divorced from Christ.

We are here dealing primarily with matters of practical behavior, presumably. This is the way to settle torts within the community without taking the debasing step of going to public law for settlement. The issue is not a doctrinal one. However, the practical advice laid down here for the resolution of a certain kind of difficulty is likely to pattern the community's assumptions about a proper way of dealing with other kinds of difficulties as well—even leaving aside the likelihood that the Jewish-Christian understanding of "binding and loosing" made far less division between the power of teaching and the power of excommunication (or even between offensive behavior and offensive doctrine) than I have here allowed.[29] If they are all brethren, and are not to call one another "Rabbi" because they have only one who so leads them, Christ; if their one leader, Christ, continues to abide with them all days, and is in their midst when they gather in his name;[30] if there is ordained some mysterious way in which agreeing Christians participate in the authority of Christ, perhaps by sharing in the mind of Christ, then I submit that the logical conclusion of the general thinking about Christian common law evidenced in Matthew's treatment of internal disputes is that a similar procedure should obtain in determining points of Christian thought-law: the ultimate appeal to both understanding and authority is to the community's sense of what is right. It is, at least sometimes, only at that level that there can be a definitive practical determination of what belongs to Christ. What the assembly can assert or deny in common is also thus bound or loosed in heaven, because the mind of the assembly manifests the mind of Christ who is in their midst as they are in his name. They have prophets and scribes and sages to assist their discernment, but they have all been baptized into the Holy Spirit as well as the Father and the Son, and it is finally there—where no blasphemy is tolerable—that they enact together the ultimately discerning Christian mind.

The synoptic Gospels are ostensibly dealing with a time when one did not have to be concerned with providential arrangements for determining what belongs to normative Christian understanding. The answer to such questions was visibly there among the askers, and by the time the story is over they have found a way of hearing and understanding him. The synoptic Gospels are also, less ostensibly, about the later time when unanticipated problems and questions concerning the Christian truth were arising, and the means of resolution were not so convenient or clear. But the synoptic Gospels, for all the importance of their compositional *Sitze-im-Leben,* are remarkable not for how much they tell us about the workings of that later time, but for how little. That, I take it, is a significant datum. They are not worried. They boldly postulate concrete manifestations of the mind of God through the mind of Christ, tell us of the investment of this understanding in the closest disciples of Jesus, and set the church on its way as if they have said virtually all that needs to be said. Do we judge this to be their inadequacy, their regrettable insensitivity to needs for which they ought to have taken greater responsibility? Or their romanticism and escapist nostalgia? These are options to the critical historian. But there is another, and more economical, way of assessing the curious complacency with which they reconstruct the Christian foundations: things are working out well enough. Christ abides; and between the faithful memory in which his people preserve the essential Gospel, and the faithful life through which they continue to belong intimately to him, he makes his guiding presence felt. Their fidelity seeks first the kingdom of heaven; whatever needs to be added, be it a response to persecutors or a prophecy or a wise understanding, will somehow be given—and will somehow be received. Apparently, they *have* said virtually all that needs to be said: that is, the essential Gospel, founded on deeds which have, after all, been *"fulfilled* among us." Their understanding has been well and graciously founded. Whatever refining or developing it is to do will presumably be an orderly by-product of what they already understand to be Christian fidelity. The cumulative understanding that is rooted in their devoted faithfulness discerns the mind of Christ.

3

The Acts of the Apostles

*T*he synoptic Gospels do not take us explicitly into the post-ascension period. They arrive at the point where the light apparently breaks most fully for the followers of Jesus, and then are over. The hints they give of later times—the times of their own literary formulation—are too slight to permit much more than crafty guesswork about what their compilers took to be the means of determining normative Christian thought in their own day. Implicitly, of course, the Gospels offer themselves as a norm, to the extent that their representations attempt to establish an understanding of what has taken place by God's plan enacted through Jesus. There are also practical implications in the fact that they identify the earliest authorized and informed agents of the publication of that understanding. One must be wary of projecting conclusions, however. All three synoptic Gospels establish that an understanding of God's work through Jesus had come about, but they do not define what it was; and when Matthew adds to this some more detailed suggestions about later procedure for determining what is to be said, it is notable that the method of appeal partially transcends even the most faithful apostolic memory. If we look for something, correlative with the synoptic tradition, that directly attempts to represent the working-out of Christian understanding in the post-ascension world, all we can find is Acts. It is there that we must turn in order to get a further check on the theory that appears to inform the synoptic tradition.

In Acts, one may find replicated most of the general synoptic scheme of a cumulative unfolding of the Word. It is to be found not directly urged, as if it were a pet theory or a polemical counterposition, but represented casually and desultorily, in the manner of a pattern taken for granted. Neither are its evidences mere repetitions of the matter already given in Luke's Gospel: new hints emerge, new strokes are added to the sketch of the underlying habits of mind.

This is most especially evident in the glances at the first stage of the Word's definitive unfolding, at the level of the Expectation based on the Promise. Peter uses this as a point of departure in his first public preaching: "the promise is to you and to your children" (2:39), and Paul later follows him by characterizing his good news as being the fulfillment of "the promise to the fathers" (13:32), and by claiming that his persecution in Judea is on account of "the hope of the promise made by God to our fathers" (26:6; cf. 28:20). But the understanding of the content of "promise," somewhat vague in the Gospel of Luke, is here more directed and particularized.

Its content in Acts varies significantly with the context. Acts alludes once (1:6) to the political version of the Promise that is sometimes reflected in the Third Gospel's portrayals of popular understanding. But this version is not seriously entertained thereafter, and may be only a last show of apostolic misunderstanding before the coming of the Spirit enlarges the Christian vision. The dominant motif by which the ur-gospel of the promise is interpreted is rather in terms of the world to come, and especially the resurrection. Paul makes to Agrippa the claim that he is judged on account of the hope of the Promise. What may seem abstract here is concretized in his other pleading: to Felix he confesses specifically a hope for the resurrection of the dead (24:15), just after he has objected to the Sanhedrin that they are judging him "concerning hope and resurrection of the dead" (23:6). Although at times Acts connects the hope and promise directly and simply with the resurrection of Jesus (13:32–33; 26:7–8), more characteristically it associates them with the doctrine of general resurrection—indeed, the appeal to Agrippa in 26:8, on closer inspection, shows the same concreteness within its abstract invocation of the promise, and apparently means to argue that Paul's having preached the risen Jesus is inoffensive precisely because it is a particular instance rooted in and legitimated by a general hope of resurrection among the Jews generally, but especially among the Pharisees.

Accordingly, when Paul splits the Sanhedrin with his insistence that he is being judged for preaching resurrection, I think it would be seriously inaccurate to take this as a successfully time-gaining bit of sly politics on his part. He perceives that his charge will have the desired effect. But this is not because he is simply using the Pharisees: he sees them as the agents of the true understanding of the Word, albeit only at a relatively elementary stage of its emergence. It is typical of Acts that Paul speaks well of his Pharisaical training in general and of Gamaliel in particular, and that the narrator represents Gamaliel generously in his intervention in 5:34–40. It is typical of the underlying reason for this that Gamaliel is represented as being open to a revelation beyond that which he already knows. The Pharisees are the true inheritors of the seat of Moses, at least up to the point that their stage of understanding is incorporated into, as well as corrected and transcended by, later revelation. When they respond affirmatively to Paul's plea before the Sanhedrin, they have not been seduced but reminded of themselves. Their judgment as a result is both just and open-minded. Whatever difficulties they may cause for the Christian way by their practical applications of the Law, it is clear that in their more speculative understanding of what it says about the world to come they are the most enlightened of its sub-Christian interpreters, and have in their own manner prepared the way of the Lord at this preliminary stage. It is worth noting that the qualities that permit them to play this role, and recommend them to Luke, are especially their learning, their righteous strictness of behavior, and their openness to the workings of the Spirit —or at least of spirit. Such are the main constituting factors of adequate understanding at this first level, and such is the foundation on which higher understanding is built in Luke's view, both for Christian individuals and for the universal historical unfolding of the Word.

Luke's second stage of the Word comes with John. I have previously indicated Luke's reluctance to yield as much to John's stratum as the other synoptists are willing to grant. In Acts as well as the Third Gospel, the Baptist stage of revelation is subdued, and tends to be acknowledged only along with a careful assurance that it is subsumed, fulfilled, and rendered effectually obsolete by the mission of Jesus. John's baptism is the starting point of Peter's little Gospel in chapter 10; but it is passed over quickly. Jesus acknowledges it at the beginning of Acts (1:5) but points to the greater spiritual baptism that is yet to come. Paul in Pisidian Antioch is careful to insist that John pointed beyond himself to the more worthy one (13:25). Still, the acknowledgement is there. Paul allows that God gave Jesus to Israel "with John having previously preached a baptism of repentance before his appearance, to all the people of Israel" (13:24). In more inadvertent moments, Luke yields still more. Apollos may know "only" the baptism of John, and need more instruction, but he is not much faulted for that; and if the curious dozen Ephesians are even more uninformed, evidently ignorant of Jesus as well as of the Holy Spirit, Luke nevertheless calls them disciples, *mathētai* (19:1): apparently, one who has gone as far as John can take him is already well on the way to the kingdom, and at least something of a fellow-traveller of Christians. Acts adds nothing to what Luke's Gospel tells us about how John's mission was to have made its claim, and says far less about such matters than the Gospel does. But what it says is congruent with the scheme suggested there, and with the further particularization of the Promise contained in John's more pointed references to the one who is coming, to the need for repentance, and to the imminent judgment that is the link between them. This state of understanding is still closer to the truth than that of the Expectation, and an important introduction to the place of Jesus in the scheme of things (even though the heightened place of the first level in the representations of Acts show yet more clearly than in the Third Gospel that even those who have not accepted John may nevertheless find in their own Expectation-theology a basis for entertaining seriously the claims of the Christian preaching). If the Pharisees of Jerusalem may be moved to suspend judgment while they watch and wait, the Baptists of Ephesus are readily enlisted into the new baptism that explicitly concretizes and fulfills elements of John's forecast. However muted, the level of News is still, for Acts, the effective starting point of the Gospel itself (1:21–22).

If Luke's representation of the first stage is more ample in Acts than in his Gospel, the contrary is true of the third stage, the gospel of the kingdom. Not with respect to the fact of its presence, for references to such a gospel occur intermittently up to the final verse of Acts, where Paul is said to be "proclaiming the kingdom of God and teaching the things about the Lord Jesus Christ." But aside from the reference to post-resurrection instruction in 1:3, Acts has essentially nothing to say about the role of Jesus in making the kingdom known. The various kerygmatic sketches of Jesus' career point to his suffering and death and resurrection, and occasionally to his power and good works, but not to the gospel which Luke elsewhere credits him with preaching. In part, the omission is a conscious avoidance of redundancy: Luke begins by reminding his reader that he has invested in the Third Gospel his account of "all the things which Jesus undertook to do and teach" (1:1), and need not repeat either the deeds or the teachings in Acts. Still, the speeches of Acts at least glance occasionally at the signs and wonders done by the pre-crucifixion Jesus, and it is therefore remarkable that there is no reference to his gospel of the kingdom.

The explanation for this, I believe, has a great deal to do with the relaxation of Luke's perspective that occurs when he represents the Gospel from a temporal point of reference that lies after its full revelation. Once the secret is out, it no longer matters so much precisely what Jesus did or said, or to what extent his pre-crucifixion mission was an evident advance on that of John the Baptist, or even whether he had explicitly anticipated his own crucifixion and resurrection in his teachings. The pattern is plainly there in the scriptures, and Jesus has plainly fulfilled it: that, the kerygmatic practice represented in Acts repeatedly implies, is all one really needs to know. If one knows that much, it should be decisive. Philip's adventure with the eunuch is procedurally paradigmatic. When the historical arena lies after this fullness, only the curious *need* pry further into the earlier and more primitive unfolding of the Word, interesting and encouraging though it may be. Luke therefore allows himself a foreshortening in Acts, and gives us a time of fulfillment in which the content of Jesus' own gospel may be bypassed, his ministerial distinction from John may be blurred, and his predictions of his own providental fate may be omitted altogether. In the Third Gospel, Luke is treating the earlier—and more primitive—phase of this history, and is serving the legitimate curiosity of his Theophilos. It is therefore of some interest to him not only to give the content of Jesus' gospel but to emphasize that it was more than that of John, and that Jesus operated as a new departure rather than in continuation of John's gospel. That, after all, is what one might ordinarily expect from the visible ministry of the Messiah himself. But in Acts, Luke does not have to address himself to that expectation or directly to that ministry, and does not. The consequence is a picture rather more like that offered by Matthew, where the difference between the main outlines of John's News and those of Jesus' gospel is not evidently great. This is probably, given the other synoptic evidence, a bit more faithful to the tradition Luke was using than the Third Gospel's more exaggerated distancing of Jesus from John—though even there, Jesus' gospel admittedly reaffirms John's, and the populace may be readily forgiven if they suspect Jesus to be the risen John. Under pressure, the synoptic tradition manifests a distinction between the second and third stages of the Word —but evidently does not regard it as a crucially important distinction or consider the gap between John's News and Jesus' gospel of the kingdom to be nearly as great as the gaps between the other stages. Jesus advances on John more as heir and historical realizer than as preacher. Similarly, the tradition evidences a confidence that Jesus' teaching anticipated his eventual passion and resurrection (though in this case Luke is significantly less insistent than his synoptic colleagues), just as one might fairly, though hardly necessarily, expect from the appointed and surprising Messiah. But this is apparently taken to be the least impressive of the evidences for the Christian case. The point is not urgent. Consequently, Luke treats it lightly in his first work and does not seem to find it awkward to omit it altogether in his second.

One reason why the point is not urgent is because the all-important emergence of the final and quintessential Gospel overshadows all other considerations, and can be more readily and universally established in other ways. In a close look at the career of Jesus, it is interesting to see the progression of the Word and the richness of the interlocking ways in which its final stage is revealed and guaranteed. The grateful apostles may well cherish and savor the fullness of it. But if the quintessential Gospel is, as Luke would have it, the present Lordship of Jesus and the possibility and necessity of forgiveness in his name, demonstrable by the testimony of Scripture and eyewitnesses, it is of relatively little kerygmatic or instructional use to insist in post-resurrection flashbacks that Jesus himself foresaw and predicted all this before his passion, especially when one can cite the more impressive phenomenon of post-resurrection teaching. And Acts' orientation is decidedly keryg-matic, concerned to represent the breakthrough of the Gospel rather than the reflective rumination of established Christian communities. What counts for the apostles is to establish Jesus' basic credentials in a publicly and universally convincing way. What happens is therefore that normative understanding, the understanding that forms the basis for salvation from the judgment to come, is repeatedly defined by Acts' missionaries on the simpler basis of a firm and compelling coincidence between Scripture's promises and the actual career of Jesus. The one messianic and saving plan of God may be manifest in four different ways, but kerygmatic efficiency specialized in the two which most con-vincingly interpret each other: Scripture, the most conveniently au-thoritative of the four (because among other things it is the only one whose authority is independent of faith in Jesus), and the career of Jesus as suffering and risen Messiah, the historical answer to and fulfillment of the Law and the Prophets. That, evidently, is where Luke also saw the dominant factors defining Christian understanding. It is not un-likely that Luke found in this specialization a convenient refuge from the problem of representing Jesus' predictions of his passion and resur-rection. Even more than his synoptist colleagues, he evidently had difficulty in representing these predictions to be both clearly made *and* either quite uncomprehended or otherwise ineffectual. Acts suggests by omission that these predictions never were among the most impor-tant considerations, and shows where the most important investment lay.

It is obvious that for Christians themselves, the career of Jesus estab-lished the controlling norm by which Scripture was to be properly read —though I shall add a substantial qualification to that remark presently. But once the right reading is thus found, and the Scripture and career are perceived as mirror-image and original, the order of proceeding may be casually reversed. Faith's easy commuting back and forth be-tween them consequently results in occasional misjudgments concern-ing the force of argument. Peter's reasoning in chapter 2, for instance, is essentially that Jesus had to be resurrected because he is the Messiah, which is satisfying to the mind of the believer but hardly a persuasive tack to take with those who are not ready to grant either premise on Peter's bare say-so. The more circumspect procedure is the one at-tributed to Paul as his customary method: working from the scriptures to show that they point to a Messiah who is to suffer and rise from the dead, and arguing that Jesus is the one in whom all this is finally proved by being fulfilled (17:2–3). Any Jew who is sufficiently open-minded may possibly be led, as the Jews of Berea were led by Paul, to "examine the scriptures daily, if these things be so" (17:11). Not all of them found that the scriptures attested these things to be so, of course. Even those who did, had thereby only half the picture. The kerygma claimed that Jesus had indeed fulfilled these scriptures by having died, risen, and been appointed eschatological judge. On what evidence?

On the evidence of witnesses. True to the position taken in the Third Gospel, Luke's later apostles are uncompromisingly literal-minded about this. Admonished not to teach about Jesus, Peter and John reply that they cannot be obedient to men and disobedient to God, and therefore they cannot forbear to speak about that which they have "seen and heard" (4:18–20). The vulgar literalism of this is explicated not only by Peter's assurance that the specially appointed witnesses saw Jesus after the resurrection, ate and drank with him, and heard him command them to preach his election as Judge (10:40–42)—but by their being brought into position to watch Jesus ascending into the clouds (1:9). Little is left to the imagination. Stephen, though his vision is admittedly (and necessarily) a less palpably verifiable one than that of the Twelve, is even taken so far as to witness the post-ascension state of affairs, to see Jesus standing at the right hand of God (7:55), and can thus testify to his perceived Lordship. Even Paul has been allowed to see the Lord and hear his voice so that he too can witness to things that he has literally seen and heard (22:14–15; cf. 26:16). The conservatism of Luke's criteria for witnesses is especially suggested in 1:21–22, where candidates for Judas' vacated office must be legitimate observers of Jesus from the time of the baptism of John through the resurrection to the ascension; and in 13:31, where Paul invokes the authority of the Jerusalem witnesses, who had come with Jesus from Galilee (and presumably therefore knew him well enough to give unimpeachable testimony of his identity with the risen one?), but modestly declines to mention his own less thoroughly grounded seeings and hearings. Paul is a legitimate witness in his own right as he is also a legitimate apostle (14:14); but Luke evidently feels more secure with the utterly unequivocal apostleship and witness of the Twelve, and can thus be somewhat gingerly about Paul. As in the Third Gospel, the accent falls upon the most unquestionable proof, the most public evidence, the most unimpeachably reliable witness.

The trustworthiness of the eyewitnesses *ap' archēs* is further enhanced by their being able to manifest the marks that had commended Jesus to the people during the development of the Gospel of the kingdom. They work signs and wonders (2:43; 5:12; etc.), which (as Peter reminds the crowd in Jerusalem) was a way in which God had shown his approval of Jesus (2:22). This is rightly grasped, at least by the more perceptive and pious, as the Lord's witness to what they preach, as a sign that they should be heeded (8:6; 14:3). The apostles can sometimes inspire in others holy fear and reverence, as Jesus had done to them (5:11; 10:25; 28:6). But on the whole, I venture to say that in Acts, as in the Third Gospel's representation of the pre-crucifixion Jesus, the real center of gravity in the effectiveness of the mission lies in the non-miraculous and relatively unspectacular evidences. The apostles are impressive. They speak with boldness and power, as with wisdom (4:8; 4:29–31; 6:10). They find favor with the people (2:44–47; 4:21; 5:13). With good presences and good fruits, they continue on the way of their Master, and make similar impressions on the open-hearted. They speak with authority, and those who have ears to hear, hear.

It is never forgotten, however, that their authority and their message are both given to them by Providence. The apostles are authoritative witnesses not because they happened to be in the right place at the right time, but because they were foreappointed by God to be witnesses through whom the truth might be known (10:41). And the truth is not simply the resurrected Christ as they saw him. As Ananias explains it to Saul, he has been foreappointed to see and hear the risen Lord, and to witness to what he has seen and heard—but also *to know God's will* (22:14–15). Witness to the resurrection is an indispensable part of the process of establishing publicly Jesus' claim to messiahship and thus his place in the hidden messianic plan of God. But that hidden and unconventional plan is not entirely, in its totality, given with the fact of the resurrection itself, even the resurrection of the Messiah. The apostles must therefore take on the further job of interpreting and defining God's further will for men, making known the right way of understanding the plan of salvation and our relationship to it.

In the first instance, the apostles may be supposed to be in possession of this definitive understanding of God's will through the special instructions which they received from the risen Lord, making up what their observation alone cannot supply. The apostles, including Paul, may thus be witnessing to what they have heard—directly from the mind of Christ—when they proclaim his Lordship, forgiveness in his name, and the still more radically challenging doctrine that salvation comes no other way (3:23, 4:12, 13:38ff.). But in fact, the evidence on which to base such a supposition is not without counterpoise. That the apostles were instructed by the risen Jesus concerning the kingdom of God, we know (1:2–3); but we do not know the content of this instruction. If we try to infer, it is striking that Jesus' quoted remarks pertain primarily to the coming gift of the Spirit; and that the apostles' subsequent witness to him throughout the world is connected with the gift of the Spirit; and that neither their question to the risen Lord about the restoration of the kingdom of Israel (1:6) nor the somewhat patronizing reassurances of the two men in white at the ascension (1:11) is suggestive of a very deep state of insight on their part at the time of the ascension; and that the only item mentioned for their witnessing, as they replace Judas with another fully experienced and informed witness, is the resurrection (1:21–22). The quintessential Gospel does not clearly show itself in Acts until after the sending of the Spirit. When it does come, it seems to transform as well as augment the earlier stages of understanding. For when Jesus refers to the Promise in 1:4, he refers to the gift of the Spirit. The apostles do not understand, and inquire about political restoration. Only after they have received the Spirit do they make the correlation of the Spirit with Promise. Then Peter can assure his audience that they too can receive this gift, "for to you is the Promise" (2:38–39). The Pharisaic glimpse of the world to come and resurrection was deeper and more authentic than the popular dream of political success. But the inspired understanding of Spirit, earnest and instance of greater life, is a "knowledge of salvation" as much deeper than that of the Pharisees as the baptism of Spirit is deeper than the water baptism of John. When the apostles have received Spirit and Gospel, and are in a position to speak boldly to the effect that "God exalted Jesus to his right hand as a ruler and saviour, to give repentance and forgiveness of sins to Israel" (5:31), they also add "and we are witnesses of these things, and the Holy Spirit which God gave to those obeying him" (5:32). We, and the Holy Spirit. It is a formula to which I shall inevitably return later; but in this instance, its implication is that the Holy Spirit gives independent and confirming testimony.

The implication may in fact be that the Holy Spirit is specifically the source of that deeper understanding of God's plan and accomplishment which the apostles do not show in the first chapter of Acts, but preach openly once the Holy Spirit has empowered them to utter "the great deeds of God" in every tongue (2:11). Acts never plainly alleges this, never plainly denies it. The Spirit is evidently regarded as the source of power in bearing witness (1:8; 4:8), expressing itself in boldness, *parrēsia* (4:13; 4:31). But to what extent, if any, is this power a power of understanding, this boldness the boldness of the knower?

The indications are somewhat oblique, but they are that the Spirit contributes the full measure of insight, and finally establishes the locus of normative understanding. It is notable that such insight is, in Acts, a property of spirit generally: the possessing evil spirit who beats up the seven sons of Sceva does not recognize them, but can say "I know Jesus, and I understand Paul" (19:15); and the divining spirit of Philippi perceives in Paul and Silas "servants of the most high God, who announce to you a way of salvation" (16:17). Can it be supposed that the Holy Spirit would be less communicative about the things important to understand? Not by Ananias of Jerusalem, whose attempt to deceive the Church was an attempt to deceive the Holy Spirit, who in turn gave the understanding that made it transparently unsuccessful (5:1–11). Nor by Ananias of Damascus, who was sent to Saul not to teach him but so that he might receive his sight and be filled with the Holy Spirit (9:17). Nor by Stephen, who was full of the Holy Spirit and wisdom (6:3, 5, 10), and when filled with the Holy Spirit saw the glory of God and Jesus as the Son of Man at his right hand (7:55–56). The Spirit, like the apostles, bears witness; like the apostles, the Spirit teaches and shows what Christians are to understand.

Like the apostles: for there is no question throughout Acts of a spiritual revelation entirely independent of the basic apostolic teaching. The commendation of the Jerusalem community in its early days is that it remains steadfast in the teaching of the apostles (2:42), and what the angel of the Lord calls "all the things [words? *rhēmata*] of this life" are taught by them to the people (5:20–21). The basic teaching of the messiahship of Jesus, the resurrection, the coming judgment by him and the possibility of forgiveness and salvation in his name, is given in every Christian beginning. The understanding must first be formed by teaching, and then the Spirit may work with what has been given. The basic teaching, and the Spirit—two foci that between them define the boundaries of normative Christian understanding.

The apostolic teaching cannot in itself stand permanently alone, even with the leaven of the Spirit. I have already suggested that Acts seems to acknowledge a degree of deficiency in post-resurrection understanding, corrected only with the gift of the Holy Spirit. This is not the only sign in Acts that the post-ascension period is importantly formative for Christian understanding. Acts makes it abundantly clear that there are things to be learned between the ascension and the Roman mission of Paul. Paul is in fact told in the course of his commission that he is to witness to what he has seen and to what he *will see* through future appearances of the Lord (26:16); Peter shows how much that can involve when he must reunderstand the workings of the Lord in a fairly radical way in the course of his eye-opening adventure with Cornelius. It is not that the apostles were simply too dull to grasp the full Gospel through Jesus' post-resurrection teaching. The further realization may in fact have been potentially available in that teaching, even if not fully explicit until a later historical moment; but it was not, it seems, easily available. Peter's realization that God is no respecter of persons seems to come as the full dawning of an only partially grasped truth, but there is no suggestion of self-reproach. The inadequacy of understanding at the time of the ascension derives rather from the fact that the time of the ascension does not mark the upper limit of the time of revelation. All the prophets, says Peter to the Jerusalemites, have spoken of "these days" (3:24). To wit? Not the days of completion of Jesus' earthly ministry in direct person, but the days of the completion of his full ministry through those whom he has sent. For Scripture, it turns out, has spoken of the events of Jesus' career, but also of the events succeeding: the election of Matthias (1:20), the outpouring of the Spirit and of prophecy (2:16), the mission to the Gentiles (15:15–17). Thus the Lord has said, who *is doing these things* that he *has known* from the age (15:17–18) —and thus the "fulfilled deeds" that lie at the foundation of Christianity include those fulfilled well after the ascension, according to the eternal plan and knowledge of the Lord. We must therefore have a way to move beyond even what once seemed to be the full Gospel, and to add to what the apostles first enjoined the Jews to "know assuredly" (2:36), so that our understanding may keep adequate pace with what God, having known from the beginning, now wishes to press upon our minds. How do we discern God's saving knowledge?

The most instructive instances to examine are those in which the greatest internal tension was produced within the Christian self-understanding. The two best candidates, both involving a substantial shift in the conception of the nature and scope of God's saving plan, are the incidents surrounding Peter's visit to Cornelius and those of the Jerusalem council.

The former is staged in elaborate detail. The first target for a change in understanding is Peter. And although the process begins with a perfectly private vision, it is notable that it moves in the direction of maximum publicity. The vision is too parabolical for Peter to understand until he can perceive it as a confirmation of what has been revealed more openly and to others. Even the private instruction to visit Cornelius is not left alone, but is given an open confirmation by Cornelius' coordinated vision and dispatch of messengers. Peter knew that he was being sent by the Spirit (10:19–20). The way in which it was arranged made it possible for others to be fairly sure that this was the case. Surprising as it may seem, the Spirit has directed a mission to the Gentiles. But still more surprising is the Spirit's open and visible-audible designation of the Gentile believers as acceptable, just like the earliest believers (10:47), through God's giving them the equal gift (11:17). The Jewish witnesses are understandably astonished (10:45), but there can be no question about what they have witnessed. God, through the Spirit, has redefined the Christian reality, and they must change their understanding accordingly. It remains only for this shift in understanding to be communicated to the rest of Christendom. Peter therefore meets the skeptical objections of the Jerusalem conservatives with a telling of his story—obscure vision, Spirit's instructions, correlating vision of Cornelius, accompanying witnesses, gift of the Spirit, and all. The visible evidence is overwhelming. The opponents glorify God and draw the proper conclusion: "then God gave repentance unto life even to the Gentiles!" (11:18). God's foreknowledge has realized itself in fulfilled deed, so plainly that mere memory and a sense of appropriateness are sufficient to interpret the meaning.

The Jerusalem Council affair is, as far as the reporting of Acts goes, a still more significant test case—for here it is not a matter of the instruction of unanticipating ignorance by a clear sign in due season, but precisely a direct conflict between one asserted law of thought and its rejection. Some say that salvation is dependent upon circumcision according to the Law; Paul and Barnabas dispute this (15:1-2). The matter is brought—not appealed or submitted, but brought—to the apostles and elders in Jerusalem, where the objection is repeated by Pharisaic converts. Peter again tells his story; Barnabas and Paul tell theirs; and James offers his judgment on the matter, appealing to the confirming correspondence between the testimony of Scripture and the testimony of Peter's experience; and so the issue is concluded, with the objecting view overthrown formally and definitively.

Precisely how does this come about? A cursory reading suggests that James was in a position to dictate the decision as constituted judge, after hearing the opposed advocacy of the Pharisaic and Peter-Barnabas-Paul parties. Such an interpretation does not altogether abuse Luke's presentation. A certain hierarchical prepossession flows through the account, beginning with the determination to take the question to "the apostles and elders" in Jerusalem, running through the hearing for which "the apostles and elders" are assembled, and reaching a climax when James "answers" the depositions and "concludes" what is the appropriate thing to do. This is in harmony with a hierarchical drift that runs through Acts generally, from the assertive leadership of Peter and the dominant role of the apostles—to whose ministry the others "did not presume to join themselves" (5:13)—to the elders appointed in the early Pauline churches (14:23) and the elders of Ephesus who are placed as overseers to shepherd their church (20:28).

A degree of institutional authority is taken for granted in Acts. But it is, nevertheless, only one of two foci in the discernment of the truth. The leaders themselves derive their authority from the express will of the Lord, beginning with the foreappointment of the providential Eleven, through the divine election of Matthias and of Paul, to the elders of Ephesus, who have been so placed "by the Holy Spirit" (20:28). This is the Spirit who, according to the testimony of Peter to the apostles and elders, made no distinction between them and the Gentiles (15:9), the Spirit that is given to all who are obedient to the faith (5:32). More delicately, but no less persistently, Luke attributes a role in discernment to the agents endowed with the Spirit, be they Gentiles of no previous standing or the community of otherwise undistinguished believers. Peter does not overbear those who are suspicious of his comportment with Cornelius, but comes with witnesses, tells his story, and thus secures their assenting recognition that God has indeed acted. He behaves as if trusting in their authority as well as their discernment. When the dispute about the service to the Hellenist widows arises, the Twelve call "the multitude of disciples" together and make a proposal that turns out to be pleasing to them, involving their own appointment of *diakonoi* whom they are able to recognize as "full of spirit and wisdom" (6:2–5). A closer look at the account of the Council reveals the same alternative focus at work. Paul and Barnabas, whose news of the conversion of the Gentiles has been received with joy by "all the brethren" en route, are received by the Jerusalem apostles and elders—and the church (15:3–4); and Luke's specification of the apostles and elders for the council (15:12) is modified by his reference to "the multitude" (*to plēthos*, 15:12) who receive Peter's argument with the assenting silence that had greeted his explanation of the Cornelius affair (11:18), and by the definitive response to James's intervention: "then it seemed good to the apostles and elders with all the church" to send forth the decision (15:22). The Pharisaic Christians are not simply overridden. Luke's reference to their silence indicates that they accept what Peter has said. The decision is the decision of all the church.

The text of the decree contains two virtually appositional phrases which summarize the final position of Acts on how we are to understand what belongs to Christ. "It seemed good to the Holy Spirit and to us," says the letter (15:28). The conjunction of the two is to be explicated by the parallel phrase three verses earlier. "It seemed good to us, having become of one mind" (15:25). As Luke indicates repeatedly in the reports of the earliest days of the Jerusalem church, the phenomenon of being of one mind, *homothumadon*, is the seal of its uniform reception of and submission to the faith and the Spirit that perfects it. The leaders of the churches are evidently especially empowered to indicate the ways in which the Spirit leads men's understanding; but what they have to say is finally guaranteed and ratified by that broader manifestation of the Spirit that lies in what seems good to all those who believe. *Homothumadon:* the discernment of the mind of Christ.

The possibility of authentic agreement is limited in the first instance by the ground of the apostolic teaching, which communicates the quintessential Gospel as perfected through the infusion of confidence and understanding given with the Spirit. Thus Acts' insistence on the essential kerygma, to which the Spirit too bears witness along with the apostles. This may not be violated. If it is augmented by the later unfolding of God's will through events, it is in no particular rescinded. Hence Paul, instructing the Ephesians that there will come from among their own members those who will pervert the word, warning them against the violence their misguidance shall effect, at the same time assures them that the Word he has given them is capable of building them up and giving them an inheritance among all the sanctified (20:29–32). Not the elders themselves, but the shared Word rules and builds. Paul himself has only echoed the earlier, if obscure, disclosures of the Spirit, "saying nothing apart from what the prophets and Moses said was about to happen" (26:22). But that message, which included both the original kerygma and the further news of the invitation to the Gentiles (26:23), emerged from the scriptures only gradually. Even after the ascension, Christian understanding required the further offices of the Spirit to discern what the Spirit had really revealed about what belongs to the plan of God, the mind of Christ.

The characteristic modes of disclosure are not the more spectacular and dramatic spiritual phenomena. Paul could claim a private vision that told him that he was to bring light to the Gentiles, that they may receive forgiveness and a share among those sanctified by faith in Christ (26:14–18). But nothing important in Acts remains private. The Gentiles' fruitful response establishes what God has done. Fruits are a canon of discernment throughout. When Paul preached the faith, and enjoined works worthy of repentance (26:20), he reaffirmed the standards by which the Spirit defined the fruits by which its participants might be known—for he taught about righteousness and self-control as well as about resurrection and judgment (24:25). Throughout the book, good men are honored, and by virtue of their goodness accorded some measure of authentic and self-limiting discernment, from the apostles to Gamaliel.

It is in fact Gamaliel who most decisively confirms, albeit from his less privileged first-level command of the Word, Luke's ultimate canon of discernment for what God has in mind for men to know. If they are inauthentic, they will scatter and disappear. Untruth self-destructs. And if they do not scatter—well, from Gamaliel's perspective as well as Paul's, the truth is to be perceived and obeyed, *homothumadon*. Where the obedience is properly given, the Spirit follows; and where the Lord guides through the Spirit, the truth may be found through what "seems good to the Holy Spirit and to us," to what "seems good to us, having become *homothumadon.*"

Founded in the apostolic teaching, where the plan of God is grasped in the coincidence of Scripture, Jesus' career, and Jesus' instructions, the normative understanding of those who are to be saved is further unfolded during the time of salvation's spreading, as the Lord continues to work with his people. Prophets are helpful in this process, but they play only a marginal role in Acts, exhorting and predicting minor events. Scholars are useful, and are given much respect; but their office is mainly to persuade the unbeliever and to confirm what has already been discerned. Apostles are extremely important as pioneers of new understanding; but they are the first word, not the last. The decisive test comes in the bosom of the Christian church, whose loving unity and righteous behavior are complemented by a one-mindedness that is readily persuaded of the Spirit's true workings, however surprising. Like an apostle writ large, the church lives in the Spirit and is open to its disclosures—and these become decisively normative in and through the members' faithfully cumulative communal recognition of what is in fact happening in and among them.

4

John

*I*t is an apt irony of historical accident that the various ways of arranging the canon finally stabilized with the juxtaposition of Luke and John. I am not thinking of Boismard's thesis that Luke himself was John's final editor,[1] but of the more usual view that emphasizes the differences between them. The two Gospels with prologues: one has only to look there. From Luke's own homely (if stylish and self-consciously learned) voice, which speaks to a probably real and certainly verisimilitudinous Theophilos about journeyman predecessors and historical deeds and the business of research and composition, we turn to a content of utterance and a tonal sublimity that may properly belong to the Holy Spirit alone, though it eventually goes so far as to descend into the midst of an extraordinarily privileged human "we" which forms the final locus of celebration. This "we" becomes the addressee, to the extent that there is one; but it is notably a "we" purified of historical association, of any longing for any evidence besides glory, purified even of fleshly begetting. Luke's prologue opens the subject to rather ordinary human understanding; John's fairly closes the subject, and clearly implies that ordinary human understanding is both inadequate and rather beside the point. Between these two, one may evidently test the coherence of early Christian suppositions demandingly —and perhaps to the breaking point.

Such a test may be conducted at various stages of the hypothetical formation of the Fourth Gospel, and I shall eventually attempt to deal with the implications of some of the source-theories for the reconstruction of forms of earliest Christian understanding. But the first and soundest level at which one must work is the one which is unequivocally attested: the Fourth Gospel itself, in the form known through discriminating textual criticism. That document was apparently thought by its final editor to embody a more or less adequate representation of Christian understanding—for even if we may suppose the editing unfinished, the text nevertheless gives us materials accepted as belonging to the process. No hypothetically reconstructed prior stage may have

100

quite so much said for it, since all such posited documents are not only in themselves hypothetical, but also subject to the same charges of incompleteness. Indeed, they must face more forceful charges of incompleteness: for in each case, what we know even more firmly than the hypothetical earlier text is the fact that it did not survive alone but only in redacted combination with supplementary and qualifying material. There is some reason for supposing that there was a signs-source,[2] and that it represented one authentic early Christian mode of understanding; but there is incomparably greater reason for acknowledging that there is a Fourth Gospel, and that it represents an authentic pattern of early Christian thought, perhaps authentic even in its inconsistencies. At any rate, that is what we must start with. Whether or not the Fourth Gospel was deliberately left in the form in which we find it, it was accepted in that form. We do not know for certain that it or any of its sources was ever accepted in any other form. That, therefore, is where one must begin.

One thing that is immediately striking is that the terms of the Christian Gospel, even of the ultimate Gospel, seem here to be unlike the synoptic accounts. If the synoptic quintessence places Jesus as the eschatological judge in a final cataclysmic scenario, the Fourth Gospel generally ignores the apocalyptic version of the kingdom, and is at pains to insist that Jesus does not judge (3:17, 8:15, 12:47), that judgment has taken place already (3:18), and that eternal life, rather than succeeding the general resurrection, has already become available (5:24; 11:25–26).[3] Small wonder that communities whose sense of the content of Christian thought were formed on synoptic models entertained suspicions about the orthodoxy of the Gospel reputed to be of John.[4]

But the issue is not content. Content is a secondary matter, because it is determined by a prior consideration. The issue is that prior consideration: what is the Fourth Gospel's sense of the court of appeal by which true content is to be decided? On that question, and no other, hangs the essential problem of original theological authenticity, and the possibility that there may have been a procedural consensus that antedated the emergence within the Christian fold of trial theologies theoretically subject to its test. The question that must be addressed to the Fourth Gospel is therefore: What does it have to say about normative Christian understanding, especially with respect to the criteria by which it may be determined?

I turn first to the pattern and theory of revelation contained in the Gospel's account of Jesus' public ministry.

What makes revelation so crucially important is the jeopardy of man's existential situation. The Fourth Gospel does not bother to explain how this precarious state has come about, but the fact of the matter is that despite the divine creation of the world (1:3, 10), that same world has somehow fallen under an evil domination, be it styled the ruler of this world (12:31), the father of the devil (or, though less gramatically, the demonic father, *tou patros tou diabolou*, 8:44), or the less personal agencies of darkness (1:5, 3:19) or sin (*tēn hamartian tou kosmou*, 1:29). Whatever the structure of this disadvantaged condition, it results in a sharp cleavage between the world and God, such that the natural character of the former is evil. The works of the world are evil (7:7); men, being of the world (8:23), thus tend to do evil works (3:19), as if following the direction of a diabolical and lying father (8:38, 41, 44). But the world is not radically evil: it was divinely created, and is still capable of being divinely loved (3:16). However steeped in darkness and sin and death, the world may yet be saved (3:17, 4:42), may be given life (6:33, 51), may be rescued from sin (1:29), may be illuminated (1:4, 9; 3:19). Therefore the possibility exists that men, though of the darkened and death-bound world, may come into the light (3:31), be rescued from their sins (8:24), receive life (3:16, 36; 5:24). The benevolence of God would have it so: he acts so as to save rather than condemn (3:16–17). But condemnation is the automatic alternative to salvation (3:36; 5:24, 29; 12:48), and men are not readily inclined to recognize and accept the offer of rescue, because the accustomed darkness of their lives leads them to resist and hate the light that reveals and judges them (3:19–20). The slave of sin hates to hear the truth, when the truth is that he is a slave of sin (8:34, 40). How then shall he come to see beyond this dreadful judgment to the deeper discovery that in this same revelation is a truth that has the power to make him free (8:32)? Paul saw the dilemma of God's benevolence in dealings with Israel: wanting to give life, God gave his word to men that their obedience might secure it—but the weakness of men was such that the instrument of life became an instrument of judgment and of death. The Fourth Gospel faces the problem in its newer form. How shall God reveal in order to save? How may benighted and perverse men be addressed and engaged so that salvation may fall within the reach and capacity of their cooperation?

The key question is posed in 6:28: "What shall we do that we may work the works of God?" For the alternative is to work the works of the world, which are evil and deadly. The answer to this question can be given only through the mediation of the Son. We have never heard God's voice nor seen his form (5:37). No one has seen the Father, except the one who is with God (6:46). No one has gone up to heaven, except the one who has come down from heaven (3:13). Thus although the Jews may profess the Father as their God, yet they have not known him (8:54–55; 7:28). Neither do the Samaritans know the object of their worship (4:22). But the Son knows him (8:55; 7:29). No man has ever seen God—but the only begotten has revealed (1:18), and has revealed what he has seen with the Father (8:38).[5]

The Son may be the light of the world, and reveal the unseen and unheard Father, because of his direct knowledge and his total obedience, by which he becomes for the world a faithful imitation of the Father. He comes into the world not on his own, but because he is sent by the Father (8:42). He is here therefore only in the Father's name (5:43), seeking not his own glory but that of the Father (7:18; 8:50). He accordingly does nothing of himself (8:28), and follows not his own will but that of the Father (5:30; 6:38). Indeed, he *can* do nothing of himself, but only what he sees the Father doing—for the Father loves the Son and shows him all the things he does, and what the Father does, the Son does likewise (5:19–20). The true nourishment of Jesus as the Son is therefore to do the will and the work of the Father (4:34). His works are not only the works the Father has given him to do (5:36) but effectually the works of the Father in the world: therefore the Father wills that the Son be honored as himself (5:23). Believing in the Son is equivalent to believing in the Father, in the most literal way: "he who believes in me believes not in me but in the one sending me" (12:44). This is so in three ways. In the first place, the Son's obedient enactment of the will and the works of the Father makes him effectually the Father's way of acting in the world, the Father's earthly mode of self-revelation. In the second place, the Son has not only been sealed by the Father (6:27) and thus authorized in his obedient agency to be a visible manifestation of the Father's will and work, but moreover he is himself endowed with divine life, "for just as the Father has life in himself, so he gave to the Son life to have in himself" (5:26). The Son is therefore not just a faithful imitation of the locus of true life and light, but in him is life and the life is the light of men (1:4). And in the third place, the Son is not alone, but the Father who sent him is with him (8:16, 29): and indeed is *in* him (10:38), so that in this sense too it may be said that the Son and the Father are one (10:30) and that he who has seen the Son has seen the Father (12:45).

Believing in the Son is believing in the Father. And that is what men are called to do. The Son comes to do the will of the Father; but the will of God is precisely that everyone seeing and believing in the Son may have eternal life (6:40). The Son manifests the works of God, so that men may come to work the work of God rather than the works of the world; but the answer to the critical question, "What shall we do that we may work the works of God?" (6:28), is precisely "This is the work of God, that you believe in him whom he sent" (6:29). The existential issue therefore draws to a sharp and efficient focus: believe in the Son and have the life which God's love offers, or disbelieve and fall into the automatic condemnation to destruction (3:16, 18, 36).

But what is it to believe in the Son? And how does such belief come about?

There are, in the first portions of the Fourth Gospel,[6] two levels of belief in Jesus. The first has to do with his basic authenticity, and works itself out through the divisions among the Jews about him. Some think him to be a deceiver; others maintain that he is a good man (7:12). Some suppose him crazy; others insist that he neither speaks nor acts like a madman (10:19–21). Some take him to be a sinner; others say that he must be from God (9:24–34; cf. 9:16). Despite initial wavering and uncertainty,[7] this division tends to push to stark alternatives. Those who believe in him—that is, in his authenticity—tend to conclude that he is perhaps the Christ, or the expected Prophet (7:31, 40–41); those who, for one reason or another, will not accept this conclusion are ready to have him arrested (7:32, 44). The same signs lead some to believe in him, and some to plot his death (11:45–53).

It is presumably at this level that those believers arrived who saw and were convinced by the signs Jesus did during the first Jerusalem Passover visit: "many believed in his name, beholding the signs which he was doing" (2:23). Is this then identical with that belief "in the name of the only-begotten Son" (3:18) from which life and rescue come? Apparently not; for despite the similarity of formula, there is something significantly incomplete in that first stage of belief. The incompleteness is hinted, I think, by the succeeding two verses in chapter 2: "But Jesus did not entrust himself to them, because he knew them all, and because he had no need of testimony at the human level—because he knew what was in man" (2:24–25);[8] and it is surely indicated by the next passage, at the beginning of chapter 3, in which Nicodemus' acknowledgement of Jesus' signs and of his authenticity as a teacher sent from God (3:2) is immediately answered with an assurance that a rebirth of a sort that Nicodemus does not even understand is indispensable to entry into the kingdom (3:3–12). The Prologue indentifies belief in his name with just such a begetting from above as Nicodemus lacks (1:12–13). One must, for a start, believe in Jesus; but there are ways of believing in him which are not sufficient.

Perhaps the clearest example of the two-layered character of belief is not that of Nicodemus but that of the man born blind. After the miracle, he is quite prepared to acknowledge that Jesus is a prophet (9:17), and that he obviously is of God and does his will (9:30–33). But when subsequently posed the key question by Jesus himself, "Do you believe in the Son of Man?"[9] he must answer helplessly, "And who is he, Sir, that I may believe in Him?" (9:35–36). Jesus informs him; and the man then announces his belief, and worships. The moral is clear. He

believed in Jesus, but did not yet believe in the Son: and the difference
was important.

The will of God is that everyone who sees the Son and believes in him
may have everlasting life (6:40). Seeing, *theôrôn*, is here surely equivalent to *diakrinôn*, discerning.[10] The man born blind has seen Jesus, but
had not discerned the Sonship. That is why Jesus tells him that his
presence is a function of judgment insofar as men who do not see may
see, and those who see may become blind (9:38). The Pharisees who
claim to see but rest with their suspicions that Jesus is a deceiver and
a sinner are thus doubly blind (9:40–41). But even single blindedness
disqualifies. Those who saw the miracle of the loaves were ready
enough to believe that Jesus was the expected prophet (6:14), but their
misunderstanding, however enthusiastically affirmative, requires that
Jesus conceal himself from them (6:15). When they find him again, and
learn that they have more to learn, they grasp the message enough to
move beyond the miraculous sign they have already received and ask
Jesus what sign he does that they may see (*idômen*, here the mere
observation of the sign[11]) and believe him: "what do you work?" (6:30).

The shift in language is significant. There is, admittedly, an unsteadi-
ness of usage in the Fourth Gospel, enough to suggest that, for instance,
the weight of the terms "believe" and "glory" in the verse concluding
the first miracle at Cana (2:11) is importantly different from the deepest
sense of *belief*, and from the glory which obtained only after the crucifixion;[12] but there are firm tendencies. One of the tendencies is the
distinction between *sign* and *work*.

Signs are miracles which can be established by vulgar proof: taste the
liquid drawn from the water-vessels, check out the hour of healing, get
depositions from the parents of the man reputedly born blind, smell the
decomposing corpse of Lazarus. It is probably no accident that each of
these instances is confirmed through witnesses who are either ignorant
of the miracle or motivated to disguise it: the confirming procedure is
properly scientific. Other people's reports of such signs may thus be
trusted, and it is therefore no excuse not to have witnessed them oneself
(12:17–18). But of course many did witness them (2:11; 2:23; 6:2; 6:14),
and of these, many followed the clear logic of their implication: no one
does such wonders unless God is with him (9:30–33; cf. 3:2, 9:16, 10:21).
That brings them to the first level of belief (2:11, 2:23, 3:2, 6:2, 6:14,
etc.). There, one may still be unsure of Jesus' precise status—a teacher
come from God (3:2), or the Prophet (6:14, 9:17), or at least greater than
John (10:41), or in some ways the equal of the Messiah (7:31)—but at
least one may clearly rule out the possibility that he is mad (10:21) or
sinful (9:16, 30–33), unless one blindly clings to conflicting preconcep-
tions.

There are, admittedly, those who fail to believe despite having had so many signs done before them (12:37). Such incredulity warrants the invocation of Isaiah's extreme explanation, which is prophetic of precisely this incredulity: he has blinded their eyes and hardened their heart so that they may not see and understand and turn and be healed (12:40). But however apt may be the application of this prophecy, there is an alternative way of accounting for their unbelief which more plainly discloses their responsibility for their state, and shows their blindness to be not something imposed but, literally, a connivance.

The radical disbelief in—and concomitant opposition to—Jesus is rooted in his having broken the Sabbath (5:16, 9:16) and is exacerbated by his bold claims about his relationship to God (5:18, 10:33). These are quite simply against the Law, and those who profess to be disciples of Moses, to whom God clearly had spoken (9:28–29), must oppose such inadmissible behavior: Jesus is evidently a sinner. Similarly, an appeal to the Law will demonstrate that he cannot be a prophet (7:52) and that he cannot possibly be the Messiah (7:42). Anyone who takes him seriously is obviously an accursed ignoramus, with no knowledge of the Law (7:49). Anyone who says that he is the Messiah is contributing to the delinquency of Israel (7:12), and deserves to be expelled from the synagogue (9:22; 12:42).

So far, the argument seems sound. Its fatal flaw, as Nicodemus points out, is that it violates the Law itself by judging before all the evidence is in (7:51). The opponents, faced with the virtual paradox of a wonder-working sinner, sustain their judgment of his sinfulness by closing their eyes to the wonders. But if the signs alone are not perceived as persuasive evidence against a conclusion of guilt, then the Law will provide grounds for counter-argument against each of the main points of objection. The Law requires that the work of circumcision be done sometimes on the Sabbath: so why not healing? (7:22–24). The Law itself calls mere mortals *gods:* so why should one with a still better claim to the title be forbidden it? (10:34–36). And then if the Father himself works on the Sabbath, what is irregular about the one who works the Father's works doing so? (5:17).[13] Being a disciple of Moses is little help if one exercises only fleshly judgment about what Moses has written (8:15). If one sees only that Israelites are not to be enslaved and rests content with obedience at that level, and yet fails to discern the deeper bondage that breaks the Law (8:32–36), one has significantly missed the point; if one perceives only the fleshly descent from Abraham and not the need to imitate Abraham's receptiveness to the truth (8:39–40), one loses the real sense of, and the real participation in, Abraham's paternity (8:38, 44). If one is really a disciple of Moses, and really believes what Moses has written, then far from becoming an opponent of Jesus, one must become his disciple: for Moses wrote of him and condemns those who do not believe in him (5:45–47). If he seems outrageous in making himself superior to Moses (6:32, 49), to Abraham (8:53), and to the prophets (8:53), then one should realize the deeper truth that what Moses and Abraham and Isaiah and the other prophets—indeed, the scriptures in general—saw and bore witness to was precisely Jesus' glory (1:45, 5:39, 5:46, 8:56, 12:41). Whether or not Jesus bears witness to himself, Scripture and the truth both justify him.[14] Those who do not grasp this are blind, to signs and the Law alike. If they compound their fault by arrogantly rejecting attempts to relieve them of their blindness (as the Pharisees do not only with Jesus but with the deft and simple argument of the man born blind, 9:34), then they are self-blinded. And if, with all this, they nevertheless insist that they see, then they have taken a self-incriminating responsibility and made their blindness sinful (9:41). There is no excuse for not being convinced by the signs.

But neither is there excuse for being convinced only by the signs. Jesus' observation that they do not believe unless they see signs and wonders (4:48) is clearly an objection, even though he readily accommodates the request of the royal official that his son be healed. When the Jews ask for a sign (2:18, 6:30), they are not rebuked in the way that such a request is met in the synoptic Gospels—and indeed, signs are offered in response. But signs take one only part way. They do not necessarily lead to the discernment of the only-begotten Son, and therefore are not the real stuff of life. To go there, one must see more deeply than the vulgar and fleshly level of the miraculous. One must perceive not the signs but the *works* of Jesus.

The terminology is not so sharply distinguished as to leave no occasions where *ergon* seems to mean miracle.[15] On the basis of the belief stimulated by the signs, one might plausibly propose to read Jesus' claim in 5:36 and 10:25 as meaning that his *miracles* bear witness to him. His announcement that the man's blindness is so that the works of God may be made manifest in him (9:1–4) seems to refer to the coming cure. The very shift in terms that occurs in 6:30, "What sign do you do, that we may see and believe you? What do you work?" seems to establish an equivalence between the key terms. But for all that, I think that *work* is a specially reserved term in the Fourth Gospel, significantly different from *sign* and correlative with a deeper understanding of Jesus, and that those to whom the Fourth Gospel was addressed would have perceived this difference without requiring either polemic or definitional excursus.[16]

The apparent slippage of terms in 6:30 is in fact a literarily deliberate representation of a standard piece of incomprehension, analogous to Nicodemus' failure to grasp the meaning of *gennêthênai anôthen*, or the Samaritan woman's literal-mindedness about living water, or the disciples' misunderstanding of Jesus' reference to the sleep of Lazarus. They ask for an authenticating sign, after the model of Moses' arrangement of miraculous manna, and are willing indifferently to say "do a sign" or "what do you work?" What they do not understand is how different these two are. He will not do a sign; and his *work* has to do, as he has just hinted to them, not with the literal, if miraculous, food that perishes (as manna does pre-eminently), but with the metaphorical food which the Son gives for everlasting life (6:27). He now repeats the same instruction, this time more overtly: the true bread from heaven is himself (6:32–35), and the work he works is being there, speaking the words of spirit and life (6:63), so that those who come to him and believe may neither hunger nor die (6:35, 49–51, 58). This is what the Father wills; therefore, it is what the Son works (6:38–40). To hanker after a vulgar visible miracle, a mere sign, is to stay within the boundaries of that which perishes. The truth is deeper and simpler. Jesus' audience may have been thinking of the ability to do miraculous signs when they asked "What shall we do that we may work the works of God?" (6:28), perhaps wanting to learn how to imitate Jesus' feat with the loaves. But —providentially—they chose an ambiguous language. The deeper, simpler, and more essential meaning of the question has to do not with miracles but with acting out the Father's will. The works of the world are evil and dark, because they do not enact God's will. How then to work the *true* works of God? Whichever question they had intended, they receive the answer to the more important one: believe in him whom God has sent (6:29), see the Son and believe in him (6:40). Not sign, but work—the work of the Father, the work of the Son, and the proper work of obedient men. But, however much they may have been impressed at the level of signs already, they do not manage to get past this level to the deeper belief that gives life (6:36, 40–42)—that is, they do not penetrate to the true sense of *work*, and perceive that it is not doing the works of the Law that saves, but performing that act of faith that is the *ergon alêthinon*.[17]

For it is this idea that the works of the Law are superseded, I believe, that underlies the Fourth Gospel's notion of works. It has obvious affinities with Pauline theology and may owe its origins to Pauline influences. But be that as it may, it is the principle by which one should interpret the innuendo in other sayings about works.

On the one hand, there is the matter of the "works of Abraham" in 8:39–40. This too is a new edition of a familiar Pauline idea. Salvation comes to the sons of Abraham, and his true sons are not of his flesh alone, but are those faithful to what the Law reveals in Abraham. And what is that? There are two main interpretations. From one point of view, the main work of Abraham is circumcision, by which men are made members of the covenant and participants in the Promise. According to this viewpoint, circumcision is one of the works of the Law to which one must be unflinchingly faithful. But Paul's alternative is that Abraham's chief work, which antedated both circumcision and the Law, was faith. Thus faith, and not the works of the Law, is what saves. The Fourth Gospel is a branch from the same root.[18] Abraham rejoiced to see the day of the Son (8:56), and his works are characterized by contrast with those who would kill the one who has told the truth which he has heard from God (8:39–40). That is, Abraham as believer is the true model for those who would work the works of God, those who would do God's will —in contrast with the works of the Law, which are only speciously linked with Abraham. You search the scriptures, because you think to have eternal life in them: but ironically, their true work is to point to the true source of life, the one who shows himself above what they seem to enjoin as works. Again, fleshly judgment leads the understanding astray.

On the other hand, it is against the same background that one should understand the contention about the man healed on the Sabbath. In the first instance, the Jews are angered because Jesus has violated the Law, failed to do the works of the Law. Jesus says: "I did one work, and you all are amazed" (7:21). He does not mean that they are favorably impressed, but that they are surprised, nonplussed, shocked—the context makes that clear by going on to argue that if the Sabbath can be used for circumcision, they should not be angry (thus the specific value of *thaumazete*) if it is used to heal (7:22–23). The concluding admonition to judge not according to appearance but according to righteous judgment is basically cognate with the reminder not to judge according to the flesh or the rulebook but according to a deeper discernment. Jesus did one work. What was it? In one sense, it coincides with the sign he did, the miracle of healing: but it is not identical with the sign. More exactly, the word sets up a confrontation between Jesus and an understanding which, although especially characteristic of the Pharisees (7:45–49, 8:13, 9:16, etc.), is typically attributed by the Fourth Gospel to the Jews in general (7:1, 8:22, 9:18, etc.). By doing a work on the Sabbath, he has failed to do the works of the Law. But the point is exactly in the transfiguration of the term *work,* not only in the punning sense that the work proper to the Sabbath is non-work, but in the deeper implication that points to Jesus' non-miraculous revelation of the work of God and the end of the works of Law as a way to life: his deliberate and benevolent violation of the Sabbath is his own work. As the text's earlier discussion of this event also shows, the miraculous character of the healing is scarcely in editorial sight: attention is focussed only on the breach of the Sabbath, which Jesus accounts for by reminding his opponents that the Father works on the Sabbath (5:17). That he should both violate the Sabbath and make himself equal to God only worsens his standing with the unbelieving Jews, of course, but the two are inextricably tied together. Jesus works not the works of the Law but the works of God. He works on the Sabbath because that is what he has seen his Father do (5:19): the work that is not a work of Law is therefore precisely for that reason a revelation of Jesus' higher order of working. The verdict is exactly the one invited by the Sabbath-breaker whom Jesus addresses in the logion inserted by the Codex Beza after Luke 6:5: *ei men oidas ti poieis, markarios ei.* And he knows, perfectly. His Father works, and he works. And his Father will show him still greater works, that you may be amazed (*thaumazête*, 5:20).

So, I think, is to be interpreted the cryptic introduction to the later Sabbath cure. Is the man blind because of his own sin or that of his parents? Neither, replies Jesus, but in order that the works of God may be manifested in him (9:2–3). Superficially, this reply appears to refer to the cure itself. But I think it more plausible that it refers to the deeper level of God's work that lies beyond the miraculous sign, even if connected with it: the freedom from the Sabbath restriction, and the eventual belief of the man born blind in the Son of God (9:38). That is why the event can then be summed up in the terms of 9:39: "I came into this world for judgment, that the unseeing may see and the seeing may become blind." The man born blind has seen not only in the vulgar literal sense, but in the more important sense. Jesus has just told him that he has seen the Son of God, and the man responds with belief and worship (9:37–38), but those with literal sight and professed reverence for the Law of Moses have undergone a fatal closing of the mind's eyes on the same occasion, and have put themselves under judgment.

The irony is thus double when Jesus asks for which of his good works which he has shown from the Father do they wish to stone him, and they reply that it is not for a good work but for blasphemy, that he makes himself equal to God (10:32–33). What they take to be a Law-breaking bad work is indeed a good work—the supreme work of God among men, the revelation of the Son. His works bear witness to him (5:36), more perfectly and thoroughly than his signs can do: the signs leave confusion about whether he is a prophet, a teacher come from God, or even more, but when the Jews would resolve their uncertainity by asking him directly if he is the Messiah, he simply tells them that the works he does in his Father's name bear witness to him, but they still do not believe (10:24–26). If they could only discern the works, they would see. "If I do not do the works of my Father, do not believe in me; but if I do, then even if you do not believe in me, believe in the works, that you may know and understand that the Father is in me and I in the Father" (10:37–38). As Nicodemus insists, the final judgment even under the Law comes only after a man has been heard out and his deeds known (7:51). If one really knows what Jesus does, one may perceive that his works are the works of God, and bear witness to his having been sent by God to bring to completion the works God has given him to complete (4:34, 5:36). The one who does the truth comes to the light, that his works may be manifest, that they are worked in God (3:21). But how can his works be known by those who shun the light? And thus the very works that are the work of God, and reveal the truth about Jesus, and make it possible to see and believe and therefore to live, leave those whom the darkness has mastered not only unable to grasp him but ready to brand him a sinner contemptuous of the works of the Law— and thus, ironically, of the works of God. For the Fourth Gospel, Jesus is the Work of Contradiction.[19]

The norm of Christian understanding is, thus far, the Son, particularly as he is seen through the discernment of his works as the manifestation and enactment of the will of the Father—Christ as the effective expression of the mind of God. Looking back now to my summary remarks on the sense of the constitution of Christian thought found in the synoptic Gospels, I discover—with no small measure of surprise—that most of the claims may be repeated here. "The pattern of right understanding that is the ultimate wisdom of God for men may be found in the scriptures, properly read"—for even if the Fourth Gospel is not especially preoccupied with this dimension, it nevertheless makes it clear that the revelation in Jesus is what Moses and Isaiah are all about, and what Abraham saw, and what was promised in the Law and the Prophets, and in the scriptures at large, which bear witness concerning him (5:39). "Or in the pre-crucifixion teachings of Jesus of Nazareth, properly grasped" —for despite the difficulties even the disciples had in understanding altogether what he was talking about, it is clear enough that this was his message and that only his enemies' dogged incapacity to be detached from their presuppositions prevented them from getting the basic point. "Or in a discerning appreciation of the career of Jesus up through the time of his taking up"—but in the Fourth Gospel, one can say as much even setting the temporal limit at the end of his public teaching, for his works have just this function. I omit for the moment the remaining function of the synoptic theory, the post-resurrection teaching, and find once more that the next description continues to fit: "and these manifest one and the same messianic saving plan and Word of God, to which one may submit in belief and be saved, or withhold assent and die." Some of the emphases might be adjusted to characterize the Fourth Gospel more exactly,[20] but the formula holds.

It is with the concluding part of the summary on the synoptists that the coincidence dies away: "all of these are immediately accessible, or accessible through reliable witness, to ordinary human capacities." At this point, that cannot possibly stand as a characterization of the Fourth Gospel's underlying assumptions. This much is true up to the level of signs, perhaps; but that is not sufficient. When it comes to the discernment of works, it may be granted that there are ways of sustaining eligibility that may be said to fall under ordinary capacities (a willingness to hear reason, an avoidance of evil works), but it is by no means clear that what is in man, with or without the assistance of trustworthy intermediaries, is necessarily capable of approximating the necessary discernment on its own.

What has the Fourth Gospel to say directly about such matters? The verdict is not readily encouraging to the ordinary capacities of men. It is heavy with the potential arbitrariness of election. No one comes to the Son unless drawn by the Father (6:37, 10:29). Those who are so given will hear and follow (10:27), but those who are not given are simply not his sheep and do not believe (10:26). Those who are given by the Father, the Son will keep, because such is the Father's will (6:39). But those who are not given—well, as John the Baptist attests, it is only from heaven that one gets a following (3:27); and as Jesus himself attests, the begetting Spirit, like the wind, blows where it will (3:8). Those who believe in his name are not of the ordinary stuff of mankind, but are begotten of God (1:12–13), begotten from above by the Spirit who blows where he will (3:8). If one wishes to construct a desperately arbitrary theology of election, the Fourth Gospel will provide texts to support it.

All the same, it would falsify the Gospel's drift to settle for the complex of texts cited above without qualifying them by another compatible (if not obviously congenial) group that returns the responsibility for non-election to human capacity. The ultimate locus of salvific decision lies in the will of God, but that will is not necessarily formed without reference to human desert or normal human capacity. This is a subtle but important aspect of the Fourth Gospel's theology, and its lineaments can be perceived—can be glimpsed on a more specific and concrete level in the case of the man born blind. Is he being punished for his parents' sin, or is his blindness because of sin foreseen in him by God? The former proposition could be interpreted in a way not uncongenial to the Fourth Gospel, as referring to a general condition of human sinfulness by which suffering might generally be explained. The latter proposition more readily and obviously corresponds to a theory of justice sustained by the Fourth Gospel's theology as a whole. But neither proposition is really applicable to this case, precisely because the blindness is about to be graciously removed and therefore need not be accounted for as a punishment but only as a setting for a dramatic event that is so remarkable and rewarding as to make the problem of the blind man's previous discomfort seem trivial. The awkward question of justice is neutralized accordingly, as one virtually forgets what it had been about.

The analogue on the larger scale, for which the story of the man born blind is deliberately modelled, is the problem of the relative darkness in which men are forced to struggle until the revelation of the Son. There are two importantly different varieties of this darkness. The lesser is the darkness of simple ignorance. It is possibly not culpable, though that issue (like the question of the blind man's sin) is never really resolved. It does not have to be resolved. We do not have to care, because the issue of culpability is made trivial by the triumph of the light in which the darkness is banished. Men were left darkling so that God might be glorified in the Son's disclosure. If such darkness can finally be traced to God's will, those who are dramatically rescued from it will rejoice at his wonderful works rather than complain about the unfairness of the way he set them up. Darkness is not an important theological problem with respect to those who have already escaped it, or are about to do so. And as for the others, it is notable that the Fourth Gospel does not concern itself much with those who lived and died before Jesus' ministry, and it is still more notable that when it adverts to them, as in the case of Abraham (8:56), it makes them somehow equal partakers in the same revelation enjoyed by the contempories of Jesus.

The other darkness is deeper, and it is the darkness of ignorance as invincibly fortified by the darkness of sin. In addition to the uninformedness that God offers to remove, there is in all mankind a perverse streak that is wantonly followed by some. Men tend to love the darkness rather than the light, not because they are sentenced to darkness by a divine decree or a withholding of revelation, but because their works are evil despite what God has revealed (3:19), and they do not want to hear the truth that says so (3:20). They are attuned to the glory of men in preference to the glory of God (5:44, 12:43). The judgment of Jesus is just, because he seeks after the will of the Father (5:30); the same right judgment is available to men, and if they really seek the will of the Father, they will know whether Jesus expresses the ways of God or some unauthorized quackery of his own (7:17). Those who are really obedient to God as their Father, rather than to their own lusts, will love Jesus (8:42); being of God, they will hear God's words in him (8:47). But if the love of God is not really in them (5:42), they will not hold within them the word of God that brings discernment (5:38). They become the servants not of God but of sin (8:34). confined by their own neglect to the works of this world, which are evil (7:7). There, they do the works not of their true Father, but of their father of lies and lusts (8:44). There is no appeal to the arbitrariness of a divine election: God has offered to release them from the provisional darkness, and they have no one but themselves to blame if they love the darkness more than the light (3:19).

If the Jews of the Fourth Gospel are concerned to give proper credit to God (9:24), the Gospel itself is even more concerned to do so. Its theological theory is, like Paul's, ready to ascribe man's right understanding to the gracious work of the Father, but not at the expense of human responsibility, or even human capacity as the locus of that responsibility. Those who believe and find life are the recipients of a divine benevolence that goes well beyond what is in man (2:24–25), but it is founded in what lies within human abilities. Despite all the darkness that surrounds the human condition, it remains possible to love and pursue the light of God. It is, in fact, required—not by an arbitrary divine decree, but by the nature of reality. It is, quite simply, a matter of life and death. Those who stifle their natural inclinations to life and truth and light, in order to remain comfortably self-deceived about the dark falsehood they are acting out, must die. That is the way that they have chosen. Those who respond otherwise will see the light and accept it, will know the truth and be freed, will have life more abundantly. All are called. They choose themselves. That is why Jesus does not have to judge. Belief in the Son lies, if not within, at least accessible to what may be called the natural capacities of man. The Fourth Gospel is insistent that these "natural capacities" are so only graciously, on permanent loan from the Father wherever they are not squandered; but it insists also on the fact of human squandering as against divine withholding. It does not represent that the possibility of loving light and truth is simply a function of arbitrary election.[21]

Thus there is, up to this point in the Fourth Gospel, a strong measure of coincidence between its theory of thought-law and that of the synoptic tradition. I shall attend presently to the Fourth Gospel's views on post-resurrection teaching and post-ascension witness. But it remains to attend to another critical matter. The coincidence of the synoptic constitutional principles is in the mind of Christ, as expressive of the mind and will of God. In a sense, that formula too may be applied to the Fourth Gospel; but there appears to be a significant difference. The term "mind" is, as it applies to the synoptists, fairly unequivocal: it suggests a more or less broad content of understanding reflected in pronouncements ranging from the Sermon on the Mount to the apocalyptic predictions of Jesus. Thus far, "mind" appears, if applied to the Fourth Gospel, to be without evident content: either metaphorical or opaquely hidden in the mystery of the Son. The Gospel seems to be efficiently reduced to: believe that Jesus is the Son of God (viz., that he is in effect the presence of the Father) and you are saved. Is it, as it may appear, a question of a single law of thought, the identity of Jesus with the Son?

That is surely the main norm, just as the gracious power of the Father is the main consideration in explaining how some men come to accept it. But as in that case, there is more to be said.

There is more to be said because, in the first place, there was more that Jesus said. Even if Nicodemus did not discern everything about him all at once, he perceived him as a teacher come from God (3:2)—and the teaching that inspired this observation was evidently, from Nicodemus' confession, not confined to Jesus' proclamation of his identity as the Son. It seems rather to have been a disclosure of the Father, of the kind that may lead a Pharisee to discern an authentic interpreter of the Word, or an *am ha-arez* to recognize an authentic prophet who may announce in a less derivative way that "This is the Word of the Lord." He speaks the words of God (3:34), as rabbis and prophets may be said to do. His teaching is the teaching of the Father (7:16), because he teaches as the Father has taught him (8:28). Thus the proper response for one who hears his word is to believe in the one who sent him (5:24). Such an act of faith, as in the case of rabbis and prophets, entails a coordinate act of faith in the bearer of the word himself, but only as a consequence of appropriating the word as truly the Lord's. The basic level of unbelief is therefore not disbelief in Jesus, but disbelief in his word, in the word of the Father that is spoken through him. The same resistant *epithumia* which impeded the effectiveness of other men sent from God, and was accordingly denounced by them, is at work in the resistance to Jesus. Men do not hear his word because their deformed dispositions resist the truth. They do not hear the word of the Father, because they are not faithful to him, not genuinely people of the Father (8:43–47). In one sense, the role of Jesus is accordingly transparent. Because he speaks as the Father has directed him to speak, the Word he transmits is itself an agent of judgment, just as the Word delivered through Moses stands in judgment over those who do not keep it. Jesus himself does not have to judge (12:47–50).

The bearer of the Word, however, is not merely an unconscious medium of communication. He says what was given to him to say, but also what was given to him to understand. The judgment implicit in the Word he bears is thus echoed in his own judgment. The Law accuses; but Moses also accuses (5:45). The Word from the Father judges; but Jesus also judges, and his judgment is just, precisely because it conforms obediently to the will of the Father (5:30). He not only transmits the Father's teaching and the Father's will, he recapitulates them in himself. He says not merely what he has been told, but what he has *seen*

(3:32, 8:38), and what he *knows* (3:11). And he has many things to say and to judge (8:26).

Many things: not only the central message concerning the identity of himself with the Son and therefore with the Father, but other teachings and judgments that apparently are to define normative understanding in ways that supplement the more rarefied mystical intuition of his Sonship. The Samaritan woman expects that when the Messiah comes, he will tell us "all things" (4:25). Jesus' acknowledgment that he himself is the one appears to ratify her supposition, further reinforced when he not only tells her "all things which I have done" (4:29, 39), but spends two days with her townsmen giving to them what they find to be a belief-inspiring *logos* (4:40–42). We may note Jesus' analogy between the writings of Moses and his own words (5:47): it is important to realize not only that he is the Son, but that he has the words of eternal life (6:68). If his sayings occasion belief in him (4:42, 7:40, 8:30), they also occasion belief in themselves (5:47), and they sometimes occasion disbelief in themselves (6:60) which results in unbelief in him (6:61–66). Believe him, believe his words. If his word has no place in you, you are alien (8:47). True conformity to the revealed norm of understanding is not confined to an indescribable intuition of the Son, but involves keeping his word (8:51). To those who believe in him, he tells what there is further to do: "If you remain in my word, then you are truly my disciples" (8:31). It is his *words* that are spirit and life (6:63); it is in abiding in his word that the true disciple will come to know the truth and be made free (8:31–32).

The shifting of tenses in the last-mentioned passage signals a matter of profound importance in the Fourth Gospel's sense of, and need for, a constitutional basis of understanding that goes even beyond what the disciples had seen and heard in his public ministry. It also stands as a warning against making too much of Jesus' diverse pre-crucifixion teachings. Jesus does not say that they know the truth, but that they are going to know it; not that they are free, but that they shall be freed. Despite the apparent implication of the Fourth Gospel's representation of the public teaching of Jesus, his words and works had not yet revealed all the truth. Despite the various breakthroughs of insight and understanding, and the attendant confessions of Jesus' Sonship, he can say that these are not yet the realizations that he has come to bring about: "When you lift up the Son of Man, then you shall know that I am the one, and I do nothing from myself, but just as the Father taught me, so I say these things" (8:28). In the meantime, you must, like true disciples, abide in my word (8:31)—such of it as you already have—and wait for the liberating truth that is to come (8:32).

But how much of his word did they already have? The Fourth Gospel is frustratingly evasive on this point. It respectfully alludes to various teachings of Jesus, and suggests that they were important for the proper governance of pious understanding, but it does not reconstruct them for us. Jesus is characterized as the Teacher of Israel, and spends two days teaching the Samaritans, but we are not told much about what he taught. The evangelist does not seem to think that our right understanding requires a detailed look into that phase of revelation. Why? The most likely answer, I should think, lies in a balance of three factors. The first is that all other doctrine pales into relative insignificance next to the all-important issue of realizing who Jesus is. The second is that all other doctrine was likely to have been inadequately, even misleadingly, understood until the season of illumination that was yet to come. The third is that the illumination is probably supposed to have held other teaching implicitly within itself, making it unnecessary to detail the lessons.

The level of Signs is not repudiated by the Fourth Gospel, but it is put firmly in its place. It is a useful steppingstone on the way to that leap of faith which alone brings full understanding. But the steppingstone becomes a stumbling block when one fails to accept the invitation to that leap. The attitude of the Fourth Gospel appears to be that the instructions to the Samaritans, important though they may have been at the time, probably constituted a temporary form of understanding somewhere near the level of Signs, and needed not only to be adhered to faithfully until the fuller illumination but also to be transformed by that illumination and surrendered in their now obsolete senses. Everything in the Fourth Gospel suggests that the pre-crucifixion works and teachings of Jesus were important, but also that they were bound to be misunderstood. From his double perspective, the evangelist hints consistently that the words of Jesus, like his works, must be known and kept —but cannot be fully known or kept until that post-crucifixion time in which their intelligibility will first completely emerge.

His works have been impressive, indeed somewhat shocking; but the Father is going to show him still greater works than these, that you may be amazed still more (5:20). After telling Nicodemus of a begetting from above, and of the sight of the kingdom of heaven, Jesus can still say to his puzzlement: "If I told you earthly things and you do not believe, how will you believe if I should tell you the things of heaven?" (3:12). Nathaniel sees that Jesus is the Son of God and the King of Israel, but a still greater vision lies ahead of him (1:49–51). The disbelievers do not understand at all what Jesus says (8:43–47), and those who are still open enough to wonder who he is (and to be ready to believe) do not understand that he is telling them about the Father (8:25–27); but even those of most advanced belief and understanding remain partially unable to

grasp his meaning (10:6; cf. 11:11–13, 23–24). If in individual instances
this opacity can be corrected by plainer explications (10:7ff., 11:14,
25ff.), there remains a way in which Jesus does not entrust himself and
his secrets even to believers (2:24–25). In fact, he cannot. The greater
works by which this can happen are not yet done. Those who believe
will see his glory (11:40), and in a limited sense, they have already done
so (2:11); but there is a deeper sense still hidden in the uncompleted.
He is not yet fully glorified (7:39). Only when they lift up the Son of Man
will they really know (8:28). Only when they behold his glory, the glory
as of his Father's only-begotten, will they grasp the fulness of truth in
him and be made completely free (1:14, 8:32). By the end of chapter
12, his disciples have been offered, and have begun to participate in, the
mind of Christ: but a fuller participation, and the first arrival at a
completely adequate understanding, still lie ahead: these things his
disciples did not understand about him at first, but when Jesus was
glorified, then they remembered that these things were written about
him and they did these things to him (12:16). We must therefore move
further into the Gospel if we are to discover how it is that they came
to know, and how other men shall know, the truth that makes men free.

If we move to the end of the Gospel, and treat what transpires
through the narratives of the passion and resurrection, we may expect
to see, in one sense, the point of greatest enlightenment among the
disciples, and with it, theoretically, the most developed grasp of the
constituting factors by which Christian understanding is to be governed. But that expectation must be qualified, and in two ways.

In the first place, the narrative does not extend all the way to the
point of the greatest promised illumination, even if it may be expected
to leave the disciples in better condition than at any moment in the
previous span of history. The earlier portion of the Gospel connects the
peak moment with the glorification of Jesus and the giving of the Holy
Spirit: but the Gospel itself, like the Gospel of Luke, does not carry us
as far in its narrative as to that point of promise. In the representation
of the disciples, therefore, we should not necessarily expect a great
advance in understanding over the earlier breakthroughs, and we
should certainly not expect an illustration of the deepest and most
perfect Christian knowledge.

But the second qualification is less obvious and more curious. Various
levels of realization emerge in the first twelve chapters. They are somewhat inconsistently attributed. To be sure, the Jews and their Pharisaic
leaders remain, for the most part, steadily convinced that Jesus is a
sinner; and large numbers of the people take him to be some sort of
authorized agent of God but remain confused and uncertain about just
who he is; and disciples believe that he is the Messiah and the Son of
God, whatever the exact weight of those terms may be; and there are

glimmers here and there of some believers' approximation to the understanding of the deeper senses of Jesus' sonship, his essential identity with the Father. But personages within this drama seem to stray back and forth across the boundaries of these strata of understanding. Unbelievers come to believe, become disciples, and subsequently lapse; and even after Simon Peter has made for the Twelve what appears to be the ultimate confession of Jesus' messiahship and sonship, Jesus remarks that his absence from Lazarus at the time of his death was to their advantage, "that you may believe," whereupon Thomas rallies his colleagues in a clear state of non-comprehension (11:15-16). The reader who sees what Jesus says of himself and what he does to illustrate and demonstrate his claims may readily presume that the disciples' confessions of faith are recognitions of and assents to just what he himself has perceived. But if he looks more closely, he will see that even in the first twelve chapters, the Fourth Gospel teases us with shifts in awareness. To some extent, these shifts are the legacy of a redactional process that incorporates signs-level sources into a grander scheme that relativizes what they undoubtedly meant to be ultimate. But I do not think that the main results are due to mere editorial clumsiness. The later redaction clearly means to exploit the unconscious inadequacy of its sources' understanding, attributing both its achievements and its limitations to the pre-crucifixion world, and thus representing a pre-Spirit phase in which it was possible for even the most enlightened disciples to have much of the right language but miss its fullest legitimate meaning.

The reader who has not perceived this in the first twelve chapters will not be prepared for the comportment of the disciples in the passion-resurrection narrative—for here it becomes on the whole quite clear that their assent must have been on a much lower level than Jesus' revelation, and that the picture of the disciple who now hears his words but will know only in the future what they really mean (and indeed, does not yet quite grasp that he is speaking of the Father) is, in the course of the story of passion and resurrection, much more characteristic of the state of the most advanced disciples than one might have guessed from the outspokenness of Jesus' earlier teaching.

I refer to Peter's misunderstanding in the garden, and his subsequent confusion and cowardice; to his and the Beloved Disciple's ignorance of the place of the resurrection in the scheme of things, and their failure to believe until they enter the empty tomb; to the astonishing spectacle of Mary, after all she has been through, turning from an empty grave in mere distress, and then rising from an interview with angels to inquire of the gardener about the transportation of the body. These are not evidences of having known what one said in confessing that Jesus was the Son of God.

The last few chapters only intensify the general problem of understanding implicit in the first twelve. That problem may justly be summed up by applying not only to the disbelievers but, in another sense, even to the disciples the familiar formula: seeing, they did not see; hearing, they did not understand. The truth is revealed in the scriptures—but the closest disciples, confronted with the empty tomb, still did not understand the Scripture (20:9). It is revealed in the teachings of Jesus—but the disciples do not understand his metaphors (4:32–33, 11:12) any better than the Samaritan woman does (4:15), and will not understand them fully until after the resurrection (2:19–22). It is not by any means clear that his explications are grasped more satisfactorily than the parables they mean to decode, and the general indications—especially the sequence of misunderstandings in chapter 6—seem to be that they are not. The truth is revealed in Jesus' career, especially in his works—but "the disciples did not understand these things about him at first, but when Jesus was glorified, then they remembered that these things were written about him, and that they did these things to him" (12:16). They recognize that he has the words of eternal life (6:68), but they do not yet know what those words mean. It is as if the unbeliever hears only thunder while the believer hears the voice of an angel, yet must wait until later to realize what it was the angel said. In the meantime, one must remain in Jesus' word (8:31), waiting to understand it fully; and one must follow him (12:26), without yet understanding where he is leading one. Even after the resurrection, all is not immediately clear. Even the meaning of a post-resurrection saying may be subject to disputed interpretation (21:22–23).

Indeed, at times even the perspective of the narrator's voice seems scarcely better off. Jesus' conduct in his first appearance to the disciples after the resurrection is obviously designed to prove the material identity of his body with that of the crucified Jesus they had known—thus also the terms of Thomas' skepticism, and of Jesus' subsequent proof to him. The disciples rejoice to see him, but the weight of the scene does not establish a larger realization than that the man whom they had thought to be the Messiah is alive again, despite his crucifixion: indeed, bears still the wounds that did not definitively triumph over him. Theology can find grounds for arguing that the promised glorification of Jesus is written there in his hands and side, but sober criticism cannot readily accept that the expectation generated by earlier references to glorification and the gift of the Spirit is adequately fulfilled in his showing his wounds and breathing upon them. The words to Mary about his ascension are cognate with the more ambitious dimensions of the earlier themes, but it and they sort awkwardly with the scene that follows. And if Thomas' confession likewise seems to break beyond the palpable evidence to an insight reminiscent of the highest claims of earlier chapters, it is belied and betrayed by the vocabulary of the narrator's sum-ming-up immediately afterward: he speaks only at the level of signs, where it is possible to say "Messiah" and "Son of God" and "life in his name," but not to mean by these terms more than Luke's Peter means in the third chapter of Acts. Even a Gospel narrator may show himself in his account of the resurrection not yet to have accepted Jesus' invita-tion to a deeper understanding. In its last chapters the Fourth Gospel seems to betray unconsciously a need for that revealing Spirit it has promised will come. It is possible to propose that the final redaction is deeply artful, and ingeniously leaves the narrative voice in a partly benighted pre-Spirit condition, with the confidence that the reader will recognize that the narrator does not have the authority to define the level of understanding but surrenders it to the Spirit and its recipients. That is an attractive hypothesis, but the over-all management of the text does not suggest to me that such a procedure is really at work. The inconsistency is striking, and I cannot see a plausible resolution that would render it genuinely coherent. I think it much more likely that the redaction is simply incomplete. The editor has not got around to taking a signs-level source into the higher realization.

However one is to attribute them, there emerge in the Fourth Gospel clear indications of two quite different levels of understanding: a basic stratum, in which Jesus may be recognized as the divinely ordained and wonder-working Messiah, albeit paradoxically (though also, it turns out, providentially) an obediently suffering Messiah; and another stratum, arrived at only through a quantum exaltation of understanding, where the usefulness of the term *Messiah* drops away,[22] and only terms more immediately expressive of his intimate relatedness to the Father will do. The over-all thrust of the Fourth Gospel suggests that while the first level is true, the fullness of truth that makes us free comes only at the second level, which entered the world historically only (except in the person of Jesus) in unstable glimpses until after Jesus was taken up.

Before attempting to come to terms with the implications of all this for the Fourth Gospel's disclosure of the means by which the truth is released and validated, it remains to consider the problematic chapters which I have advisedly skipped over until now. I say advisedly for two reasons. The first I have already mentioned: it is useful to consider the more public teachings and deeds of Jesus separately from the private discourses of chapters 13–17, so that a clearer picture can emerge of what the Gospel represents to be the open revelation, as distinct from that which was delivered to more esoteric circles. And one of the strik-ing results that emerges—especially striking in comparison with the synoptic treatment—is that there is remarkably little difference be-tween the position of the disciples and that of the others. The Twelve are singled out only at 6:67–71, and the disciples in general are rarely given privileged audience (and even when they are, they are not given very significant teaching): they hear what is addressed to the Jews or to The People, and if they do not respond with the hostility that Jesus' remarks sometimes inspire in those larger audiences, it is not because they have been specially briefed. The representation in the first twelve chapters justifies Jesus' later claim that "I have spoken openly to the world; I always taught in a synagogue and in the Temple, where all the Jews assemble, and I said nothing in secret" (18:20). At least it seems that he said nothing in secret that he did not also say more publicly— unless, perhaps the content of chapters 13–17 is a significant advance on the already remarkable disclosures of 1–12.

Perhaps: because one must hold reservations about the original placement of the main body of material in chapters 13–17, and that is my second reason for treating them separately. There is some reason to suppose that their original native habitat was precisely at the most advanced point of understanding, just before the return of Jesus to the Father.[23] If it was once so, that would account in part for the evident disparity in the disciples' understanding, between this section and the final chapters of the present text, not only insofar as these chapters would then have been seen as the most advanced stage of a cumulative understanding, but also insofar as their placement as an ample and climactic conclusion would have made it less necessary for the redactor to rework further his inherited and only paritally transformed passion-resurrection source material. (Some further transformation would of course eventually have been in order—the defectiveness of the narrative would have needed attending to, even if Peter and Mary might have been left unchanged—but the problem would not have seemed as starkly odd and redactionally urgent as it now does.) But that is not, however, the way in which the Gospel comes to us. No matter how special or privileged the disclosures of these chapters may be, they are given as the substance of discourses at the Last Supper, and it is within that frame that they must first be dealt with.

The state of the disciples' understanding is, to be sure, not free from its earlier limitations. Peter sees only the surface of Jesus' action in the feet-washing, and is told "What I am doing, you do not yet know; but you will know after these things" (13:7). No one is sufficiently privy to the hidden workings to interpret rightly Jesus' remark to Judas (13:27–29). Like the larger group of hearers earlier (7:33–36), Peter does not know what Jesus means by saying that they cannot come where he is going (13:33–36): and even when told that they do know where he is going, and know even the way, Thomas assures Jesus that he does not know (14:4–5). Told that they have seen the Father, Philip asks to be shown (14:7–8). Neither do they grasp what Jesus means in saying "a little while" (16:16–18). And even when, momentarily beyond their earlier difficulties with metaphors and parables, the disciples assert that Jesus now speaks plainly and without indirection, their confession of belief is not significantly beyond that of the Samaritan woman: Jesus knows all things and has come forth from God (16:29–30).[24] Jesus underscores the relative inadequacy of this state of belief by assuring them that they will shortly scatter and desert him (16:31–32). The over-all assessment of their understanding is signaled by Jesus' disappointed remark to Philip on the occasion of his request to see the Father: "I have been with you for so long and you have not known me?" (14:9).

If they had known him, they would have known the Father (14:7). But evidently, they did not. Jesus therefore repeats the teaching of earlier episodes, and the Last Supper discourses recapitulate virtually the whole pattern of teaching contained in the first twelve chapters. The world has not known the Father (17:25), and has been under the domination of an evil ruler (16:11). Those who remain immersed in the world hate the truth and its bearers (15:18–20), because they do not know the Father (15:21). The world loves only what is like it (15:19). But there is a chance of rescue. The Son has known the Father (17:25) and the Father has given him everything (13:3, 16:15, 17:7) and sent him into the world (17:18), where the Son, obedient to the Father's commands (14:31, 15:10), declares his name (17:26), speaks his words (14:24), works his works (14:10), and brings the presence of the indwelling Father (14:10–11, 17:21). No one can come to the Father by any other route (14:6). The world has a chance to believe and accept (17:21), but may fail to rise above its perversity, and thus reject the words, the works, the Son, the Father (15:22–24). The latter response brings sin (15:22, 16:9) and self-condemnation. The former leads to eternal life (17:3). In one sense, those who come to believe do so only because the Father has given them (17:2, 6, 9) or because the Son has chosen them (and not they him, 15:16). But another sense, the initiative and responsibility are theirs once the Son has appeared in the world: the Father loves the disciples *because* they have loved and believed in Jesus (16:27).

To know the Son is to know the Father (14:7), and eternal life is to know the Father and Jesus whom he sent (17:3). At one level, the pre-crucifixion disciples have accomplished this; but at a deeper level, they have not. Therefore, the fulfillment of their understanding, and the life that corresponds to it, lie in the future: "you shall live; in that day you will know that I am in the Father and you in me and I in you" (14:19–20).

It is important that this fulfilling moment come, since they are being sent to bear witness (15:27), to bear fruit that will remain (15:16), to go into the world, sanctified in truth, to bring about the belief of others through their word (17:17–20). They are being sent just as Jesus was sent by the Father (17:18), and are to be received as Jesus himself is to be received (13:20), so that all may be one—the Father and Son in the believers as in each other (17:21). But before the sending-forth is fully effectual, they are to be sanctified in truth; and coordinate with their bearing of witness is the witness-bearing of the Spirit of Truth. It is by sending of the Spirit that their understanding will finally be exalted and stabilized enough to arrive *for the first time* at the state that is to be normative for Christians.

For unlike the synoptics,[25] the Fourth Gospel points beyond its own narrative boundaries for the achievement of genuinely Christian understanding even for the closest disciples. It does not, and apparently cannot, happen before Jesus goes. The Spirit is the factor that accounts for the transition between their present unperfected state and the anticipated future when they will be sanctified, glorified, and brought into all truth. This cannot take place until Jesus goes, for otherwise the Comforter cannot come: he is to be sent by Jesus (16:7). But the coordination between the work of Jesus and that of the Paraclete runs far deeper than the fact that Jesus sends him to fulfill predictions. It is, in fact, almost total. The Holy Spirit, as a factor in the proper constituting of Christian understanding, is essentially identical with Jesus.

The main theological pattern in chapters 14–17 reasserts the centrality of Jesus. Jesus is the Way, the Truth, and the Life (14:6): one must remain in him. He is the true vine (15:1f.): one must remain in him. Then one may come to the Father, one may bear fruit; but without him, one can do nothing (14:6, 15:5). Those who love him will keep his word (14:23), will keep his commandments (15:14). Those who do not love him will not keep his words (14:23–24). Jesus has loved them, just as the Father has loved him (15:9). If they keep his commandments, just as Jesus has kept the Father's, they shall remain in his love, just as Jesus remains in the Father's (15:9–10). The special commandment is that they love one another just as Jesus has loved them (13:34, 15:12). Those who do love him, and keep his commandments, will be loved by him and by the Father; and he and the Father will come and remain with them (14:23) and Jesus will manifest himself to them (14:21). He goes, but he will return to them (14:28); he will come and receive them unto himself (14:3). He will not leave them orphans. He will come to them, and they will live, and then they will know that he is in the Father and they in him and he in them (14:18–20). Then he will tell them plainly concerning the Father (16:25) and their joy will be full (16:22–24)—and they will see his glory (17:24).

This pattern unfolds without reference to the Holy Spirit. The Gospel's alternative way of formulating it, with reference to the Holy Spirit, is essentially a theological doublet. In this pattern, what the world does not know or see or receive is not the Father or the Son, but the Spirit of Truth, which the disciples know because it remains with them and shall be in them (14:17). This same Spirit of Truth is a Comforter and/or Advocate[26] whom the Father will give them at Jesus' request, to be with them forever (14:16). Because they keep Jesus' commandments, he will arrange all this. Does this mean that they will then have the Spirit of Truth *instead of* Jesus? At first it appears to be so: the Father will give them "another" *paraklēton*. But over the next few verses, it seems less clear: I will come to you; the world sees me no more, but you see me, because I live and you shall live (14:18–19).

The unclarity and inconsistency leave the problem irresolvable. But from a theological perspective, there is scarcely any problem at all. For functionally, the office of the Spirit is essentially identical to that of Jesus, and a perfection of his work. He is, in effect, "another Jesus," and it matters little whether or not that means precisely the same Jesus in another mode of presence. The Spirit is to guide the disciples into all truth, by speaking not of himself but what he hears (16:14–15), and will thus testify of Jesus and glorify him (15:26, 16:14). The Spirit will teach them all things, and will remind them of the things Jesus has said to them (14:26)—and this time, they will understand, and will see his glory as of the only-begotten of the Father, full of grace and truth. The Spirit fulfills the self-revelation of the Father through Jesus. He is essentially the resolution to the problem of Jesus' self-effacement, inconsistently thematized in the Fourth Gospel, in which Jesus reveals the Father but is reluctant to testify to his own glory and mediatory importance. The Spirit in fact fulfills all that Jesus reveals, for he will teach all things (14:26), including the things to come (16:13). He even extends Jesus' revelations since what they cannot yet bear in Jesus' pre-crucifixion disclosures will be supplied later through the Spirit (16:12–13).

The identity between Jesus and the Spirit may be perceived even more clearly within the Fourth Gospel's theology of the Word. Jesus, in his works and in his words, has revealed himself and has revealed his Father through himself. As the revelation of the Father, he is the Truth and the Word of God. Those who know this truth will be freed; those who understand this Word will have eternal life. But throughout his earthly career, Jesus did not succeed in being known fully or in having his words completely understood. As far as men were concerned, his words were not yet spirit and life; for although they may have been so in themselves, they could not release that spirit and life to men until they were more completely appropriated. His disciples could only keep Jesus' words without having fully grasped them, and wait for the time in which the light would fully dawn. In that interim, are they aware of the incompleteness of their understanding? Probably not. At least they are not aware of the degree of incompleteness, since Jesus' meaning could seem to resolve itself at a level far more modest than the amazing truth that they had not dreamed. But when, in the course of the faithful keeping of his words, they really come to understand, then at last they will see him, will see his glory as the only-begotten of the Father—and that is where the Spirit becomes a reality in their lives. And what is spirit? It is that which gives life. When Jesus' words finally achieve their goal of communicating life, they have begun to act as spirit: only then, in the fullest sense, are his words spirit and life. That which gives eternal life is the eternal Spirit. When the remembrance of Jesus, the Word sent from God, is transformed into full understanding, the faithful disciples receive the Spirit sent from God; when the remembrance of his words is similarly transformed, the disciples receive the Spirit sent from Jesus; and this transformation may as aptly be described as the returning to them of Jesus in full life, to abide with them and in them.

Faithful memory, transformed by insight, becomes living and life-giving presence. At that locus, the theological strands of the Fourth Gospel converge. From there, they may be developed in a variety of more mythic modes of expression—and so the Fourth Gospel develops the themes of the sending of the Spirit, the return of Jesus, the teaching and the abiding and the Life to come. In one sense, the Spirit of Truth may continue to dwell with the disciples after Jesus departs from them, even though it is not yet able to execute its life-giving office, and is therefore not yet (as Spirit) in them (14:17). In another sense, the word remains, but because it is not yet vivifying the Spirit is not yet there, and so must be sent later, and may be said to be sent either by Jesus (16:7) or by the Father at his request (14:16). And yet in another sense, it is Jesus himself who becomes manifest again within them, (14:21) returns in life to them after having left them (14:28). In one sense, they will then be taught or shown or told more completely (14:26, 16:14, 25); in another sense, they will simply remember well, and will finally know and see what they have already imperfectly known and seen (14:7-9, 17). In one sense, the Jesus whose reassurance and advocacy established the righteousness of his own scandalous works during his earthly minis-try, and accordingly established the righteousness of the disciples' imi-tation of such works, is different from the presence and knowledge by which they will know comfort and justification. In another sense, how-ever, that later *parakletos* is the same presence and knowledge as before, only more deeply and ultimately experienced.[27] The underly-ing theory reaffirms the identity between the pre-crucifixion and post-resurrection teaching of Jesus.

That same locus of convergence is also the Fourth Gospel's own solution to the potential problem of its own redactional history. Whatever the theological differences of the different sources it has absorbed or of the different strata of its interpretations of the sources, it does not admit, or evidence, a substantive discontinuity. The ambitions of the isolable signs-source appear to have been relatively modest, by comparison with those of the full Gospel: to bring us, at the level of signs and through the logic that obtains at that level, to the confident conclusion that Jesus was the Christ, the Son of God, so that we may have in his name the life that is thus made available to us (20:31). Whether or not the basic source behind the passion-resurrection narrative was originally part of the signs-source, it too does not seem to go much beyond that level of understanding. But why should one suppose that this level of understanding is necessarily final? The Gospel traditions in general make it clear that the disciples did not, in the course of Jesus' pre-crucifixion ministry, understand fully what he was doing and saying, and that they were sometimes quite unaware that they had misunderstood. The constitutional theory implicit in the synoptic tradition not only allows for but requires growth in the understanding of the scriptures, of the career of Jesus, and of his pre-crucifixion teaching, at least to bring understanding to the level achieved in the light of the post-resurrection teaching. But nothing requires that significant growth must stop there, even if it is unanticipated. The synoptic Gospels, like the variously reconstructed signs-source, obviously suppose that their authors have arrived finally at complete Christian understanding; but nothing internal to them guarantees the adequacy of that supposition. The recognition that a miracle is intended to be a *sign* entails the possibility that its signification may be incompletely understood just as the notion of *parable* entails the possibility that a plausible interpretation may nevertheless be significantly deficient (a principle implicitly recognized in the synoptic tradition's treatment of the parabolic saying about the Sign of Jonah). Why not then a significant incompleteness also in the disciples' understanding of "Son of God," or "life in his name"? Nothing requires that the understanding even at the moment of the ascension be definitive. The continuation of divine guidance makes it unnecessary that it be so. That is why it is theologically more important to discern the court of appeal than the specific content.

The Fourth Gospel does not admit or evidence a discontinuity. It does not repudiate its signs-source: on the contrary, it is of the greatest significance that it conserves it.[28] It merely insists that the understanding at that level, and at the level of the passion-resurrection source, is importantly incomplete and needs to be supplemented by a higher discernment. Even if the last-supper discourses originally stood as a post-resurrection instruction of a higher order than that reported in the synoptic accounts, they nevertheless point beyond themselves to a later time in which not only the earlier career and teachings of Jesus but even their own imperfectly grasped disclosures will be better remembered and better understood. Even when read as post-resurrection utterances, these discourses only give in explicit though ungrasped form the true content of the disclosures that all the Gospels suggest were given by Jesus to his followers on that occasion: but they do not claim that these communications were accurately understood, any more than the synoptists claim that the equally plain predictions of the passion and resurrection were properly grasped. Quite the contrary—only in the future will they be remembered and fathomed. In a post-resurrection setting, these discourses claim that the disciples only *thought* they understood at the time of Jesus' departure, and thus account for the synoptic tradition without rejecting anything but its ultimacy. In their present setting, they point equally to the unfinished character of initial post-ascension understanding, and promise that Christians are eventually to go well beyond what the disciples thought they knew at that point. But even that "well beyond" is firmly conservative. It keeps and is faithful to what had already been learned. It learns it more deeply and completely, even as it extends and amplifies. The Fourth Gospel resolves the potential problem of its own redactional history by honoring and accounting for the sources it absorbs, while explaining why it is necessary to go beyond them, and how it is possible.

That this is the case is further reason why the law of Christian thought cannot necessarily be limited to the basic grasp of Jesus as the Son. The Fourth Gospel is careless of detailing the judgments and teachings of Jesus which it indicates were variously given, but its assurance that they will be re-expressed and augmented through the Spirit constitutes its warrant for this carelessness. The Gospel does not undertake to circumscribe or delimit the content of normative understanding. It means to establish the conditions of its achievement, while pointing beyond itself to the later season when these conditions will be realized.

The Fourth Gospel is itself written from the perspective of that later time. It represents the confusions and misapprehensions endemic to the period of incomplete realization in which it is set but, like the synoptics, seasons them with glimpses of that more complete understanding which its more privileged audience would be sure to recognize. It is clear that the distance between the two species of realization is here much greater than in the synoptic Gospels, requiring a more radical reinterpretation of what had been understood before. There is some, although not complete, warrant for Bultmann's conclusion that in the final analysis, the Fourth Gospel represents that "Jesus as the

Revealer of God *reveals nothing but that he is the Revealer.*'[29] But, once again, the key issue is not the content of revelation but the means of arriving at it; and the Fourth Gospel does not reject the synoptic theory of the constituting conditions of Christian understanding. It applies them more daringly, and from a different perspective. But it does not much limit or preordain what they may yet disclose or what their application may render obsolete. Instead, it pointedly refuses to limit their legitimate reconsideration to the period immediately succeeding the triumph of Jesus over death.

The perfected norm of Christian understanding for the Fourth Gospel is therefore the state of understanding that will obtain once the Word has come to full life, once the Spirit has been received. This may be said to be a participation in the mind of Christ not only insofar as it is especially a recollection and deep comprehension of the teaching and works of Jesus, but because he himself, the Word, will dwell within and give life as well as truth. But how can one pursue such a deep participation in the mind of Christ?

The transfiguration of mind effected by this indwelling is obviously beyond unaided human powers. Still, the condition of understanding which it encompasses is persistently alleged by the Fourth Gospel to be fully coordinated with ordinary ways of knowledge. It is the resolving place of convergence for the proper human understanding of the various public evidences: the scriptures, the public teaching of Jesus, the career of works through which he showed himself. And although the Fourth Gospel attributes its achievement to the gracious and miraculous intervention of the Spirit, it represents that intervention as essentially a more perfect mode of appropriating what was already within human understanding. Moreover, it has another way of looking at it from a less inspired level that makes it coordinate with a human initiative. For how shall we understand the enigmatic statement that "when you come to exalt [*hotan hupsōsēte*] the Son of Man, then you will know that I am the One, and I do nothing from myself but as the Father taught me, I speak these things" (8:28)? With his fondness for polysemous pronouncements, the evangelist may well have the crucifixion in mind—but not primarily. It is not those who crucify Jesus who come to such full understanding. The glorification of Jesus may also be in view —but not primarily. It is not his addressees who raise him back into the glory he had from the beginning, but the Father. The central sense, and the one that makes possible the overtones of the others, seems to me to be: when you arrive at a much more elevated notion of the Son of Man, then you will understand.[30] That is, his disciples must make an act of mind that raises their conception of Jesus to the proper heavenly level—then, and only then, will they recoginze who he really is and what he has really been doing. This is not an understanding that is simply given them from without. They must do it themselves. By exalting him, they will see his glory, and will share in it, because they will then be where he is and participate in the eternal life that is there (17:24); the true servant will follow him, and the consequence is not just that he will be where the servant is, but that where he is the servant will be too (12:26). That is, the true servant will follow him to heavenly glory, and participate in heaven. It is the work of heaven, but its vehicle is the work of human understanding, within the reach of our capacities, if only we will lift up our minds enough to exalt him as his resumed glory deserves.

The subsequent mission guarantees the Gospel's acknowledgment of adequacy of human capacity. Those who perceived his authenticity should be ready to recognize its deepest meaning once their understandings have learned to look that far. After all, the word of the human witness is subsequently expected to be enough to lead others into belief (17:20). The words of Jesus are spirit and life. That is not true of all words. But if the spiritual and life-giving quality of the words is a supernatural grace, their capacity to give understanding and disclose the truth that releases spirit and life lies within the reach of the human mind, however clumsy or impeded may be most men's grasp of them. Seek first the true understanding, and the rest will be added unto you.

Clumsiness and impediments, however, are as much a part of the human scene as the communication of truth. The real meaning of Jesus and of his teachings, of his works and of the scriptures that point to them, is not obvious. Confusions and uncertainties have abounded. Even his last remark about the Beloved Disciple was subject to misinterpretation. Moreover, there are new disclosures yet to be made. How, in the face of the many possible ways of understanding the elusive revelations that have been given and shall be given, can one discern the true from the false? What prevents the followers of Jesus from inadvertently scattering, each to his own, leaving the true Jesus alone?

What prevents this is a protection given by the providence of the Creator and his creating Word. The constitution of Christian understanding depends upon unity, but a tendency toward unity is given with the truth itself. The condition of adequate understanding is that the disciples remain in Jesus, keep his words, keep his commandments. And of these, the most emphatically urged is that they love one another, as he has loved them. Their unity in love will be a unity in Jesus, the Way, the Truth, and the Life. What belongs to that unity belongs to the truth; what separates itself from it does not.

This is not a matter of arbitrary command. It is a consequence of the nature of the Truth, and of its rootedness in God. The Father's love for

the Son has a counterpart in his love for those who love the Son (16:27).
As the Father loves the Son, so the Son loves those whom the Father
has given him (15:9); and as the Son loves the Father and abides in his
life-giving commandments and love, so the followers of the Son keep
his commandments—of which the chief is that they love one another
—and remain in his love (15:10). It is of the nature of Truth to love the
Truth and all that is of the Truth; only the world and darkness tend to
scatter and fragment. All who are of the Truth move toward the union
of love as well as understanding, not simply because it is commanded
but because that is what the Truth is like.[31] The command is from
before the foundation of the world. Therefore those who come to grasp
the truth tend to become one just as, and for the same reason as, Father
and Son are one; and those who remain one in what they have of the
truth tend to grasp it more perfectly. Unified in love, they share in one
another, abide in one another, and know together the truth that makes
us free. *Together*, or not at all. Unity becomes a criterion of true understanding, because it is of the nature of the Truth—especially of the
life-giving Truth that expresses itself not only in the economy of understanding but in the economy of love. The form of unity that guarantees
the accessibility of true understanding is not that of organizational
order nor that of identity of belief but that which transcends and resolves both: the unity of love. Love is, in the Fourth Gospel, not only
the obedient and faithful witness to the presence of the Truth, but the
supreme mode of its appropriation.

When questions arise, as they must, concerning the right interpretation of Jesus, and of the revelation he brought, and of the Christian Way,
and of his signs and his parables and his works and of the adequacy or
authenticity of insights old and new, by what canon shall the normative
understanding be discerned from its specious competitors? The theory
of the Christian constitution implicit in the Fourth Gospel is not by any
means the Gospel's main preoccupation, but it is there and is quite clear
on this point. Normative understanding is to be discerned through the
loving Christian community, which knows and experiences the Truth
through its unity in love.

It is, moreover, to be discerned through the self-consciousness of the
community, because it harbors the abiding Truth within itself, and is
itself within the Truth. The indwelling of Jesus—the new state of completion to which the Gospel points sometimes as the sending of the
Spirit, sometimes as the return of the Son—makes communal self-
knowledge a mode of the Lord's most intimate manifestation of himself,
and even of his presence. It is, finally, to be discerned through the
fidelity of the Christian community, which remains in Jesus, remembers
what he has said and done, continues to pursue his way and keep his

words and follow his commandments. In short, the constitutional theory of the Fourth Gospel, as it looks to the future that stretches beyond the resurrection, appears to envision as the understanding's ultimate court of appeal essentially what Paul had seen. Its theological value is as the mind of Christ, communicating the intention of God through vivifying Spirit. But its sublunary face is the cumulative and faithfully remembering self-consciousness of the obedient and loving Christian community.

5

The Pauline School

I. Ephesians and Colossians

Whatever their actual connection with the apostle Paul, the epistles to the Ephesians and Colossians[1] manifest a general situation that Paul might well have found a pleasant relief from his struggles with the Galatians and Corinthians, and even his circumspect diplomacy with the Romans. Here there is little anxiety about competition from Judaizing falsifications, and no apprehensiveness about the solidity of his own authority in the minds of his addressees. The audience is implicitly made up of Gentile Christians, firmly grateful to the Gospel that has rescued them and to the apostle who has authoritatively established it as their Way. And whatever their connection with Paul himself, these epistles are clearly founded in an authentically Pauline understanding of that rescue and that Way.

Before the Gospel, the Gentiles were at the mercy of their own guilty waywardness. In the last analysis of justice, it may be said that it is their wicked works that have alienated them from God and made them his enemies (Col 1:21, 3:5–6; Eph 4:19). But in a still deeper theological analysis, that alienation lies at the root of their minds, which have misguided them into the works by which they are justly condemned (Col 1:21). The natural condition of the Gentiles is wicked because they have been too insensitive to obey the light, however faint, that has been given them: it is that insensitivity that plunges them into the works of uncleanness and greed (Eph 4:19) and permits their *epithumia* to corrupt them (Eph 4:22), because their dullness of heart darkens their minds (Eph 4:18) and leaves them to walk by the guidance of minds that are vain (Eph 4:17), according to this world and the understanding that is formed only in its image (Eph 2:2–3). Having surrendered insensitively to the guidance of this *adokimos nous* and of the dark power with which it is cognate (Eph 2:2), they became dead, the children of wrath (Eph 2:3, 5).

Their guilty waywardness of mind is one side of their movement to

133

doom, the one that falls under their responsibility and makes their condemnation just. The other and correlative side—the one that falls under God's mercy and makes their rescue possible—is their ignorance (Eph 4:18). If they really knew what God has planned for them, if they really knew his will as he has revealed it most fully, they might effectively counteract the dullness of their hearts and the lustfulness of their vain worldly minds. The rescuing solution for them is that they learn Christ (Eph 4:20). The truth is in Jesus (Eph 4:21). If they hear him and are taught by him, they will be made new in the spirit of their mind (Eph 4:21, 23).

There is, in these epistles, not much more than a hint of the Pauline insistence upon the need to *submit* to the truth, to appropriate by obedience what is not readily congenial or even intelligible to minds infected with fleshliness. We hear that the Gospel is God's mystery, hidden from before the ages and only now revealed to men (Eph 3:3–5, Col 1:25–27), and that its inheritance comes only by election and grace (Eph 1:4–5, 11; 2:8; Col 1:6), but there is little suggestion that it must wrestle with the minds of men before conferring its blessing upon them. The truth seems more humane than in the major Pauline epistles. The accent therefore falls on knowledge rather than obedience, and the metaphor of faithful marriage lies more ready to hand than that of faithful servitude.

We are exhorted to put off the old man of corruption and put on the new man formed by God in righteousness and holiness of truth (Eph 4:22, 24). But specifically, the new man which we put on is one made new in knowledge (Col 3:10). We are saved graciously, but redemptive grace abounds particularly in the pathways of our thought, *en pasê sophia kai phronêsei*, "making known to us the mystery of his will" (Eph 1:8–9).

The fundamental "word of truth" that is "the Gospel of your salvation" (Eph 1:13), the foundation of Christian understanding, is still apparently the kerygma of the redemptive cross and life-giving resurrection, for although not emphasized as firmly as in the major Pauline epistles, the elements of that kerygma lie embedded in the thought-structures of these two epistles: the redeeming blood of the cross (Col 1:14, 20; Eph 1:7, 2:13, 16), the reconciling sacrifice (Col 1:20, Eph 5:2), the dying and rising with Christ (Col 2:11–15; 3:1–4; Eph 2:5–6). This kerygma is the true foundation laid down by the apostles and prophets with Christ as the cornerstone (Eph 2:20). It is the Gospel that was preached in all creation (Col 1:23), and defines the faith in which the Christian must continue.

How can we determine the exact normative content of this faith? Implicitly, one reliable means would be collating its universal and public manifestations. The assumed consistent publicity defines a potential court of appeal, and one common to Paul and the synoptists. But a correlative court known to them is missing here: there is no hint of the possibility of discerning the true law of understanding in the fabric of antecedent history or literature. These epistles have virtually nothing to say about scriptural foundations or correspondences, beyond a vague reference to the investment of the promise in Israel (Eph 2:12). They also say nothing about the apostolic eyewitnesses. The apostolic authority, yes—but as derived neither from observation nor from pre-crucifixion ministry, but from election and revelation. That is, here they side with Paul's conviction and against Luke's tendency. The Pauline disinclination to accord a significant advantage to the understandings of those who had known Jesus in the flesh is here decisively repeated: the mystery concealed from men in earlier ages is now revealed to the apostles and prophets *by the Spirit* (Eph 3:5). Not the apostles only, but the apostles and prophets; and Paul's own reception of revelation by which the mystery was made known to him (Eph 3:3–4) establishes him as a fully authoritative knower and teacher of the Gospel, with no theoretical foothold allowed for any invidious comparison with those who had been apostles before him, since they must have become such through equivalent revelations of their own, not by privileged observational access. He has, he says, written a brief account of the revelation made to him, the reading of which will allow us "to understand my insight into the mystery of Christ" (Eph 3:4). Thus the universal published Gospel registers the basic normative understanding, but the mind of the apostle or prophet visited by the revealing Spirit is the deeper and more immediate reflection of the mind and mystery of Christ from which that Gospel derives.

This does not, however, establish the apostle as a definitive locus of understanding, as against those who have received the Gospel from him. The apostle is conscious of the gracious privilege of understanding which he enjoys; but he is also conscious of the degree to which his addressees also, though neither apostles nor prophets, participate in the same illumination. If they knew the mystery of God's will initially only through apostolic intervention, they now have received the Spirit as a result of their faith (Eph 1:13), and by the Spirit they have direct access to the Father (Eph 2:18). In him "are hidden all the treasures of wisdom and knowledge" (Col 2:2–3), and those who are joined to Christ may receive a growing participation in these treasures. Hence the apostle reminds them of what they know; and rather than giving them much further instruction, he prays that the Colossians be filled with the knowledge of God's will in all wisdom and spiritual understanding (Col 1:9), and prays that God give the Ephesians "a spirit of wisdom and of revelation in knowledge of him" (Eph 1:17). They are not dependent upon Paul for such understanding. To those who have, more is given. One of the fruits of this fuller illumination, which leads to walking in a manner worthy of and pleasing to God, is further "growing in the knowledge of God" (Col 1:10). They are no longer dependent upon any apostle. The growth of God flows directly to the body from Christ the Head (Col 2:19). The economy of understanding belongs to them now, or at any rate is firmly invested in them.

How does it work? In these epistles, even more clearly than in Paul's major epistles, the basic model of Christian understanding is essentially communal, at least in its perfected state. The apostles and prophets are the recipients of a particular grace, a special gift needed for the founding of the holy edifice—but it is all the members together who grow into a temple for the indwelling of God in the Spirit (Eph 2:21–22). It is not by the apostles but by the church that the mystery is to be made known to the heavenly rulers and powers (Eph 3:10). Because they are called into one body under the headship of Christ, and because the word of Christ (or the Spirit, Eph 5:18) dwells within them, they can teach themselves (Col 3:16), for the gifts that are given for the building up and perfecting of the church include the gifts that make teachers as well as those that produce apostles and prophets (Eph 4:11–12). In this providential economy, in Christ, realized through the unity of the Spirit (Eph 4:3), is the ultimate canon. One body, one Spirit, one Lord, one faith: and when this unity is realized fully, and the body is grown into a perfect man, there will be achieved a unity of the faith and of the knowledge of the Son of God (Eph 4:13).

The desirability of approximating to this perfect communal understanding is made the keener by the hint of present instability in doctrine. In that day, we shall no longer be "infants, blown and carried around by every wind of teaching in the sight of men, in cleverness to the craftiness of deception" (Eph 4:14). Evidently their escape from the basic vanity of mind to which the Gentiles are prey (Eph 4:17) has not been so complete as to make them immune to the deceit of vain words (Eph 5:6) or beguiling persuasions (Col 2:4) built on "philosophy and empty deceit, according to the elements of the world" rather than according to Christ (Col 2:8). The mind of the flesh, formed in the image of this world, can still endure and be self-deceived (Col 2:18). Deceiving others by their weakness and incompleteness, it makes them prey to the world again, takes them from Christ (Col 2:8). If deceit and misleading teachings abound, and the time of full knowledge has not yet come, by what means shall we be protected from the weaknesses of our infantile understanding, and from being deceived into fellowship with the children of wrath (Eph 5:6–7)?

First, we must remain faithful to the Gospel which we heard—that universal Gospel by which the mystery of God's will is disclosed—and remain firmly joined to Christ as our head, confirmed in the faith as we were taught (Col 2:7). That which does not build on Christ, but turns rather to worldly elements of human philosophy, is at best vain and at worst fatally pernicious. Christ, as preached universally by apostles, and then experienced in the Body, is the basic canon of discernment. Any understanding that is not consonant with Christ is clearly false. In fact, it is far more necessarily false than is the case even in Paul's major epistles, for the cosmicized Christ of creation and *plērōma* is by definition the norm and measure of all truth and reality. No authentic understanding could possibly be dissonant with Christ.

Initial apostolic teaching has laid down some further specific guidelines. We know, for instance, that the works of darkness bring judgment upon the children of wrath, and that one who participates in them cannot have a share in the kingdom of Christ (Eph 5:3–11; cf. Col 3:5–6). We know this because we were taught it along with the Gospel (Col 2:7). But we also have insight into this truth independently, through our renewed and edified minds. Having once lived in the world-oriented vain manner of the works of darkness and of darkened mind, we see how differently the Spirit now summons us to the things above and to the goodness, righteousness, and truth that are its fruit (Eph 5:9, etc.). Though our minds were once darkened, we now understand what it is to be, and to live as, one whose truth is according to the image of God (Col 3:10). We are now to be followers of God and of Christ (Eph 5:1–2). That means that we must do God's will, and walk as Christ walked. This is apparently not an obscure command. Risen from the death of our sins, we are illuminated by Christ (Eph 5:14), sufficiently to make our practical choice one between what we see as wisdom and what we see as folly. Walk carefully, not as unwise but as wise; be not foolish, but understand what the will of God is (Eph 5:15, 17). It is apparently within our power to determine what is acceptable to the Lord (5:10), simply by applying our reformed sense of appropriateness to see what is fitting to saints (Eph 5:3). Here too, what began as apostolic injunction is now internalized, and may be discerned by introspective judgment as well as recollection.

Fidelity to the original Gospel, and walking in the good fruits to which both the apostolic teaching and the Spirit clearly point, give us a steadying basic orientation that will help to keep us from being blown away from Christ or into immoral teachings. If we clearly realize what we know about the transformation of our life and its relocation in Christ and with God, triumphant over the world, we will know what belongs to Christ and what to the world, and should be able to see through the flaws and vanities of seductive heterodoxy (Eph 4:17ff.; Col 2:6—3:3). But the capstone of the building-up of our understanding, explicitly contrasted with the instability of the *nêpioi* amid the winds of doctrine, is the simple formula: "speaking the truth in love, we grow in all things into him who is the head, Christ" (Eph 4:15). The unity of the Spirit which leads us into truth and understanding is most perfectly expressed in love, the spiritual quality that is above all others and that is the "bond of perfection" (Col 3:14). The unity of that love that excels knowledge (Eph 3:19) is the ground on which fuller knowledge grows (Col 2:2–3). True understanding, forever in competition with vain philosophy, is discerned through the self-awareness of those who join themselves in mutual love to the gospelled Christ who is their head and their mind.

Whatever their connection with Paul himself, these two epistles develop along Pauline lines. Emphatic about the unparalleled importance of the basic Gospel, they nevertheless value the greater knowledge that comes with more perfect realization of the Christian way. Confident of the strength of the understanding given in the Gospel, they are nevertheless alert to the potential danger of competing doctrines that can be destructive of life in Christ's salvation. Forthright about the advanced understanding in the possession of the apostle, they nevertheless recognize that God's way of giving the truth is such that its final discernment lies with the cumulative self-understanding of the loving Christian community. As with Paul's major epistles, these two manifest a sense of the constitution that governs Christian understanding, and offer a way of discernment within it. Remember the Gospel you received; walk worthily of it; and remain in the mutuality and unity of love. The mind of the community thus perfected recapitulates the mind of Christ.

Here, however, there is one more note of difference between these epistles and their Pauline ancestors. Paul had not quite explicitly faced the question of how far the boundaries of his notion of the Christian community might operatively extend. For the most part, he remained in the confidence that the organizing power of the Spirit of Christ could do within the individual church whatever work needed to be done in the formation of understanding, and that it would lead to no real contradictions between the minds of individual churches, since each would embody expressions of the mind of the one Christ. Implicitly, his view was more directly universalist: the same Gospel is preached everywhere by all apostles, and it is upon this one foundation that the one Spirit builds toward more perfected understanding. Ephesians and Colossians bring this implication into more overt realization. The Church is one. It does not matter that the Colossians are not Paul's apostolic children—he is with them in spirit nevertheless, because the constitutional truth of the one Body dominates over the organizational truth of its discrete communal manifestations. Does the companion epistle address the Ephesians, or the Laodiceans, or the Colossians, or none of these in particular? The uncertainty of scholarly reconstruction is ironically appropriate. Within the theory which it manifests, it does not matter. There is finally one Body, as there is one Lord and one Spirit, and one Faith. It is in the shared Gospel that true understanding is founded, and it is in the self-edifying mutuality of love in the whole Church, speaking the truth in love, that true understanding is perfected up to the very fullness of Christ, the norm of all wise knowing (Eph 4:13–16).

II. The Pastorals

Whatever the connection of the pastoral epistles with Paul,[2] it is not the same as that of Ephesians and Colossians. The latter's easy confidence about the development of true knowledge and ready optimism about the coherence of growing Christian understanding are authentic developments of one side of Paul's theology: the process of Christian perfection under the benevolent and illuminating guidance of the Spirit brings such riches as the *gnôsis* celebrated in these epistles. But Paul balanced this with a sober caution about the potential dangers of becoming too ambitious of mind, straying too far from the stabilizing humble obedience to the saving Gospel into a speculation whose value was rather indifferent by comparison with the Gospel itself and which can turn one's head disadvantageously. If Ephesians and Colossians do not join Paul in his concern, the pastorals compensate by worrying firmly.

The specific occasion of worry is the existence of competitive teachings, teachings that deviate from sound *didaskalia*, which are capable of shipwrecking the faith (1 Tim 1:19) or overthrowing it (2 Tim 2:18; Ts 1:11). We are not given many particulars about the nature of this heterodoxy, but it appears that it comes in several varieties. One is a Judaizing doctrine, having to do with commandments that pervert the truth about what is clean and unclean (Ts 1:14–15). Another is the promotion of a more metaphysical false dogma, such as Hymenaeus' and Philetus' claim that the resurrection has already taken place (2 Tim 2:17–18). Another appears to be a pandering to undisciplined *epithumia* (2 Tim 4:3–4). Another forbids even marriage (1 Tim 4:3). All are at best vain, foolish, babbling; at worst, pernicious.

God wants all men to be saved and to come to a knowledge of the truth (1 Tim 2:4). But there is a falsely named "knowledge" that opposes itself to the truth, a false knowledge whose sponsors are missing the faith (1 Tim 6:20–21), and which may be claimed to be a function of spirits of error and teachings of demons (1 Tim 4:1). The problem of discernment is acute. If Timothy can be assured that "the Lord will give you understanding in all things" (2 Tim 2:7), how shall we know the Timothys from the Hymenaeuses who falsely claim such advanced understanding? For demonic though the false teaching may be in effect, it apparently does not always smell overtly of brimstone. Some of the corrupt-minded teachers, reprobate with respect to the faith, have "a form of piety" and evidently seem quite respectable to pupils who follow them, despite the name-calling which may be indulged in by those who disapprove of their doings (2 Tim 3:1–8). It is all very well to say that their folly will eventually be exposed (2 Tim 3:9): but what about right now, when an accurate assessment of them may possibly be a matter of spiritual life and death?

The first canon of discernment is the saving and gracious purpose of God, manifested in Jesus Christ and brought to light in the Gospel (2 Tim 1:8–10), the Word of God that leads to the eternal life promised by God before time, which Paul preaches and teaches among the Gentiles by God's command (Ts 1:2–3). Fidelity to the Gospel is the first principle of stability. Hence Paul tells Timothy that he should "remember Jesus Christ raised from the dead, of the seed of David, according to my Gospel" (2 Tim 2:8)—and it is in this context that he can give the assurance that Timothy's understanding will be well-formed, for he does so not unqualifiedly, but thus: "Consider what I say; and consider what I have said, as commissioned teacher of the Gentiles," because this teaching is "a pattern of sound words which you have heard from me in faith and love in Christ Jesus" (2 Tim 1:13). Timothy must therefore "remain in the things you learned and were assured of, knowing from whom you learned" (2 Tim 3:14); and if he abides in these things, minding himself and the teaching, he will save both himself and those who hear him (1 Tim 4:16). This sound *didaskalia* is not that which the Holy Spirit gives through power from the mind of Christ, but is as homely and ordinary in its public objectivity as one could ask: it is a deposit given in a form of sound words, and although it is guarded by the indwelling Holy Spirit it is given by perfectly ordinary means (2 Tim 1:13–14). Once Timothy has received it, he can entrust it in turn to other faithful men, who will then be competent to teach still others in their turn (2 Tim 2:2). There is little problem of development. To the extent that the word has already been published, Paul can mainly content himself with saying "remember"; to the extent that there are new lives to be won, he need say only "teach what you were taught." The process of disseminating and consolidating Christian understanding is, within this scheme, extremely simple and ordinary. So far, there is little theoretical difficulty in establishing what belongs to basic Christian thought: it is whatever was in the Word that was manifested in a *kerygma* taught to the Gentiles by Paul.

From the major Pauline epistles, one might suppose that this kerygma is the salvific death and resurrection of Jesus and the possibility of gracious participation in it through faith. But even setting aside the inadequacy of such a restrictive formulation of the kerygma for the major Pauline epistles, it will not fit at all in the pastorals. Titus is typical in its manner of introducing a reference to the redemptive and purifying self-giving of Jesus Christ and the hope of the glorious parousia. "For the saving grace of God appeared to all men, instructing us that, denying impiety and worldly lusts, we might live soberly and righteously and piously in the present age, waiting for the blessed hope, *etc.*" (Ts 2:-11–13). Good behavior is effectually part of the kerygma itself, not a secondary consequence of it. Even the death of Jesus is said to be that he "might cleanse for himself a particular people, zealous of good works" (Ts 2:14). Paul's apostleship in Jesus Christ is specifically "according to knowledge of truth that is according to piety" (Ts 1:1). To behave impiously, even in so apparently inessential a matter as failing to take care of the welfare of one's own people, is to deny the faith (1 Tim 5:8)—not simply to disgrace it, but to deny it. The Christian is to walk in a piety that can be recognized and approved even by outsiders, not only to prevent blasphemous criticism of the teaching (1 Tim 6:1) that is the word of God (Ts 2:5, 8), but because what is commonly recognized as sound, decent, pious behavior is automatically and necessarily part of the essential teaching. This is the way to life through good works, the sound words of our Lord Jesus Christ and the teaching according to piety, to differ from which is to be shown up as understanding nothing, corrupt of mind, deprived of the truth (1 Tim 6:3–5). Those who have abandoned iniquity and lust and worldly desires in order to accept the truth that is according to piety should know "the things appropriate to the sound doctrine" (Ts 2:1), and should be reproved and be exhorted if they slip along the way. Any teaching that runs otherwise is self-condemned.

Normative Christian understanding is therefore mapped basically by the convergence of the fundamental apostolic kerygma with the community's own independently received sense of decorous, pious, sober comportment. Any teaching leading to the violation of either of these is *ipso facto* disqualified. So closely linked are these two, in fact, that the pastorals are clearly suspicious of any teaching that does not immediately promote decorous behavior. It is not sufficiently creditable for teaching to be merely consonant with piety.

One may readily imagine that those who were especially impressed with the more perfected knowledge alluded to by Paul and celebrated in Ephesians and Colossians might be impatient with the pastorals' anti-speculative suspicions and respectable communal morality. But there is more to the pastorals' stand than dull conservatism. The moral standards may seem surprisingly indistinguishable from what one might expect from a nice civilized Gentile community anywhere, but they are rooted in—or at least consciously correlated with—a specifically Christian renovation of understanding. "The aim of the preaching is love from a clean heart and a good conscience and unfeigned faith" (1 Tim 1:5). That, if the words are given weight, is not unworthy of Paul himself. The gentle and modest moral style that is derived from it by the pastorals may seem less vigorous and courageous than Paul's, but this is due in part to the quieter tone of the pastorals—consider, for instance, how quietly Paul is here brought to speak of the persecutions he endured and of the fact that all who live piously in Jesus Christ will be persecuted (2 Tim 3:11–12). Under the modest manner, the pastorals present the love of God as a demanding disciple.

The Pauline doctrine of love could not, however, be induced from the pastoral epistles. It is notably absent from the catalogues of characteristics by which a man may be judged fit for positions of church leadership, and has little emphasis in the general descriptions of proper Christian comportment. It is not the binding spirit that holds the church in unity. The Spirit as such, in fact, has retreated to the margins in the pastorals' sense of the way the Christian *politeia* now works, and the shift shows consequences in these epistles' notions of the constituting of Christian life as well as Christian understanding. But there remains a basic conviction about the importance of Christian unity, and although its rationale is more slack and its presence more pale than in the uncontested works of Paul, it is the way in which the pastorals make their final case against heterodoxy.

A teaching that induces what is incompatible with a good conscience is self-disqualified. So is the denial of the salvation effected through Christ. But what of the teachings that are merely vain and speculative, leading to no evident contradictions, and to neither virtue nor vice? The self-incriminating problem with them is that they lead to contention, disunity, division (1 Tim 6:4; 2 Tim 2:14; Ts 3:8–9). "Pursue righteousness, faith, love, peace with those who call upon the Lord from a clean heart. But refuse foolish and instructed investigations, knowing that they beget fights—and a servant of the Lord ought not to fight but to be gentle toward all, ready to teach, forbearing, in meekness instructing the opposers" (2 Tim 2:22–25). Factiousness is intolerable, and inconsistent with the character of the Church as the pillar and ground of truth (1 Tim 3:15); the factious man is evidently perverted and if he cannot be recalled to his senses and to the way of love and peace by two meek reminders, he should be avoided as a man dangerous and self-condemned (Ts 3:9–11).

If not exactly the way of Paul, this prudent procedure is nevertheless at least reminiscent of the way of Aquila and Priscilla. That much compromise is understandable if, as the pastorals allege, their author has seen too many instances of claimed knowledge that lead to no respectable end, too many teachers who promote idle and unfounded speculations out of scriptures that were meant to edify and discipline pious lives (1 Tim 1:4, 7–8; 2 Tim 3:15–17; Ts 3:9), too many eager learners who became victims of their own flighty instability (2 Tim 3:6, 4:3–4). If the Promethean fire from heaven which Christ had brought to the Gentiles had flourished, in the view of the Colossians and Ephesians, to a knowledge worthy of a Daedalus, the pastorals form their basic sense of propriety from gazing on the wreckage of Icarus. That kind of ambition is too unnecessary, and too risky. It destroys unstable persons and gullible communities. That kind of thought is too far removed from the sound, healthy, fruit-bearing *didaskalia* that is the normative backbone of Christiantiy for it to be definitively discerned as part of the truth or appropriately accepted as normative. And so the pastorals try even more assiduously to remember where they came from. Paul, a worthy pattern of Christian doctrine, conduct, purpose, faith, long-suffering, love, endurance (2 Tim 3:10), admonishes Timothy to be a pattern for believers in speech, behavior, love, faith, purity (1 Tim 4:12). What men like these did and enjoined and taught must define the Christian norm. Fidelity to the Way and the teaching they pursued is at the very least a safer course to steer by than the novelties of those who claim new knowledge that cannot readily be reconciled to the foundation they gave. Hence the cautious criteria for those who will hold positions of leadership as teachers and governors of the church: they must be tested, lovers of the good, holding firmly to the faithful Word according to the teaching, able to sustain order among sometimes unruly believers.

The pastorals are keenly conscious of the potential virtues of conservative and firm leadership. Paul to Timothy—not Paul to the Cretans or to the Ephesians. Paul appointing Titus to appoint elders in every city. Paul himself commissioned to take the word to the Gentiles. The sense of the communal church is there, but it is consistently disciplined by the sense of its need for guidance, by an awareness of a necessary moderating control that runs along a chain of authority from Paul to the elders and deacons of the churches to which he is distantly related. Part of the major business of this chain of authority is to safeguard the norms of Christian understanding. These are to be found in Paul himself, known and taught and lived out; but they are also to be found in Timothy and

Titus, and in those whom they have successfully taught. The norm is the deposit, the *didaskalia*, that kerygma that tells of our redemption and invitation to life, and of the righteousness that is the condition of our accepting that invitation. We must look not to its enlargement but to its behavioral concretization. Its primary locus is therefore the Christian memory—the memory of the Gospel as we first heard it, unadulterated by any later adjustments or compromises, and the memory of those whose lives showed what their teaching told. Those who can be trusted as authentic vehicles of this memory are those whose own lives witness to the sort of pious sobriety and constancy that is worthy of the Gospel, those who by their fruits have shown themselves to be capable of understanding it. It is in their recollective self-understanding seen in clear conscience that the law of Christian thought will become most plainly manifest. The community as such does not have the integrity and cohesiveness to embody the consciousness that must accordingly be found more reliably localized in its most respectable members. The pattern of human authority must make up in its own body, and after its customary manners, what human frailty leaves lacking in the power of the Word and the Spirit.

6
The Johannine School

"*A*nd we know that the Son of God is come," says what is now the peroration of 1 John, "and has given us understanding [*dianoian*]" (5:20). The body of the epistle appears to be a series of instructions, to enhance the received understanding of the addressees; but the instruction comes mainly by way of reminder, not of news. "I write to you not a new commandment, but an old commandment which you had from the beginning—the old commandment is the word which you heard" (2:7); "I wrote to you not because you do not know the truth, but because you know it" (2:21). The basic stance of the author[1] is that a sufficiency of understanding has already been given to them, and that "you have no need that any man teach you" (2:27). What he presents in the epistle is offered under such rubrics, and is essentially a mode of self-reflection for the Christian body he addresses.

He writes to celebrate and reaffirm what they know together, but he also writes to explore their way of understanding, in order to secure it —and them—against a present danger. They have heard that Antichrist is coming (2:18, 4:3), and this expectation is now realized in the form of false prophets (4:1; cf. 2:18) who will attempt to lead them astray (2:26)—and the author wishes that no one lead them astray (3:7). And that is, in a way, precisely what has happened to the false prophets themselves, for they have arisen from Christian circles, even if their present apostasy shows that they did not really belong to them (2:19). They will lead astray if possible, even the elect. Hovering on the uncertain edge between the theoretical guaranteed stability of those who are authentically "of us" and the practical possibility of deviance, the author remembers with his audience the truths that disclose the grounds for his confidence and the grounds for his concern.

The underlying theological theory is that despite the darkness and lust and untruth and unrighteousness and sin of the dying world and of the devil who dominates the world, God—who is free of all the negative features that characterize the world—has loved us (4:19) and shown his love by sending his Son into the world so that we might live through

145

him (4:9). The Son came to undo the works of the devil (3:8) and to take away our sins (3:5), to be the saviour of the world (4:14). He laid down his life for us (3:16) and became propitiation for our sins and for the whole world (2:2). His blood cleanses us from sin (1:7) and permits us to overcome the world (5:4) and to have eternal life (2:25) as Children of God (3:1) *if* we obey God's commandment to believe in the name of his Son Jesus Christ and love one another (3:23).

It is nowhere clearly stated how this commandment became manifest. Here and there are hints that it was also the commandment of Jesus (2:3), heard by those who saw him and passed on to others by their witness (1:1–3), as part of an understanding given by the Son (5:20) and that is perceivable through a right interpretation of the death of Jesus (3:16, 5:8, 1:7). But the author is not much interested in the practical etiology of that understanding: he knows that he has it, and that his addressees have entered into it, and is for the most part content to proclaim as definitive truth that which he has—somehow—seen.

His own witness is important (1:1–3). But once his readers have believed and entered into the way of light, his witness is no longer a primary constituting factor in their understanding. "If we receive the witness of men, the witness of God is greater" (5:9), and they have received God's Spirit (4:13), who is truth and who bears witness (5:6, 8). The believer now has the witness in himself (5:10). This is the anointing received from God which abides in them and teaches them about all things, so that they have no need of any man's witness or any man's teaching (2:27).

They know the truth (2:21); they know all things (2:20). They themselves are now the earthly locus of normative Christian understanding, because they have the true anointing of the Spirit. They have overcome the world; but the world remains, at least for a time, and is in the evil one (5:19). The deceiving false spirits of the world continue to threaten them (4:1–5), and their condition is not invulnerably secure. They have been cleansed from sin, but may still fall into sin (2:1, 5:16). One whose love is not yet perfect may still be timorous (4:18) and insecure in heart (3:20). Therefore the epistle undertakes to remind them of the conditions of their continuing to remain norms of understanding—and these conditions may be taken as the criteria by which the adequacy of their understanding may subsequently be assessed.

The first condition is that they believe in the Son. The most elementary level of this admonition is the confession of Jesus; and although there is much more to be said, this alone is an important instrument of discernment. They must not believe every spirit, but must test whether they are from God. The test is surprisingly simple. Every spirit which acknowledges Jesus Christ is of God; every spirit not acknowledging

Jesus is not of God but of the Antichrist (4:2–3).[2] Here at least is an absolute norm for authentic understanding, and one which reverberates throughout the epistles; whoever denies that Jesus is the Christ is a liar and Antichrist, denying both Father and Son (2:22); he who acknowledges the Son has the Father also (2:23); whoever confesses that Jesus is the Son of God dwells in God and God in him (4:15); whoever believes that Jesus is the Christ is born of God (5:1) and he who believes that Jesus is the Son of God overcomes the world (5:5).

They must "have" the Son. "He who has the Son has life; he who does not have the Son of God does not have life" (5:12), for the eternal life that God has given us is in his Son (5:11). "Having the Son" is a function of believing that Jesus is he. He who so believes may also be said to be *in* the Son (5:20) and whoever is in the Son is also in the Father (5:20), abiding in God and God in him (4:15), begotten by God (5:1) and therefore being himself a child of God (3:1). To believe in the Son is thus to "have" the Son; and it is also to have the Father (2:23). But it is not simply a matter of belief. The life that is given in the Son must be manifested and sustained by walking in the light (1:7), keeping the commandments (2:3) and the word (2:5) of the Lord—walking as he walked (2:6). This is how we can know that we are in him (2:5). Indeed, it is by this criterion that we *know that* we know him (2:3)!

The commandments and the word that are to be kept, and the example that is to be followed, are not spelled out entirely. But we know that they exclude the love of the world, the *epithumia* and vainglory of life that characterize the dominion of darkness (2:15–16); they exclude sin (3:6, 8) and the denial of our sinfulness (1:8, 10); they exclude lawlessness (3:4) and the doing of unrighteousness (3:10). But above all, they exclude the failure to love (3:10, 14–15, 17; 4:8). They include doing righteousness (2:29), doing truth (3:19), avoiding sin (3:9). But above all, they include loving: for love is of God (4:7), because God is love (4:8); and therefore genuine knowledge of God reveals the necessity of love (4:7). The message from the beginning is that we should love one another (3:11). This is his commandment (3:23; 4:21). But it is also the nature of things. Not to love God, who is love, is perverse. To love God also entails love of those whom he has begotten (5:1). Abiding in love is the way to abide in God, and have God abide in oneself (4:16). It is therefore this love that proves that we have passed from death to life (3:14); it is by loving not in word or tongue but in work and truth—a summons to practical generosity and, if need be, even to death (3:16–17)—that we know that we are of the truth and make our hearts confident (3:20). Startling as it may be, this remark presents the epistle's ultimate criterion for the discernment of Christian truth: it is by love that we were rescued by him who is love and truth, and accordingly it is by love that we remain in the understanding that has been given to us, and by the work and truth of our manifest love that we know that we know. By this one fruit, you shall know them—and know the truth, and know that you abide securely in it. It is by belief that one grasps the truth, but it is only by love that one confidently discerns it.

Directly from this follows a principle of community that further conditions the meaning of the canon of love. The community that believers have with the Father and the Son entails their love for one another, and hence their community with one another (1:3). The love that binds them brings them to abide with one another, as they abide in God and the Son. Their sharing in the truth can be grounded only in the mutuality of love: without this grounding, a claim to know God is decisively discredited (3:10, 4:20). Hence the argument used by the author against those who, having "gone out from us" (2:19), might falsely seem to be bearers of the truth. If they had been *of* us, they would have remained with us (2:19). The complement of this argument is the one urged in 4:5–6; they, cut from the community of divinely conditioned love, are of the world—but if we are, as members of that community, of God, then our truth may be communally discerned: everyone who is of God will hear us. The economy of internal self-edification and self-instruction in the loving community is total. Outside, all may be dismissed as the world; inside, whoever is of God will be heard.

It is in this spirit that the author writes. With a personal conviction of his Christian authenticity, he can intone solemnly some of the great truths which he shares with his addressees, apparently unshakably confident—and presuming their confidence as well—that these laws of thought cannot be seriously questioned. Thus he never bothers to offer a rationale for the virtually axiomatic dogma concerning the place of Jesus the Son of God in the providential scheme of things, despite the fact that this very truth has come under serious question in some circles. They have believed; they have known; they have seen. There is no backtracking. To deny what they have known, what they have experienced as confirmed in them by the Spirit, is to lie and to deny themselves. Their shared self-understanding is flatly incompatible with apostasy from Jesus. The author does not stop at the affirmation of axioms, however. He reflects with his addressees upon the structure that is founded in them, exploring the logic of it, the coherence, the experiential confirming evidences, the implications, the means of assaying both it and one's participation in it. He anatomizes the constitution of Christian understanding not exactly as a systematic theologian nor as a confessor (though there are hints of both), but more precisely as an experienced voice articulating for the community a self-scrutinizing examination of consciousness in the light of a truth that is within the reach of their transformed humanity and puts it under judgment.

1 John sketches the constitution of Christian thought in surprising detachment from the criteria dominant in the Gospels. We hear virtually nothing of Scripture, except for a glancing reference to Cain; we are given only the flimsiest references to either the career or the teaching ministry of Jesus; we have no identifiable allusion to his post-resurrection teaching, or indeed to the resurrection itself. It is clear that the epistle appeals to Jesus' life and death as foundational for Christian understanding, but it is not as clear in what way this is true, or according to what interpretative criteria. One passage opens the possibility that the fundamental interpretative canon is that of the primitive kerygma: "What you heard from the beginning, let it remain in you. If what you heard from the beginning remains in you, you will remain in both the Son and the Father" (2:24). If this is like the Lucan *ap' archês*, it signals the apostolic testimony—that which was delivered by those appointed ones who had been with Jesus from the baptism of John to the ascension (Acts 1:21–22) and were therefore, *ap' archês*, eyewitnesses and ministers of the Word (Lk 1:2).[3] That is one way of interpreting 1 John, which may accordingly be read as rather nostalgic in its back-glances to the apostolic testimony. Or it could signify that which they have heard from their Christian beginning, viz., the Gospel originally preached to them.[4]

But there is another way of reading this elusive verse that seems to me more consonant with the over-all theological dynamics of the epistle. Consider the way the phrase is used elsewhere within: the devil is a sinner *ap' archês* (3:8); you, fathers, have known *ton ap' archês* (2:13–14). Here, the phrase clearly means the ultimate beginning. What is the real beginning of the Christian Word? The tendency of the synoptic tradition is to suggest the baptism of John, or perhaps in another sense the ministry of Jesus, or in yet another and more striking manner, his passion and resurrection. The Fourth Gospel, unlike the Second, begins *en archê ên ho logos:* the ultimate beginning, the divinely planned mystery from eternity which even the synoptists would acknowledge was in another sense the true point of origin for the Christian truth. There is no instance of the phrase in 1 John that cannot plausibly be read as meaning "from the ages," from the ultimate beginning. The *ap' archês* with which it begins is, at least in the light of the Fourth Gospel (and, I believe, even without it as well), clearly suggestive of the eternal Word; and the message *ap' archês* of 3:11, commanding love, is identical with the commandment which is not really new but "old," *ap' archês* (2:7). That which was in the beginning is now revealed, for he who is from the beginning has revealed himself. I opine, therefore, that the epistle consistently intends the phrase in just that way, and that one should interpret 2:24 accordingly: that which you heard that came from the ultimate origin, that commandment of love that expresses the nature and will of the Father, must remain in you, and if it does, you shall remain in the Son and the Father. Not apostolic kerygma, but something that far transcends it.

When we put together the epistle's general neglect of the resurrection and of Scripture, which are elsewhere in early Christian testimony among the most unquestionably vital moments of the kerygma, and the epistle's relative lack of interest in the phenomenon of apostolic testimony (for it is by no means clear that the author presents himself as an apostle, and he decidedly argues that his readers are now independent of such witness), the most likely explanation for this curious use of *ap' archês* is, I believe, that it is a counterpoise to a usage like Luke's. The same root, but different branches. Luke's tendency to locate the *archê* in the period of Jesus' ministry, passion, and resurrection logically implies the Third Gospel, with its ample account of "all that Jesus began to do and teach." The First Epistle of John represents another tendency, in which the *archê* is the rarefied ultimate, and the witness to its earthly revealer is refined almost to the bare bones of his having come, given the eternal commandment, and laid down his life for our salvation. The accumulated traditions of Jesus' life and teaching are abstracted from much as Paul ordinarily abstracted from the fleshly Jesus, while an essential message is isolated in all its simple purity from what he did and said, and offered abroad with the approval of the truth-divining Spirit.

Beyond the essential message, Christianity teaches other things— about the *parousia* (3:2), about life (3:14), about sin and sinlessness (5:18). 1 John implies throughout that there are many points of understanding shared between author and readers. But he does not derive them from the sayings of Jesus or from the witness of the Twelve. That sort of criterion has little or nothing to do with his sense of how we know. His claim is rather that the truth of these things is guaranteed by the witness of the Spirit held in love. So decisive and self-sufficient is this economy that participation in this loving mutuality of understanding is itself a telling test of truth and falsity. "By this we know" *(en toutô ginôskomen)* runs like a refrain throughout the epistle (2:3, 2:5, 3:19, 3:24, 4:2, 4:13, 5:2). It points to the central criterion by which the authenticity of Christian understanding is validated. That criterion is essentially their loving mutuality, as understood in a complex of relations. God is love; God has commanded love; God has revealed love and the commandment of love in Jesus; God has given the Spirit of love and of understanding of himself; God has allowed those who have responded to abide in him. All these considerations converge in the community's life of illuminated love, which is at once the conformity to God's revealed will, the recognition and imitation of Christ, the living-out of the indwelling Spirit, and life in God. This life can be explicated with reference to the standard early Christian criteria—revelation from the beginning, the career of Jesus, the communications of Jesus, the Christian Word, the illuminations of the Spirit—but it is experienced as self-validating beyond these canons of evaluation, bringing such a sureness of exalted truth that the author can summarily use the community itself as the touchstone of true understanding in others: "He who knows God hears us; he who is not of God hears us not. From this we know the spirit of truth and the spirit of error" (4:6). Whatever belongs properly to the understanding of the true Way, the discernment of both what is indispensable and what is additionally true, comes through what the loving Christian community, faithfully in Jesus the Son and doing what is pleasing in the sight of God, will hear and recognize as truth. History as such has made itself theologically obsolete, and kerygmatically almost without significance, except as the arena in which the world made room for its own defeat. Thought has no appeal beyond the self-understanding of the loving community in Christ the Son of God.

2 John confronts even more urgently than 1 John the problem of deceivers who are, in some way, false to the teaching of Christ, *didachê tou Christou* (9). This phrase is probably to be interpreted as teaching *about* rather than *by* Christ[5] (though the two do not necessarily exclude one another) and the presbyter insists that it is indispensable to religious authenticity. One who abides in this teaching has both Father and Son; one who goes beyond it and does not abide in it does not have God (9) and is so pernicious—and so dangerous even to the faithful (8)—that he should not be received or greeted. These stern measures are urged upon a community in which abides the truth (the virtual equivalent of the Spirit) and which walks in the truth and in love, according to the commandment. Apparently, the elect lady and her children have only to remember and be faithful to the truth in which they presently walk in order to resist the temptations of those deceivers who do not acknowledge an important part of the truth. "Many deceivers went forth into the world, the ones not acknowledging Jesus Christ coming in the flesh" (7).[6] Just what do these deceivers deny? The flesh of Jesus (that is, a Docetic position), or the literal coming (that is, an anti-eschatological position), or the place altogether of Jesus in the scheme of things (that is, the un-Christian position most consistently glanced at in 1 John)? It is impossible to be sure, but on balance, I think the latter most likely. 2 John, that is, faces the ultimate test of the canon of spiritual discernment. Some claim to have bypassed Jesus, going beyond *(proagon)* the *didachê tou Christou*, to be in direct contact with God.

This is a view known indirectly from the persistent polemical thrusts of the Fourth Gospel and of 1 John. It is a view evidently developed within the Christian body, and probably the stiffest test given to early Christian thought. The "deceivers" cited in 2 John may of course have been mere charlatans; but it is likely enough that they too supposed themselves to be authentic teachers, despite the differences between their *didachê* and that cherished by the presbyter and his lady. If so, the confident conservatism of 2 John suggests that they must have claimed either further revelation or more developed understanding rather than being able to support their stance on the basis of an appeal to the original Gospel as it was originally understood. 1 John suggests a nuanced version of such a claim, by showing how the Gospel as a message *ap' archês* might be taken as a revelation from God capable of rendering the historical revealer superfluous, as obsolete as his historical biography.

Is the Diotrephes mentioned in 3 John one of the agents of this competing *didachê?* Possibly; but the only indication in favor of such a conclusion is the very weak one that he is regarded as an opponent of some sort by one who is ostensibly the author of 2 John. But there is in 2 John no indication that the "deceivers" are in command of churches, and there is in 3 John no indication that Diotrephes is teaching unsound doctrine—only that he is ambitious, arrogant, inhospitable, and has spoken ill of the presbyter and his brethern. It is unlikely that he represents the *planoi* of 2 John.

It is striking, however, that 3 John reads plausibly as a letter not *about* but rather *by* one of the opponents of 2 John. Suppose that in response to difficulties caused by the instructions of 2 John, the teachers repudiated there provided themselves with similar credentials in the form of a pseudepigraphical letter of credit—possibly in the knowledge that 2 John itself was only a work of pious (if, from their viewpoint, misguided) pseudepigraphy? It is notable that despite 2 John's concern about those who do not acknowledge Jesus Christ, 3 John never mentions him and that 3 John describes on the part of Diotrephes precisely that kind of treatment which 2 John has prescribed to his addressees to use against the enemy. Moreover, the commended Demetrios of 3 John is not cited for his fidelity to the received doctrine of Christ, but only according to the more elusive criterion of the truth's own witness, coupled with general approbation and the endorsement of the presbyter himself. Furthermore, there is an interesting coincidence between 3 John's positive picture of travelling missionaries going out "from us" and 1 John's repudiation of false teachers whose going out "from us" is interpreted to their discredit. And finally, it may be noted that 3 John was accepted by the Church much later than, and more reluctantly than, 2 John.[7]

Whether or not 3 John really derives from 2 John's "deceivers," it is a forceful reminder of the difficulties caused by the desperate tactics recommended in 2 John. Diotrephes denies a hearing. The matter is being settled peremptorily, not by appeal to tradition or consensus or discernment of spirits or the fruits by which we are to know them, but by exercise of personal authority, and in a rather uningratiating manner. Within the confines of 3 John, it seems clear that Gaius will do well, and worthily of God, if he behaves hospitably toward brethren and strangers, and it seems equally clear that Diotrephes will have to answer to the Lord for his churlish behavior. Those who do ill have not seen God; those who do good are from God. This is not *specifically* Christian doctrine, admittedly, but surely consonant with the *didachê tou Christou*, and traditionally one of its coordinates presupposed both in the general Christian principle of knowing them by their fruits and in the peculiarly Johannine obsession with loving unity. It is indeed possible that Diotrephes knew what he was doing, that he remembered who he was and what he had been from the start, and even that he had good reason to take it upon himself to settle the matter without leaving it to more harmonious and less abrupt techniques. But his comportment does not commend itself to what are otherwise attested as Christian principles for the discernment of truth. One sympathizes with the presbyter of 3 John: taking such short-cuts raises serious problems. One looks back to the presbyter of 2 John with some misgiving. Would it not have been better, and more consistent, if he had been inclined to let the lady's children perceive for themselves the falsity of this new teaching? The theories prevailing in Johannine literature suggest that this is the case. Those who remain in the truth, united in love, have overcome the world and the evil spirit who dominates it. If their love is adequate, they have nothing to fear. He who abides in them is greater than the spirits of falsehood, and will triumph over them in any encounter. 2 John is faithful to the general Johannine awareness of the stark difference between world and God, and the enmity between darkness and light; but its abrupt and strongarm tactics are unfaithful to the Johannine confidence in the power of the truth itself, known with a confidence that transcends even the human heart, to make itself normatively understood within the discerning self-awareness of the loving Christian community. Its excuse for taking this anxious short-cut is that it faced the most massive and ultimate heresy of the early Christian movement—the denial of Jesus Christ. The shared criterion of the Spirit's disclosures through communal understanding stabilized by righteousness and love, that very principle that permitted the development and refinement of Johannine understanding in the first place, has been turned even against what had been axiomatic. Johannine theology in general invites the courage to face even such an ultimate test. 2 John is not up to it. Rather than taking the more patient and trusting—and Johannine—tack, it appeals flatly to a more instantaneous criterion that is compatible with the communal one, and derived from the same constituting forces, but modally different. Though without the deftly argued Pauline base, 2 John comes down on the axiomatic principle that Christ is indispensable. The chances are that if it had been able to follow through with Johannine principles, and examine deeply the communal experience in the Spirit and truth, the theoretically threatened church would have come to the same conclusions as the Presbyter: for the meaning of the Christian experience had everywhere been conditioned by the knowledge—and experience—of Christ, however variously interpreted, and the denial of Christ is too sharp a discontinuity with experienced meaning to be readily tolerable within a religious movement that had always been concerned about coherence and respectful of the ordinary powers of human understanding. That the false prophets of 2 John did not sweep the Christian world is consistent with the way that world understood the character of its own ways of knowing. But that is hypothetical history. The fact that they were opposed in such a peremptory manner, despite the basic Johannine theory of the constitution of Christian thought, suggests a darker and sadder conclusion for the real history: one had lost confidence in the practicality of what had been supposed to be the true way to discern the true norms of thought.

7

Other New Testament Evidences

Of the remaining books of the New Testament, all but two are relatively short. The longest of them, dedicated to the apocalyptic vision of John, is too unschematic in its thought-structure to disclose much about its author's habitual conception of the constitution governing Christian understanding. The epistles of James, Peter, and Jude are too brief to yield the sort of over-all reconstruction that can be induced from the ample materials of Paul's work or Luke's or of the Johannine writings. The Epistle to the Hebrews is the only one that comes close to offering a full point of comparison. Even when these books offer only hints, however, their hints are valuable, and must be tested against the indications arising from the investigation of those more adequate bodies of evidence, even if the results are not as clear and do not provide quite as firm an insight into the relevant habits of mind.

Hebrews

The opening verses of the Epistle to the Hebrews strikingly capsulize some of the epistle's most important views on the foundations of right understanding. They acknowledge the revelations of God through the prophets, and thus the authority of Scripture, but insist that the revelation that forms the basis of Christian understanding has the evidently greater authority of being given through God's Son (1:1–2). Just how much greater this authority is appears through the characterization of the Son's vantage point, which clearly makes him, on several counts, the perfect spokesman. The Son is the ideal manifestation of God, being the radiance of his glory and the true representation of his real being (1:3). But he is also the one who best commands the character of reality, being both the agent of its creation and its ultimate heir (1:2)—and between these alpha and omega points of the cosmos, the Son is also the one whose word of power sustains it (1:3). It may be the Father who speaks

155

through the Son, as through the prophets, but the Son is in essentially as good a position as the Father himself to reveal the truth about the world.

It is not with this world, however, that his most important revelations have been concerned. It is with another world to come. The distinction is crucial to the theology of this epistle, and is variously developed throughout its text.

This world is the benevolent creation of God through his Son (1:2, 1:10) and had been in various ways the object of divine concern. But it is radically flawed. It is made of stuff that can be shaken (12:27), and will change (1:12): it will grow old (1:11–12). Unlike the stable and permanent heavenly order to which the Son properly belongs, this world is the place of mere flesh and blood (2:14), a place of infirmity, weakness, ignorance, straying (4:15, 5:2). It is a place of temptation (2:18) and, given weakness, of sin (12:1). It is, for all these reasons, a place of bondage to death and to the devil who holds death's power (2:14–15).

God has cared for the world. He has spoken at various times and places through prophets, offered promise and covenant, instituted religious service, established a priesthood to reconcile sinful men to himself. But all these attempts, because they worked through the stuff of an intrinsically feeble and flawed world, have been inadequate. The world, not worthy of the prophets, persecuted and destroyed them (11:36–38). Yet it is not in the infidelity and perversity of the world that the failure has lain, but in a sheer insufficiency that not even radical repentance can cure. The Law was given by governing angels, to restrain perversity and bring a way of forgiveness (2:2, 5:1, 9:7, etc.). It could not, however, transcend the limitations of the world for which it was designed. Its priests, trying to mediate between God and men, were themselves weak, sinful, under death (5:2–3, 7:23, 27–28). Their liturgy consisted of fleshly ordinances (9:10) carried out in a worldly place fashioned by mere human hands (8:2, 9:1, 9:24). What could be expected of such an arrangement? Little. Despite its intent, the religious service could not perfect the participants' consciences (9:9), could not, despite endless repetition, remove the conviction of sin (10:1–4). The sacrifices, which can never take away sins (10:11), were really valueless in the long run—and could not please God (10:5–6, 8). The whole law, in fact, was caught in the same limitation. It was not merely unsuccessful in restraining the disobedience of men: it was itself a law of fleshly commandments (7:16), weak and unprofitable like the flesh itself (7:18), and was able to make nothing perfect (7:19). The whole convenant between God and men was faulty and feeble, like the world it tried to rescue (8:7), and was bound to be annulled (7:18; cf. 10:9) or to grow old and disappear (8:13).

This world is simply not sound enough. Salvation, reconciliation, true rest cannot be achieved within the terms it offers. Those are things that belong to a higher order—a heavenly order where permanence, perfection, and the authentically real are to be found. That is the character of the world to come. This world, limping with impotent fleshliness, is only a shadow by comparison.

It is a fairly literal shadow, in fact. It is by means of that conceptual strategy that the Epistle to the Hebrews manages to underline the dramatically new and superior character of the Christian dispensation without repudiating altogether that older covenant which it perfects. The Israelite liturgy, for instance, was ineffectual; but that is not because it was wrong, but because it was put together out of inferior materials. The true tabernacle, the true instruments, the true actions are the ones in the heavenly order. Moses was shown these, and the revelation was true. But he did not have access to them. He could only copy them according to the materials of this world, and that fleshly and hand-made imitation was simply not good enough to work. The Law points to the truth—but it is the truth to come, the truth of the heavenly order. It is useless and misleading to apply the Law to the present fleshly level of things, as if that were its true reference.

There are two conflicting tendencies in Hebrews' treatment of pre-Christian developments, however. One uses them as significant shadows, with the participants either (like Abraham) aware of the shadowy character of the literal level and the transcendental character of the real referent, or (like the priests of Levi) pitifully mistaking shadow for substance. The other is a more short-circuited and discontinuous way of preferring the new order: the old one failed, became obsolete, and was written off by God as he instituted a new covenant that at last was adequate to heaven's true possibilities (7:19–22, 8:6, 10:16).

The religion of Israel was thus either an allegory or a parody. In either case, it was thoroughly defunct with the arrival of the Christian dispensation, and in either case it had no chance of succeeding on its own terms. The new covenant, which has to do with the reliable heavenly world to come, is the only real form of religious security.

The author of Hebrews is not entirely insensitive, however, to the theological implications of leaving Israel's religious life nothing but a gross misapprehension of the truth. Even when he is inclined to treat it as pitiful parody, he makes room for more heartening meeting points between God and Israel, and allows the possibility of salvation. The prophets were not deceived; Abraham knew in what direction the Promise points; Enoch and Noah and Moses and all the faithful ones of Israel earned a reward.

They earned a reward; but they did not receive it. Abraham took on the promises (11:17), but he did not receive them. All the holy ones of

Israel died without having received (11:13, 39). The old order was ineffectual in cleansing sin, in perfecting the faithful, and in fulfilling the greatest promises. It was capable of offering promises and allowing steadfast trust to become eligible for eventual fulfillment; but such fulfillment must transcend the limitations of this shabbier world. Accordingly, it had to wait until the time when the Son took on the flesh of suffering and weakness and death in order to triumph over it on our behalf and make us participants in the heavenly order that will be fully realized in the world to come. That is where perfection is to be found, for the ancients as well as the moderns, and entry into it is only through faith and the work of Christ (11:40).

In one sense, therefore, God's saving plan had been there from the beginning and was disclosed in a shadowed allegorical way through the prophets and the mediating angels. In another sense, God has in effect changed his mind and his offering, having first given a dispensation tailored to the limitations of this world and now offering another dispensation that transcends it. Hebrews shifts between these two ways of formulating the relationship between the old order and the new, the one way placing them in two levels of reality, the other in two periods of history. In neither case is the old order sufficient, but in neither case is it a trap from which men cannot escape. God spoke to men, even in the old order. If they believed in him and trusted what he said, within the restricted scope of his old-order communications, they became eligible to participate in the coming rescue from this world into the world to come.

God's various communications to the ancients were sometimes direct, as in his warning to Noah (11:7), and sometimes in the oblique shadowed way by which the Law and the Prophets prefigured the heavenly order that is to be constitutive of the world to come. Some communications had to do with the regulation of present behavior (2:2), but their more typical character was that of promise: the revelation of the future. Luke's sense of "gospel," the disclosure of good things that have not yet appeared, is shared by the author of Hebrews; and so is his sense of the right response—an assured understanding that these things are so and shall be so. To arrive at this response, one must first believe that God is, and that he rewards those who seek him (11:6). Without this, it is impossible to please him (11:6)—not, I think, because it is insulting not to trust him, but because without this it is impossible to attune one's life to his plans and thus to draw nearer by cooperating with him (11:6). Without Noah's cooperative belief, there would have been no salvation from the flood; without Sarah's, Isaac could not have been conceived. God's work sometimes depends upon our cooperative acceptance of his news about what is to be, and he rewards those who respond properly.

Not all God's appeals to faith have to do with his future projects. In some cases, he would have us know the truth concerning his past works, and to know it with a confidence not otherwise accessible. Hebrews glances at erroneous ideas about creation and points out not merely that we should believe otherwise, but that "by faith we understand" (*pistei nooumen*, 11:3) how it really came about. The most important realities are those of the invisible order of heaven, in both its past and its future works. When we are called upon to grasp and accept these, it is the office of faith to consolidate our understanding with assurance, despite the fact that its object remains unseen (11:1).

The most urgent and perfect of God's revelations is simultaneously information about the heavenly order and a proffered promise—the good News of the world to come and of our invitation to it. The more shadowy understanding offered through earlier revelation, never completely given nor completely understood, has now been replaced by the more direct communication through the most perfect revealer, the Son (1:1–2), who reveals in full what had been shown only glancingly before. Despite the author's fondness for spiritual and allegorical modes of expression, he is evidently persuaded that the revelation that founds the new Promise, the new hope, the new covenant, was directly given by the Son. Its foundation, its *archê*, lay in what was spoken by the Lord (2:3). Hebrews is not concerned to explain how that speaking was recognizable as authoritative, any more than it deals with how the prophets were known to be speaking the truth. But the epistle does not neglect to deal with how that revelation made itself felt in the subsequent stages of its transmission. What the Lord spoke was heard by others, and they have confirmed it to us (2:3).

We receive this word of revelation by responding with faith (4:2). What we then have is characterized by Hebrews not simply as proper trust but as right understanding, the knowledge of truth (*tên epignôsin tês alêtheias*, 10:26). The foundation (*archê*) of this knowledge, delivered by the Lord and faithfully passed on by witnesses, is also the foundation (*archê*) of our assurance, and if we hold firm to it, we become sharers of Christ (3:14). We must therefore attend assiduously to the things we have heard (2:1): to keep them is salvation, and to drift away from them is perilous.

Hebrews spends considerable space elaborating on the ways in which the career of Jesus fulfilled what the scriptures shadowed, and made it possible for us to break beyond the bounds of this limited world into a sharing in the world to come. But although it thus witnesses once more to the standard conviction that one important source of assured right understanding comes from the coincidence between scriptural revelation and the work of Jesus, it is interestingly emphatic about locating the center of our confidence in the teaching of Jesus as reliably communicated by those who followed and heard him. This is, of course, consistent with Hebrews' inclination to emphasize the difference between the testaments: if the new dispensation is much better and quite other than the old, as if God had changed his mind, the teaching of its initiator provides the truest foundation.

The teaching of Jesus provides the truest foundation, but it does not exhaust the matters that we are called to know. We may not stray from the *archê* given in that teaching; but neither are we to be confined to it. We are called in fact to leave the word of the foundation of Christ (*ton tês archês tou Christou logon*, 6:1) and move on to maturity. However indispensable and irreformable may be these foundational disclosures—repentance, faith in God, teaching of baptisms and of laying on of hands, and of resurrection of the dead and eternal judgment (6:1–2) —the rudiments or *archê* of God's oracles are only a milk diet, suitable only for those who are inexperienced in the word of righteousness (5:12–13). We are called to maturity and to solid food (5:14).

Whence comes a true maturity of understanding? One initial source is an imitation of the faith of one's Christian leaders, who have spoken the word of God and shown its good fruits in their comportment (13:7). The author of Hebrews implicitly takes on this role himself. He acknowledges his clear conscience and readiness to behave well (13:18); and he instructs his addressees in finer points of understanding and complains that they are not yet ready to receive the many more difficult interpretations he is prepared to transmit (5:11). But his impatient disappointment in their immaturity derives in part from his conviction that they should not be dependent on such teaching. The time has come when a less artificial achievement of knowledge is possible, when the laws of the Lord are written in the minds and hearts of the faithful, and they do not need to teach each other to know the Lord (8:10–11). They have been enlightened; they have received a share of holy spirit, and have tasted the heavenly gift and the good Word of God and the powers of the age to come (6:4–5). By now, they should themselves be teachers rather than needing to be taught (5:12). Maturity, with God's gracious permission, is something they are already equipped to achieve: they can be borne on to it (6:1) simply by doing faithfully what they are called to do (6:3). All they need beyond what they already have is further exercise in the discernment of good and evil, and they will be ready for solid food (5:14). If they live obedient to the leaders responsible for them (13:17), contented (13:5) and in brotherly love (13:1), sharing, assembling together, and fostering mutual love and good works (10:24–5, 13:16), in the way of peace and holiness (12:14), holding fast to the profession of faith (10:23) and looking steadfastly to the one who speaks from heaven (12:25) as to the founder and completer of faith

(12:2), they will grow towards maturity, and God will work in them that which is pleasing to him (13:20–21).

The essential norm of Christian understanding is to be found in what they heard with faith as they first entered into Christian life and Christian illuminative knowledge. The truth and importance of this understanding is guaranteed by its having been spoken by Christ, who is the founder and leader of salvation and the ruler over the world to come, and further guaranteed by its having been faithfully transmitted, with heaven's endorsement given by visible signs. Its truth has made itself felt by the reception of gifts, and continues to show itself in the good fruits produced by those who live in faithful conformity with it. Anyone who wishes to discover the truth in which salvation is given should find, in all this, grounds of certitude capable of resolving the most skeptical hesitation.

The development of perfection beyond this foundational stage consists primarily in living it well, and it is not clear that any further understanding is indispensable. It is, however, desirable. As one grows in maturity, how does one discern the difference between legitimate enlargements of one's enlightenment and the competing strange doctrines that lead one astray (13:9)? Hebrews is not especially concerned about this level of development, and its hints are not entirely sure. It is obvious that we must not compromise that foundational hearing that derives from the Lord himself: that is one sure touchstone. We may search the scriptures with a spiritual eye, and find richer ways of understanding Christian truth. The author's example leads the way in this: know Scripture as an allegory of the truth of the higher order, and you will find both confirmation of the basic truths and new disclosures that augment them.

The method of further discovery is only obliquely implied. But as he celebrates the *kenôsis* of salvation, the author of the epistle shows his habit of mind in a word that seems to be representative of his method: *eprepen*, "It was becoming" (2:10). Throughout the epistle, his style of argument and presentation is tuned to this key. Whatever seems to build appropriately on the true foundation has at least a claim to attention and probably a claim to truth. Only the perfect can discern for sure; but after all, what seems appropriate to a mind well founded in the Christian beginning and faithfully developed through Christian life is likely to turn out to be consonant with the ways in which God has designed his mystery of salvation. To live well and faithfully is to enhance one's discernment of good and evil. To listen well to the voice that came from heaven, and to conform mind and heart and life to its bidding, is to be ready to discern the knowledge of God's ways.

Christian scholars of the West have been inclined in the last few centuries, as in the first few centuries, to deny connections between the Epistle to the Hebrews and the Apostle Paul. Certainly, many stark differences exist between Paul's acknowledged epistles and this one: we need only consider the place of the teachings of Jesus in the scheme of things, or the quite un-Pauline catalogue of essential Christian truths in 6:1–2, where the cross is not so much as glanced at. Granted that the author of Hebrews may have been willing to add the cross if questioned about whether his list was really quite complete, and that Paul, under pressure, might have conceded (however grudgingly) that the more perfect revelation granted to him had been amply foreshadowed in Jesus' teachings to his earthly followers. Maybe. But it is difficult to imagine Paul carelessly omitting the cross, or putting such a premium on what Jesus said.

Given such differences, it is remarkable that there is so much coincidence between Hebrews' and Paul's sense of how Christian thought is constituted. The foundational Gospel (whatever the boundaries of its particular content) as it is faithfully preached everywhere coincides with Scripture and with what is revealed through Jesus' career. The evidences by which its truth may be known include faithful witness, heavenly confirmation by signs and wonders, and the believers' experience of the Spirit. The necessity of understanding the basic Christian Gospel in the way that it is here understood can be demonstrated by evidence available to all Christians, and to most reasonable outsiders. It is indispensable to accept and keep faithfully the terms of this foundation. It is desirable to move beyond them to a greater perfection of understanding. And the means of discerning the further reaches of understanding? For Hebrews as for Paul, it appears to be the sense of appropriateness generated in the cumulative self-consciousness of the community living out in loving mutuality its life in Christ. The community of the Epistle to the Hebrews may be less charismatically vivacious than Paul expected a Christian community to be, with a less vivid awareness of the presence of the Holy Spirit and of the risen Christ— but the sense it shares with its correspondent concerning the ways in which its understanding has been constituted and offered growth is strikingly like what Paul expected to find, and encouraged, in the minds of his churches.

James

The thought-structure underlying the Epistle of James is firmly rooted in non-metaphysical traditions, at some distance from the Epistle to the Hebrews. Its author is an intellectual kinsman of Jesus ben Sira, and eludes as if by pre-established design any attempt to derive a systematic theology from his writing. His focus falls not on thought but on conduct. Even his most metaphysical streams of reflection turn aside at last to nourish our practical understanding of the Way rather than our speculative grasp of the Ultimate. Thus his early emphasis on wisdom (1:5) is left mysteriously incomplete at first—God will supply it directly to those who ask: is this gnostic illuminism?!—only to become eventually another way of appealing not to consciousness but to conscience: the wisdom that comes from above is pure, meek, peaceable, gentle, and thus scarcely distinguishable from Pauline charity. Its distance from the wisdom of insight into reality may be gauged roughly by another item in the catalogue of its qualities: it is easily persuaded, *eupeithês* (3:17). There can be little surprise when the following verse moves from fruits of wisdom to fruits of righteousness, as if there has been no important shift in the key term, or when the definitive counter-indications of wisdom are identified not as error or doubt or ignorance but as rivalry and strife (3:14–16)—which in turn are condemned for producing not darkness and confusion, but instability and wicked deeds. This is a firm advocate of orthopraxis; but orthodoxy is not his preoccupation. To some extent, it may be argued that James embodies a degree of polemic against taking the notion of orthodoxy very seriously. The opposition set up here between faith and works may be primarily concerned with faith as trust or personal confidence, but its one illustration nevertheless pushes in the other direction, towards characterizing faith as belief: 2:19 sets up the exemplar of faith not by *su pisteueis en theô* but by *su pisteueis hoti ho theos heis esti,* representing faith as a sort of understanding of reality which may be quite similar in men and devils and is therefore insufficient. The difference comes in whether one acts in the light of this understanding. To behave according to earthly low-mindedness and lust and demonic temptation is perverse. Such a one, if he really has right understanding, will tremble with the demons, or will reform in accordance with the wisdom that comes from above, in patient obedience, according to the light of the indwelling spirit.

Likewise, the distinction between hearers and doers. The former category undoubtedly appeals to those who regarded the law as possessing *hê morphosis tês gnôseôs kaitês alêtheias* (Rom 2:20), through which they may know the divine will and discern matters discriminatingly (Rom 2:18). But as in Paul's own criticism of the Jew who draws a false conclusion from this privilege, so in James' the "enlightened" student of the Word is warned that he is self-deceived if his knowledge does not bear fruit in living out the implications of what he has learned. The truth is to be remembered in action, not merely in mind.

Despite his disinclination to worry about the refinement of doctrine —indeed, because he is suspicious of overemphasis on such matters—

James bears witness to the importance of right thinking in early Christian values. On the one hand, he testifies to the existence of believers who locate their salvation especially, and perhaps exclusively, in their right belief, the way of the Christian *philosophos* whose wisdom consists simply in what his understanding has gleaned from the revealing word. James criticizes this position not as wrong but as incomplete: one does well to believe truly (2:19), and one evidently does foolishly to suppose that the word can be taken lightly (1:21) or that Scripture speaks falsely (4:5). That these are not self-sufficient does not make them dispensable; it is only their distorted exaggeration that needs objection. Knowing the right way is useless if, but only if, it is not accompanied by doing (4:17). On the other hand, the structure of James' own thought gives clear indications of an inclination to put a premium on right understanding. God is introduced as the Father of lights, and the operation of his plan of salvation is described in terms that ground it in obedient understanding. He willed to make us a kind of first fruit of his very own creatures, and to effect that adoption, he begot us *by a word of truth* (1:18). From this, James concludes that we should be quick to hear (1:19), and that we should receive in meekness that implanted word which can save our lives (1:21).

This implanted word is a source of revelation, apparently identical with the law of freedom with which it is aligned in the course of the simile of the mirror-gazer (1:23–25). One may reasonably suppose it to be also identical with James's sense of the gospel—that "faith of our Lord Jesus Christ of glory" which we are subsequently admonished to hold pure from respect of persons (2:1). But there is evidently more to it than this, since the perfect law of freedom includes the commandments against murder and adultery, and perhaps all law that is according to Scripture (2:8–12). Thus we are returned, as always in this epistle, to the regulation of the Way. Still, although the begetting Word of truth undoubtedly has strong affinities with the ten commandments (just as the sense of "truth" in the last two verses of the epistle seems much more strongly bent toward conduct than understanding), it most likely has even stronger affinities with the basic kerygmatic invitation. The faith of our Lord Jesus Christ of glory, in the thinking of James, leads us properly and firmly into a fidelity to a perfect law of freedom; the implanted and begetting word is fulfilled in living according to the commandments of Scripture. But they are not identical. The Gospel completes and establishes the true understanding of the Law.

Where is such true understanding to be found? The most important hint is that which falls upon us abruptly at the beginning of chapter 3. "Do not many of you become teachers, brethren," quoth the preacher. Thus far, one might expect that the reason is likely to be that not many teachers are needed; that this enterprise is relatively unnecessary, if not downright misleading; that it might distract from the real business of religious living. Instead, we are promptly told that "we shall receive a more severe judgment." The *we* is not surprising, since it has been clear from the beginning that the author has been teaching, and teaching according to a well-worn scriptural manner. What is slightly surprising is that he characterizes himself in this way—not merely as a fellow Christian reminding us of what we are expected to know already any-way, but as a teacher who is therefore importantly on the spot. His little excursus on the human tongue which immediately follows winds up characteristically in an invective against the evils of the unrestrained mouth, and characteristically settles on cursing rather than lying (or false teaching) as the example of the perverse misuse of speech. But in the meantime, it has touched on some other illustrative comparisons which are probably meant to reinforce his remark about the respon-sibilities of teaching. "We all trip over many things; if any one does not stumble in word, this is a perfect man, able to bridle even the whole body" (3:2). Eventually, the loose chain of thought that follows gets around to remarking that the tongue of man simply cannot be con-trolled; but such cynicism is not in play at the opening of this little discourse. The force of the first two similes, that of the bit in the horse's mouth and the rudder of the ship, are of an opposite bent, stressing not the wildness of the tongue but its capacity, if properly controlled, to tame, order, regulate. It may be that, in the general looseness of con-struction that prevails in the whole passage, the connection with the original subject of teachers has already disappeared. But it seems at least equally probable that these two analogies are reflections of a com-monplace but significant complex of ideas in the mind of the author: the tongue, as the agent of man's reason, stands in a powerful position; as the mind of a man directs and restrains him, so the tongue of the teacher directs and restrains others. For good or ill, the influence of the tongue of an ecclesiastical teacher is great, and warrants a more severe judgment.

Whether these teachers occupy a formal office or are merely those who offer instructional advice spontaneously, we cannot tell; but we know that James numbers himself among them, and we see him at work. He admonishes, warns, encourages; he draws lessons from Scrip-ture, interprets the law, tells us what will and what will not do; he instructs us in matters of worship, healing, and forgiveness of sins. In short: James the Christian teacher, if his example may be taken as typifying the comportment of those whose judgment will be more severe, indicates that the Christian teacher was one who took it upon himself to give instruction in every aspect of Christian life and thought

—one who interpreted the meaning of the way, the truth, and the life. Especially the way and the life, but as founded on, and stabilized by, the truth.

And what are the credentials of the Christian teacher, if it should come to question? Since it does not come explicitly to question, we can only surmise from the general content of James's doctrine. He who still participates in rivalry and strife will speak against the law—*viz.*, the perfect law of freedom, by which we are perfected (4:11); those who murmur against one another will be judged (5:9), and no one may judge another except God (4:12). Evidently, the teacher must propose himself as a totally devoted servant of Christ (1:1), whose harmonious relations with his brethren guarantee his participation in that wisdom that comes from above, the only wisdom fit for teaching. The community, if it bears the marks of holy life, can be self-regulating: the elders of the community heal; the members of the community confess to one another and pray for one another, and are restored; the brethren are admonished to turn back the one who wanders from the true way. The standard of normative Christianity is tested out in the quality of life as lived within the Christian community. If we are not to go astray, we must remember that every good gift is from above (1:17), and will show itself in the fruits of righteousness within the brotherhood. One must be slow to speak (1:19), but when the time comes, the necessary wisdom will be given from above (1:5). The test of that which is spoken is evidently its consonance with the saving Word which has come to life within the Christian community, and the consonance of the speaker as well.

James, like the pastorals, discourages the pursuit of bolder speculations. We are therefore not told how to verify them. The essentials of true understanding, on the other hand, seem to lie ready to hand in the Law, the remembered Gospel, and the Christian life. James seems to expect no disagreement on this, nor any difficulty of access to it. Right understanding rests in the conscience and the consciousness of the faithful *ekklêsia* as it sees itself in the perfect mirror and remembers clearly by enacting its true face. It should not be ambitious after curious speculations, but satisfied with the knowledge that gives life. And that can be discerned through its self-understanding, if it has been faithfully obedient—as in a glass, brightly.

1 Peter

We are begotten again to a living hope through the resurrection of Jesus Christ, this epistle tells us at the outset (1:3). But before the first chapter is over, the author specifies the way in which the resurrection touches us. Returning to the same verb *(anagennaô)*, he says that we have been begotten again through the living and abiding Word of God (1:23), and that this is the Word that has been proclaimed to us (1:25). At the root of Christian life lies not Christ himself, but the doctrine of Christ through which it is made possible for us to believe in him whom we do not yet see (1:8) and to hope in the glory which is yet to be revealed (4:13–14).

One does not sense in 1 Peter any concern about divisions within the Christian body. The sense of their inappropriateness is strong enough, but not the sense of their likelihood. Instead, the epistle considers repeatedly one fundamental division: that between Christians and non-Christians.

One of the ways in which this division is conceived is in terms of knowledge and ignorance. Those who criticize the Christian way and speak in its disfavor are ignorant and thoughtless (2:15); and the addressees are exhorted not to conform themselves to the desires which they formerly had in the days of their ignorance (1:14), having been called out of darkness into light (2:9). But even more characteristic of the thought of 1 Peter is a conception of the same division from a more engaged point of view, emphasizing not merely the differentiating knowledge but the proper response to it. Not possession of truth but obedience to it—*hupakoê tês alêtheias* (1:22), Christians are children of obedience (1:14). Accordingly, the usual way of describing the condition of the unconverted is in terms of their non-obedience. They are unobedient to the word, and thus stumble (2:8; cf. 3:1); they are unobedient to the Gospel of God (4:17), and will thus perish. The begetting Word has the force of law, and all the sanctions thereof.

The two ways are presented as two traditions. On the one hand, the former unbelievers are reminded that they have been redeemed from foolish conduct that was a tradition from their fathers *(patroparadotou)*. But on the other hand stands a tradition far more ancient, beginning with the election of God from before times and codified through the inspiration of the prophets, who not only foretold the grace which the addressees enjoy but even carefully investigated the nature and appointed time of the sufferings and glories of Christ, and thus became aware that they were proleptic ministers of that Gospel which has now been preached through the Holy Spirit (1:10–12). As the elect for whom those saving events, and that begetting report about them, were destined, we are admonished to gird up the loins of our minds (1:13) and to conform ourselves in obedience to the Gospel Word.

Despite the modest meekness with which we are to follow Christian conduct, refraining from reviling those who revile us (3:9), hoping to win others by wordless example (3:1), the author does not advise us to be entirely silent about the Word of truth. For anyone who asks an account of our hope, we are to have an *apologia* ready (3:15). Every Christian an apologist! If we could recover the content of such an apology, we would probably recover with it the lineaments of an early normative pattern of understanding.

The general content is indicated throughout the epistle. God's plan of redemption for the elect, though hidden in his own will from earliest times, was disclosed in the prophets. There, we may find foretold the sufferings of Jesus Christ and his subsequent glorification, and the salvation thus made available to men. This, having now emerged in history, has become the Gospel Word by which salvation is offered and received, as the Gospel is preached through the Holy Spirit and received in obedience. Obedience entails the abandonment of the ways of desire in which the ignorant Gentiles live, unaware of the truth of God and of his will, and entry into a purified and regenerate new life, sanctified in spirit, which waits in confident patience for its future glorious fulfillment. Another sort of *apologia* of example is also enjoined upon Christians (e.g., 2:12, 3:1, 3:16, 4:4), but it is to be backed up by a more explicit one which would point to the outlines of the Gospel and the grounds of its credibility in Scripture, history, and the begetting effect of the Word preached through the Spirit to obedient ears.

Even if every Christian is to be an apologist, there is likely to be a considerable degree of uniformity in their apologies, not only on the ground that individuals could not be expected to concoct one on their own without reference to a common base, but also on the more explicit evidence of the mutuality of the Christian body. We are to be of one mind (3:8). As the *diakonia* of the prophets was freely given to us who come long after, so we are to minister God's gifts among ourselves like good stewards, speaking as oracles of God (4:10–11). Submission to one another is enjoined by the will of God, and especially submission of the younger to the elders (5:5). Indeed, the elders hold a paid office, and are charged to take it with the utmost seriousness, offering their example as patterns to the flock who follow them, just as Christ himself is the great shepherd under whose directive care we are saved (5:2–4; cf. 2:25).

There is one further clue to the foundations of harmonious orthodoxy. Peter identifies himself as a fellow elder. The general pattern of humble submissiveness and charitable attentiveness which he enjoins upon the flock in general in their responses to their elders is very clearly the stance which his letter invites from its addressees. Offering himself as a pattern of patient endurance and hardy faith, freely offering the encouragement of his insight and the wisdom of his direction, he exhorts and testifies as an elder should. He feeds these distant co-elect flocks like a good shepherd, like an imitator of the Arch-Shepherd. As he admonishes his addressees to be like-minded with Christ (4:1), so he himself attempts to manifest the common understanding of the girded-up mind, with that apologetical alertness to the Word of truth and consciousness of faithful obedience to it that characterize the participated mind of Christ.

Jude

The Christian faith is in some danger, the author of Jude warns his addressees. In fact, the ostensible reason for his letter is precisely to exhort them to meet this danger—and not merely by standing firm and faithful, but by contending actively (*epagônizesthai*, 3).

These are formulations which might well be used to encourage constancy itself, especially in time of persecution. But Jude's conception of faith is not Paul's. The faith he advocates is one which was *delivered* to the saints, and delivered once for all (*hapax paradotheisê*, 3). It is a stable foundation on which true Christians may build themselves up (20), while those who do not have it may be likened to various unsettled and unstable things: wandering stars (13), wild waves (13), dry clouds swept along by the wind (12). These latter, however, are not outsiders. They are false insiders—pseudo-Christians, who have crept in secretly (*pareiseduēsan*, 4) and attempt to pervert the true faith from within the fold.

As Jude attends to the tension between the true and the false brethren, we can glimpse his notions concerning the normative in Christian belief. To begin with, it is clear that true faith is original, not something developed. It was given once for all (3), and its false forms are associated with changes and denials of what was original (4), rather than with unreconstructed backwardness. It is rooted in a confident assent to the teachings of the apostles (17–18), and in a knowing assent to the lessons of Scripture (5ff.), both of which are understood to be a sufficiently integral part of formed Christian understanding that Jude needs not to inform his audience but only to remind them of what they have known (5, 17). Deviation from this sturdy foundation can be explained only by lapses: as some of the angels unaccountably deviated from their proper fixed places, as Sodom and Gomorrah went bad, so these false brethren have fallen away, become corrupted, are lost.

The specific charges against them are not entirely clear, being wrapped in metaphor and generalized scriptural allusion. They pollute the flesh (8, 18, 23), which is a source of considerable indignation for the author; but it is not so much their sinfulness as their threat to the faith that concerns him. They not only engage in what appear to him to be inauthentic and unsavory practices, but evidently encourage and teach others to do the same, both by their dangerous example (which is presumably what is meant if *spilades* has the sense of *rocks* rather than *spots* in 12) and by their blasphemous teaching (4, 10–11, 18), which condemns and mocks and dismisses the truth. The meaning of verse 16 is difficult to fix, but I believe that its most compelling sense points to a charge that these internal enemies are being paid to teach their corrupted views—or, to put it more precisely from the point of view of the author, are being rewarded for gainsaying the true doctrine (which is undoubtedly the sense of verse 11's reference to their rushing into Balaam's error for a reward). Some of the people thus affected can still be saved, snatched out of the fire (23), but evidently the main body of the internal opposition is lost forever.

Indeed, Jude's theological view of these false Christians is consistent enough to keep him from acknowledging that they are really Christians at all. The Christians are the saints (3) who keep the faith; these are only "some men who have sneaked in" (4). Far from being evidence of a shakiness within the faith, their very comportment becomes a further evidence of the truth of the received understanding, for these false Christians are anticipated in Scripture (5ff., 14–15), were specifically predicted by the apostles (17–18), and are part of the plan of God, having been earmarked from of old to incur judgment in this way (4). Accordingly, they are what they are not merely because they have forgotten what the others remember, or because they have failed to keep what the others keep, or because they have been corrupted by their uncontrolled desires. These senses are present in Jude's accusations, but the more fundamental theological judgment lies deeper: these poor doomed infidels simply do not know any better. They are merely *psuchikoi*, and do not have the Spirit (19); they are therefore confined to that which they know naturally, as if they were irrational animals (10), and accordingly follow their natural desires (16, 18) and are thus corrupt (10). They are characterized as impious (4, 15) and are apparently insubordinate (8, 12), and are clearly considered blameworthy (though there are those who are merely to be pitied, according to 22). But they are above all deficient. They do not understand the higher things, and that is why they blaspheme against them (10). The God who is able to keep Christians from stumbling (24) has apparently not seen fit to establish these reprobate cases in the enlightened security of spiritual understanding, and has let them slip back into the limits of the merely fleshly mind.

Jude clearly assumes that his addressees share all his convictions about the true basis of the Christian faith. This assumption may be nothing more than a rhetorical strategy: although the enemy is obviously still mixed within the group, it is spoken of in third person only, while the direct address is to the true faithful. Those who have ears to hear will apparently hear, and will know themselves to be among the elect, the beloved of God, the kept-for-Christ, even if they know themselves to be in the company of others who share in their exodus but share defectively and falsely, and who will not survive. That, of course, is essentially what this epistle sets out to teach. If the truly saved were as clear about their difference from their reprobate fellow-travelers as Jude supposes them to be, there would be little point in writing. The problem is precisely that they are not. Jude writes not only as exhorter but as doctrinal umpire, to galvanize congregations to take a stand against those heterodox deviants of whom they are still too tolerant, and under whose influence they are apparently in some danger of falling. The nature of the appeal is such as to suggest that the author could afford to suppose that his addressees would recognize the rightness of his theology—that they would accept the normative principles of original teaching, apostolic authority, scriptural witness, respect for the tradition. He could afford to suppose agreement about norms; what he could not afford to suppose is that his addressees would spontaneously apply these norms with the urgency and rigor which he thought in order.

It would be useful to know what doctrinal positions were being promoted by these enemies within. Alas, most of what they were is buried in hazy polemic. We can be sure of their relatively libertine views, and of their willingness to live in cooperation with their desires; but it would be far more helpful to discover what the author means by denying Christ, setting aside lordship, blaspheming glories. Some commentators have argued that this is only more of the same—that the point of controversy is really only behavioral, and that it is their sinfulness that denies Christ. That this is part of the charge is evident; but it is not the whole of it. I think that the epistle makes far more sense if it is taken quite straightforwardly: there are evidently some among the flock who not only scoff at the moral conservatism of the official leadership and deny the authority of others to establish behavioral restrictions, but who deny that Jesus is Christ the Lord, or at least shrug off this tenet of faith as doubtful or insignificant.

It is commonplace to suppose that the term *doxai* in Jude 8 (as also in 2 Peter 2:10) refers to angels—thus, for instance, Kittel as well as standard commentaries. The fact that the following verse in each instance turns explicitly to the subject of angels seems to lend support to this reading. But there is in fact no plausible ground for this. Jude's subsequent reference is in fact not to angels but to the Michael of (presumably) the Assumption of Moses, and the purpose of the reference is to illustrate restraint on the part of one who might well take it upon himself to curse: the illustration has only marginally to do with what has just been said, linking itself in no evident way to *doxas* in verse 8. The parallel instance in 2 Peter is derivative from Jude, and seems in part to be a misconstruing of Jude's sense. At any rate, the term *doxai* is by no means fixed by the behavior of the following verse in either instance; and if a reading contextually more plausible than "angels" can be found, it would have a better claim.

Such a reading is suggested by the juxtaposition with *kuriotês* as another of the things reviled by the criticized brethren. This too has been arbitrarily associated with angels, but its singularity weighs strongly against the probability of such a reading. The key to the meaning of the verse rather lies in Jude 4 and 2 Peter 2:1—the heretics in question deny the Lord Jesus Christ. Thus it is *his kuriotês* that is denied. The most plausible reading would suggest that *doxai* is also a reference to the dignity of the reigning Lord. That the word was sometimes used in precisely that sense is clearly attested by 1 Peter 1:11, where the sufferings of Christ are paralleled with the subsequent culmination of his career and of the prophecies that foretold it: and that culmination is characterized precisely as *tas doxas.* The word has nothing to do with angels here. The opponents, in Jude and 2 Peter, scoff at the lordship of Christ and those hidden glories in which, the faith of the true believer claims, the once humiliated Jesus now participates.

There is no need to suppose that the scoffers are either visionaries or gnostics. There is no suggestion that they claim a higher understanding than the true Christians. Nor is there any hint that they consider themselves to be especially endowed with the Spirit, for in that case we could surely expect a strategy totally different from verse 19's simple categorizations of them as psychic and non-spiritual. It is more likely that they questioned the existence of the Spirit than that they claimed it preeminently. They are "dreamers" presumably because they are out of touch with the higher spiritual reality, spiritually asleep. What we can fairly infer about them is, I believe, totally consistent with a picture of a sub-group within the Christian body who are confidently responsive to the notion of behavioral emancipation in the Christian faith, but carry it rather further than conservative tradition would have it; and who are presumably satisfactorily theistic, but who have grown vocally impatient with other doctrinal ideas concerning higher powers, probably including the present lordship and glory of Jesus.

If this reconstruction is accurate, it suggests that the Christians to whom Jude is addressed related to the notion of normative understanding in a slightly more complex way than the author himself would prefer. They apparently were able to recognize that there was such a thing as the true faith, with identifiable content, taught in the churches from the beginning. They could be appealed to according to such cate-

gories of discernment without much in the way of supporting or elaborating argument. Yet this faith has apparently not made *all* the difference to them. They accept among them others who do not entirely
affirm it—who even deny aspects of it. For the author of Jude, such men
are discredited and sealed for doom *ipso facto*. For his addressees, they
apparently remain at least accepted fellow-travellers, somewhere in
the spectrum running from imperfectly enlightened brethren to the
Liberal Progressive Party on campaign. Where they are to be distributed on that spectrum, we cannot know. But the most significant
conclusion that can be drawn for our present purposes is that Jude
seems to be confident that he can afford to dismiss and condemn them
on the ground of their non-conformity of understanding, and that he
clearly believes that when the chips are down, his addressees must insist
on the importance of the enlightened knowledge of their own exalted
conservatism, and place communal purity above tolerant hospitality.
Whether too unreconstructed or too carelessly progressive, the non-
traditional are not really authentic members of the group with whom
they might mingle: they are marked, by flaws in comportment and flaws
in understanding, for doom.

2 Peter

There is no book of the New Testament quite so clear about the
existence and the evils of heterodoxy as this epistle. The danger is internal, and is urgent: "there will be false teachers among you who will
introduce, on the sly, heresies of destruction" (2:1). The future tense
here is, of course, retrojective: apostolic Peter is made to testify in
advance concerning the sub-apostolic reality, in which "many" follow
the lead of these false teachers, bringing destruction to themselves and
ill repute on the way of truth (2:2).

It is fairly clear that these false teachers are institutionalized, at least
informally. They are said to be motivated by covetousness, and to exploit the unwary for gain by means of their deceitful words (2:3): obviously, their office is a remunerative one. It is also a successful one, for
they have seduced many. There is therefore small advantage, except
rhetorically, in characterizing them as being slaves of corruption (2:19)
or as speaking turgidities of folly (2:18), or in repeatedly predicting for
them a destruction which, like the parousia itself, loses credit by its
delay (2:1, 2:3, 2:9, 2:12, 3:7, 3:16). The falsity of Balaam was demonstrated by the miraculous restraining act of the reproving beast (2:16).
In the absence of such a sign, how are we to tell the true teachers from
the false, the sound doctrine from that which conduces to destruction,
the real Gospel from its perversion?

The problem is in fact more acute within the thought-horizons of this epistle than in most other cases, since 2 Peter gives an extravagant place of honor and effectiveness to true knowledge: "all things relating to life and piety have been granted to us from his divine power, through the knowledge [*epignôsis*] of the one who called us" (1:3). Again, if we have faith, fortitude, knowledge, self-control, patience, piety, brotherly love, and charity, we shall not fail to be fruitful "in the knowledge [*epignôsis*] of our Lord Jesus Christ" (1:5–8), and our election will be certain, beyond the possibility of falling (1:10). No false teacher identifies his doctrine as such. If an extreme premium is placed on knowledge of things unseen, what can prevent a conflict of claims between the true and the false doctrine impossible to adjudicate this side of the parousia?

In the first place, we may know them by their fruits. Even with the emphasis on true knowledge, 2 Peter is careful to keep track of the way in which that truth must be manifest in comportment. Hand in hand with the destructive heresies will go—that is, presumably, now goes— impurity of action (2:2), whose character and value are suggested by moralizing glances at the sins of angels, the antedeluvian impiety, the licentiousness of Sodom and Gomorrah, and lawlessness in general (2:4–8). It is the familiar libertarian story: they think themselves free and promise their followers freedom (2:19) but they are themselves really slaves of corruption, sinners, luxurious and lawless (2:14, 2:19, 3:17). Not that they share this view of themselves, any more than they acknowledge the falsity of their teaching; but at least there is an initial rule of thumb that might be applied to distinguish those who, with the author of 2 Peter, emphasize self-control, purity, moral law, and aloofness from the pollutions of this world, from those who, with the envisioned enemy within, emphasize freedom, accommodate themselves rather more comfortably to natural urges and desires, urge the triumph of the Way over the Law (especially in appeal to Paul), and are at ease in revelry.

But the fact remains that the moral liberals *can* appeal to the writings of Paul. For their critics to claim that they distort the meaning of difficult passages is hardly to deprive them of the chance to make precisely the same criticism in return. Presumably, they made it; presumably, their having made it is one of the grounds for 2 Peter's claim that they scoff and revile things they do not understand (2:12, 3:3, 3:17). But, of course, that charge too can be reversed. The author of 2 Peter does not appreciate the "freedom" which these others enjoy and encourage, and does not read Paul "and the rest of the writings" (3:16) in the same way. Is there anything to prevent his being repudiated as a reviler and scoffer at things he does not understand, dismissed as "unlearned" (3:16) and "blind" (1:9)?

Probably not. His thundering threats might even be held against him on the grounds provided by his own canons of self-control, patience, brotherly love, peace. But there is another pattern of thought in this epistle that provides another way of getting at the question. 2 Peter, strong on moral conservatism, is conservative also about doctrinal priority, and offers two test cases by which doctrine may be discerned.

One is the cataclysmic parousia, the Day of God. The faithful cling loyally to the expectation of the great judgment, to the fulfillment of the promise of a new heaven and a new earth (3:10–13); the scoffers point out that it has not come, and that the world has been going on for a long time in a fairly stable way. Each can apparently support his views from authoritative texts (presuming that *peri toutôn* in 3:16 refers to the things just discussed in the previous verses), but 2 Peter seems to be making the claim that the opposition bases its stand primarily on sheer doubt, while the author's own doctrine has the backing of prophets, and of the Lord himself through the apostles. There seems to be no attempt on the part of the opposition to deny that the doctrine of the parousia is original, but merely to discredit it by arguing its implausibility. 2 Peter accordingly tries to reinstate it by undermining the arguments concerning implausibility. The weight of authority apparently rests with original doctrine, so long as it has not lost its credit on other grounds.

That style of understanding is a mainstay of the argumentative procedure of 2 Peter. Its very pseudepigraphical character is an obvious attempt to secure the apostolic authority, but it must be noted that there is little attempt to emphasize the special dignity of Peter, or to exploit the stature of the Rock, or even to argue (as the author himself does for Paul) that a special wisdom has been imparted to him. The authority of Peter is largely the authority of the one who was there at the start, the eyewitness who can attest that the glorious Christ of his faith comes not out of clever tales but out of his own history and memory (1:16). The truth can be discerned if we can get back to the earlier evidence.

Hence the emphasis on *remembering* as a key to doctrinal and moral stability. His addressees are knowing, and are established in the present truth: but Peter thinks it good to remind them of what they know (1:12), and to stir up their remembrance as long as he lives (1:13); this second epistle, like the first one, is dedicated to stirring up their sincere minds in remembrance (3:1), asking them to remember the words of the prophets and apostles (3:2). The way of truth is embodied and preserved in the cumulative memory of the Christian body. True and false consequently differ as stability from instability (3:16–17), and the one who is not stable in the knowledge of our lord Jesus Christ, in whom the stabilizing virtues are not present, has received not remembrance but forgetfulness (1:9). What is true is what was true from the beginning. To remember is to be in touch with the truth; to be out of touch is to forget.

At least it is to forget that which makes a difference—the entry into the saving way, the forgiveness of sins (1:9). Being addressed to an audience that knows the Gentile Christian experience, 2 Peter has the possibility of making a strong appeal to the decisive time of conversion as a way of locating the Christian norm, and the author does not pass up the chance. The addressees have fled away from the corruption that is in the world through desire (1:4), and have fled away from those living in error (2:18); and they have done this by the knowledge of the lord and saviour Jesus Christ (2:20). This is represented as the common experience of their Christian world: the Christian knows what it is to escape from the pollutions of the world into the way of righteousness (2:20–21). To fall under the influence of the false teachers, however, is precisely to fall back under the influence of that corruption and pollution from which the convert has just escaped (2:18–20). To the convert, a holy commandment is delivered, a knowledge of the way of righteousness is taught (2:21). Once this has happened, a departure from the new common way can be regarded only as a lapse, a return of the dog to its vomit and of the washed hog to the mire (2:22).

That is to say: the argument of the epistle appeals to the memory of the individual Christian to determine normative Christianity. Into what were you introduced, and with what was your new life known to be inconsistent? Remember both what you accepted and what you repudiated; and if you are offered an invitation to reject what you accepted then, and return to what you then renounced, you should know where you are. Unlike the epistle of Jude, whose infidels are persons who may never really have made it into a full grasp of true Christian understanding, 2 Peter takes the bolder step of acknowledging the Christian experience of the precarious ones, and drawing the line not between those who know and those who do not, but between those who remember and those who are content to forget. Once more, the cumulative Christian experience defines the norm.

This becomes all the clearer when one considers the other test case of doctrine, besides the parousia. It is, I believe, the role of Jesus. For while it is just possible that the reference to the denial of the sovereign lord who bought us (2:1) may be a fancy way of speaking of unfaithfulness to the moral commands of Christ, I think it far more likely that it is to be taken literally. That is, there are those who deny the place of Jesus Christ the lord in the scheme of salvation. It is for this reason that the author characterizes himself as a slave of Jesus Christ (1:1), as does Jude, in opposition to a similar denial; it is for this reason that the author emphasizes the importance of the knowledge of Christ (1:2, 1:3, 1:8, 2:20, 3:18); it is for this reason that he insists that the kingdom is of our lord and saviour Jesus Christ (1:11), and that he himself knows heavenly testimony to the power and presence of our lord Jesus Christ (1:16–18), in addition to prophesies to the same effect (1:19). It is probably for this reason that the doubts concerning the parousia are taken to be so threatening: they are another dimension of the "despising of lordship" (2:10), the denial of the dominion of Jesus Christ. When the author of 2 Peter claims that there will be false teachers who will "even deny the sovereign lord who has bought them," he points, I believe, to a contemporary denial, from within the Christian community, of the lordship of Christ.

Part of the basic remembering of the Christian must therefore be to recall in whose name he was rescued, through knowledge of whom he was brought out of his old corrupt ways into the way of righteousness. 2 Peter obviously knows the answer and assumes that we will know it as well. He obviously knows the process too, and it is a pity that he does not record it more explicitly. The convert has fled the pollutions of the world "in a knowledge of the lord and saviour Jesus Christ" (2:20), and has received a holy commandment which has somehow been "delivered" to him and has disclosed to him the way of righteousness (2:21). In his opposition to the false teachers, the author of this epistle is quietly pointing to the true teachers who delivered that commandment, who showed that way, who introduced the converts truly to the knowledge of Christ. They, like the author himself, presumably guard the true interpretation of scriptures and the true memory of the Christian body —all the way back to Peter's witness on the Mount of the Transfiguration—by which the truth may always be discerned.

Apocalypse

The Revelation of John, despite its length, has left us little that is relevant to this investigation. In its concern to deliver a new communication of a special character, it reports almost nothing about the more ordinary ways of Christian understanding. But before passing on to a general conclusion, there are a few hints worth noticing.

The boldest and most obvious one is that important new revelation may always be forthcoming. What John has been shown is a revelation of things that must happen shortly (1:1, 22:6), a prophecy that makes blessed those who hear and keep it (1:3, 22:7). The words of this new communication are true and faithful (21:5–6), being the Word of God (1:2), and are of such importance that God will punish severely any man who adds to them (22:18) and will close off salvation to anyone who subtracts from them (22:19). The book leaves no doubt that a rightly formed understanding is a significant part of Christian life, or that new developments in it are still possible.

The threats to a stable Christian normative understanding faced within the course of this book are very considerable. The church at Ephesus has had to deal with men who claimed to be apostles and yet turned out to be liars (2:2); the church at Pergamos has presently to deal decisively with teachers of importantly false doctrines, hateful to the Lord (2:14–15), and is called upon to realize this and act; the church at Thyatira harbors within its very bosom a false prophetess whose doctrine is destructive (2:20, 24). Evidently, deep challenges to Christian understanding were being thrust upon the churches. How is one to know a true apostle from a false one, an authentic teacher from a purveyor of pernicious error? And how does one choose between the bold assurance of a prophetess and the bold assurance of a prophet who damns her?

One procedural rule is mentioned to the church at Sardis: "remember therefore how you have received and heard, and keep and repent" (3:3; cf. 2:25). The author seems convinced that the original understanding given these Christian churches was sound and irreformable. Falsity comes with innovation: if the churches keep the words and works they already have, they will be safe from terrible error (2:5, 13, 25–6; 3:3, 10, etc.). Memory and fidelity are important weapons against demonic deceit.

A second principle runs thematically through the addresses to the churches: "He who has an ear, let him hear what the Spirit says to the churches" (2:7, 11, 17, 29; 3:6, 13, 22). Those who are properly disposed, it seems, will be able to recognize the true spiritual authority of this writer, just as Paul claimed that the truly spiritual man would recognize the truth of what Paul wrote.

At least implicitly, correspondence with Scripture (spiritually interpreted) is another way of arriving at the truth. The vision is well seasoned with references to scriptural interpretations by which the events of the present and the immediate future are foreshadowed. The references are oblique and unsystematic, too much so to indicate that this was an important independent method of discovery to the author. Scriptural echoes evidently reinforce spiritual vision, confirming rather than augmenting what is known more directly in the Spirit.

A fourth criterion is more desperate. Terrible punishment will be visited upon those accused of being false, and then all the churches will know (2:23). The book promises a variety of signs that will come to pass, some conditional upon repentance or non-repentance, some unconditional. The full authority of its claims will be clear once these things have come to pass. Although this has the persuasive power of serious threat, it is not a very useful criterion for present discernment.

"The witness of Jesus is the spirit of prophecy" (19:10). The author knows confidently that he is in the Spirit (1:10), and can be excused if he is too confident that other authentic spirits will recognize this. But the Jezebel of Thyatira undoubtedly made the same claim, and it would have been convenient if then John had offered some other criteria for sorting things out. The criterion of the future, the ratification of the prophecies now made, is not presently useful; the criterion of the past, the word and standard already preached at the beginning and still remembered, is more helpful. John obviously does not mean that right understanding is confined to that: his whole revelation is given for the purpose of adding to the sure knowledge of what is to be. But he evidently means that right understanding is disciplined by that foundation, and cannot be sustained apart from fidelity to what was received at the beginning of Christian belonging.

Would that he had gone into greater detail. His failure to do so, however, is in itself potentially significant. He seems to take it for granted that they will know what their foundation was, and that it was the same in all the churches. And as he admonishes the churches one by one, he evidently supposes that they can be recalled to their senses by a stern reminder. With some jarring to action from the outside, they will be able to find the resources to meet even the present dangers, to realize the falsity of false doctrine and repudiate it. All the same, what we find in this book is an enfeebled version of that confidence. The author relies on the power of special prophecy to guide and discipline, much as the pastorals rely, by an analogous though different sense of default, on the steadying character of tradition, institution, office, social decorum.

It is clear that John the Elder believes that there are important norms for Christian understanding; but it is not so clear that he is ready to trust that the more ordinary ways in which those norms are constituted are quite as reliable as they are found to be by other early Christian writers. He seems to share with them the more abstract theological assumption that the ultimate court of appeal is God working through Jesus Christ: the first verse of his book sets that as the rubric that governs the whole. But he is too swept up by the direct prophetic manifestation of Christ's governance to attend to the more homely modes of its expression much more than to acknowledge that the Christ who is the beginning of God's creation (*hê archê tês ktiseôs tou theou*, 3:14) had his image more or less adequately implanted in his churches at the beginning of their Christian life to which image they can perhaps be summoned in time of stress. But that is tentative. What is clear is that his trust is in the power of the Lord as revealer through the Spirit, and that these are times in which a more dramatic showdown is in order. Whatever the calmer ways of discerning, John is not in the mood or the market for them. God speaking through Jesus Christ and the Spirit is the supreme court, and when it is speaking one does not attend to the local magistrates, whoever they may be, on whom the burden of sustaining common law ordinarily devolves.

Concluding Observations on the Other New Testament Evidences

These writings bear witness to two types of radical crisis in early Christian self-understanding. One has to do with the behavior appropriate to a Christian: how does one strike the right balance between the two elements of James' felicitous epithet for this dimension of Christian understanding, "the perfect Law of Freedom" (*nomon teleion ton tês eleutherias*, 1:25)? Or, more specifically, in what ways and to what extent does the perfect law of freedom coincide with the prescriptions and proscriptions of the Jewish Law, especially in those matters that seem to be the especial preoccupation of these writings, viz., issues pertaining to dietary regulations, idolatrous cults, and sexual conduct? The other crisis is concerned with—to use another phrase from James —"the faith of our Lord Jesus Christ of glory" (*tên pistin tou kuriou hêmôn Iêsou Christou tês doxês*, 2:1). What must authentic understanding think about the place of Jesus in the scheme of things, and the kind of glory that can be attributed to him?

These are not new crises. They were there from the beginning. The crucifixion itself was the climax of the crisis aroused by Jesus around precisely these two issues, and the surviving records suggest that the conflict of early Christians with especially the Jewish communities over these same issues continued to be severe. As for internal conflict, there are various hints of substantive disagreement over the Law in early times, as one sense of the meaning of freedom collided with another; and there is no doubt that there must have been points of tension as earliest Christianity covered the distance between the kind of glory implied in the modest Christology of Cleopas, ("Jesus of Nazareth, who was a man, a prophet, powerful in work and word before God and all the people," Lk 24:19) and that greater glory in the ambitious Christology of Thomas ("My Lord and my God," John 20:28).

But this simply brings us back to our essential question. How did earliest Christians suppose such disagreements were to be resolved? When some find the thought of others dangerous, or blasphemous, or wanton, or backward, in the midst of a religious movement that is understood to be touching the very quick of the deepest truth of God for man, how is the discrepancy to be worked out and the normative understanding to be discerned?

This final group of writings suggests a pattern of implicit response to this theoretical issue. They differ from one another in their emphases, just as they differ from one another in the problems they confront and in the character of the communities from which they arise. Nevertheless, there are significant points of consistency both at the theoretical and at the practical levels.

First, they share the conviction that the issue is that of God's saving truth. What they are attempting to understand is what God has designed and partially executed by way of a plan of salvation for men, and they agree that it is necessary to understand this design at least in a basically adequate way.

Secondly, they acknowledge that it is revealed, at least in a shadowed way, in the scriptures. While they differ in practical judgments about what in Scripture is literal, what figurative, what still binding and what now obsolete, they share the general supposition that Scripture somehow describes that truth in whose midst they live.

Thirdly, they agree that it is in Jesus Christ that this salvation has been most dramatically revealed. They differ in emphases about where and how the revelation has occurred. Hebrews is much more insistent that the others on the importance of what Jesus taught; James is less insistent than the others on what Jesus did and suffered; and the Apocalypse goes much farther than the rest in representing the directness of present communication between Jesus and his followers. They do not all provide enough hints to reconstruct the full pattern of assumptions found elsewhere in earliest Christian literature, but they are all consistent with the basic one: Jesus perfected the revelation and institution of salvation by his fulfillment of scriptures, his teaching, his death and resurrection, and his exaltation to power, glory, and lordship—and salvation comes from belonging to the new order that is his.

Fourthly, they appear to share the assumption that the basic truths about this salvation and this new order—what 2 Peter refers to as that "knowledge of the lord and saviour Jesus Christ" by which one escapes the defilements of the world (2:20)—were adequately understood by the first followers of Jesus and faithfully communicated by them to those who followed them. They also seem to presume that the handing-on of these basic truths has been essentially successful up to the contemporary generation of Christians, and therefore that their addressees may take their initial normative point of departure from remembering what they themselves first heard when entering the Christian way, and can confirm it further by inquiring into such historical evidence as may still remain.

Fifthly, they allow that there is more truth to be learned, but they do not place as high a premium on it as on the basic received truths which they already possess, to which all subsequent authentic revelation must conform. They expect growth and maturing in understanding; but they do not anticipate any legitimate dramatic change (albeit, witness the Apocalypse, there may be dramatic interventions that may extend privileged understandings while reaffirming their essential foundation). This increment of further understanding will be fully coherent with what they have already received, will normally arise from those who are most thoroughly and faithfully experienced in Christian life, and should be readily recognizable by those who live in imitation of their fidelity.

This last condition is another point of general agreement: the key sign of authentic understanding is a steadfast life of virtue, peace, and love. One cannot fully trust the thought that arises from persons in whom clear good fruit of action is not found. But those who have long and consistently lived their faith into works worthy of the Lord are those to whom others should hearken in their progress toward maturity of Christian understanding as well as of Christian life.

As the last remark implies, these writings also assume that Christian life, and Christian understanding, are the work of communities rather than only of individuals. They bear witness not only to their authors' conviction that they are able to develop and consolidate their addressees' understanding rightly, but to the confidence that the addressees have the resources to work a similar edification on themselves. And how should they go about it? The assumption that seems to run through these various writings as a common substrate is that if they remember well and accurately together, living in a virtuous Christian mutuality, they will be able to rely on their collective sense of appropriateness to discern what belongs to the truth.

Once more, let me emphasize that I do not suppose that the theory underlying these documents is necessarily the result of careful empirical testing in the early church. There is undoubtedly careless judgment, romantic naïveté, and sheer wishful thinking involved in the ways in which early Christians thought the questions and crises of right understanding to be resolvable. It is not my undertaking to defend the theory's reliability (although I shall presently argue that it deserves to be seriously entertained) nor to allege that it was derived with scrupulous care. I am merely trying to determine what in fact it was. And in its manifestations within these remaining books of the New Testament, as in what I find in the Pauline, Lucan-synoptic, and Johannine writings, I am struck by the degree of consonance in earliest Christian literature as a whole. Whatever the flaws in practice or the inadequacies in supposition, there was a remarkable degree of agreement concerning the ways in which right understanding was thought to be constituted and the ways in which it could most reliably be achieved. There was an identifiable court of appeal.

Conclusion

"What you heard from the beginning, let it abide in you" (1 Jn 2:24). That may fairly be called the first commandment of the law of Christian thought. And in the beginning was—what? Faust was not wrong to falter. It is not indisputably clear. In the beginning, whether we speak of the beginning of one's own salvation or of the Christian dispensation or of creation itself, was the Word; but it may be supposed that the Word is expressive of the Thought that is prior to it, or descriptive of the Deed that gives it substance, or a manifestation of the Power that displays itself in action or in meaning. Faust thought that as he turned from one ultimate to another his shifts were guided by the Spirit. He was in each instance the heir of earliest Christianity, which also glimpsed a variety of answers as it peered through its new life into the hidden place where the light first broke upon the darkness that lay upon the face of the deep.

Johannine literature manifests one of the most explicit early Christian examples of a general sensitivity to the realization that the new dispensation must be seen as a function of the original creative intent, the recent fulfilled deeds an inheritance from the Beginning. There we see the original Word, the original Thought and Power and Deed, breaking as it must have done originally and always into the darkness that did not and cannot master it, bringing light and life. It does so not because it is a better second try, giving form once again to a chaos into which the world has lapsed from the insufficiency of an original botched job, but because it is the completion of the original creation, the last stage of fulfillment of the process that was from the beginning dominated by the Word, the Thought, the Power, and the Deed of God. The protological thrust of the Johannine literature is its awareness of what God's seemingly new Word, Thought, Deed, and expression of Power must necessarily mean and be at a deeper level of understanding.

The Johannine literature is the most explicit, but it is not alone. All of early Christian literature is written under the assumption that it witnesses to its own participation in the fulfillment of original creation.

184

Earliest Christian thought is radically protological, because it stands in the process by which the dominion of God, never broken from the beginning even if left incomplete, is to be definitively realized. It is also radically eschatological, because it stands within a project not yet completed, and attends more frequently and urgently to this dimension of its orientation, but it is nevertheless as firmly conditioned by its ultimate past as by its future. If the eschatological side is where Christian thought senses its critical timeliness and ultimacy most keenly, the protological side is where it habitually senses the ground of its validity and the certainty of its promise.

The Christian *archê* is twofold. On the one hand, and in its more naïve and unreflected form, it has to do with the more recent events fulfilled among us: the Word that came to John in the wilderness was one way of fixing the beginning, or the deed executed by Jesus, or the thought communicated in the post-resurrection instruction, or the power from on high that initiated the Christian missionary movement. These are complementary and mutually confirming and appear together as the foundational complex in the main early writing. The assumption that authentic Christian understanding is conditioned by what was, in this sense, *ap' archês* seems to have been universal in earliest Christendom.

But pointing to history for the *archê* involves two phases of ambiguity. One has to do with the relation of history to the antecedent divine will. Even if given an historical beginning within living memory, the Gospel is the plan of salvation intended by God from before the ages, enacted only at the ripe moment in time. The fulfilled deeds are essentially the concrete revelation and actualization of the ultimate beginning, the completion of the original creative intention. The distinction is not trivial in its epistemological consequences. Historically, conditioning *ap' archês* means one thing; trans-historically, it means quite another. Of course, the intersection of the two senses was presumed to be as perfect as their different domains permit. History, under divine orchestration, has made manifest the plan laid from eternity, and therefore the historical *ap' archês* is the replication, in another medium, of the super-historical one. But the latter is the ultimate *archê* in the deepest sense. The historical version is *our* original mode of access, and is sufficient. But the norm is more deeply embedded in the true heavenly original which history translates.

And here arises a second phase of ambiguity. History is the medium of disclosure, but it is not quite the message. The message is, in fact, concealed in it as well as revealed. Earliest Christian understanding was convinced that the *archê* definitive of God's invitation to human possibility had been made intelligible and active through Jesus, but does not show a univocity about just where and how it was to be discerned. In his teaching? In his cross? In his exaltation? Earliest witnesses are not entirely agreed in their choices or their emphases. The *archê* has entered human history and has been expressed through Jesus—but how do we trace out what truly belongs to its historical manifestation, and discriminate this from the ordinary history in which it is embedded? and when its lineaments are known, how is it to be understood?

The definitive locus of understanding is in the proper place of the *archê:* the mind of God. It is his mystery, his saving plan, his inscrutable and unpredictable wisdom. Its manifestation in Jesus meant that early Christian thought was obliged to attend to Christology as a more central theological enterprise than it had normally been, and to find either that Jesus had proclaimed the mind of God in a privileged way (essentially as the prophets had done: thus the attempts to record and interpret his public teachings) or that he had enacted it (as the prophets had occasionally done, as Israel had done: thus the attempts to record and interpret the resurrection, the troublesome scandal of the cross, the circumstances surrounding his birth). In either case, or beyond both, it was axiomatic that Christ is the primary locus of the earthly expression of God's mind, the vehicle for the intelligible historical disclosure and enactment of the saving *archê* as formed in the mind of God. This axiom leads readily, if not inevitably, to conceptualizing the canon of true understanding as the mind of Christ.

That formulation better represents the conceptual center of gravity in earliest Christian theology, probably because it brought the matter closer to home. Participation was very much of the essence. Christian thought reached to more dramatic categories only after realizing that it already belonged to them. It was protological, as it was eschatological, as a logical reflex of self-understanding in the pursuit of its own fullness. Its self-reflection led to these two bounding limits inevitably. But the first responsibility of earliest Christian thinkers was not to discern either the *archê* or the *eschaton,* but to grasp the character of that which had been begotten between these and born among them through the intervention of Christ: the Christian *kairos,* the ripe season of salvation in which all men are called to share, but to which the Christian already deeply belonged. The basic style of early Christian understanding is the search for the character of this season of salvation. Such a preoccupation asks its questions out of practical concerns, and is particularly eager to know where and how we are called to live. But where and how lead inevitably to the conditioning whence and whither, and the fact that we must live under the power and the will of the conditioning Lord raises to practical moment another pattern of speculative questions. Rethinking and reformulating the world in the image and likeness of Christ was perhaps more a matter of grateful celebration than of speculative research, but the two were complementary. The basic joy at being incorporated into God's capstone work of salvation leads to seeing it writ large throughout the universe. The basic concern to belong well to the *kairos* of salvation begets a concern to understand its shape and nature. The basic style of early Christian thought is accordingly kairology, the attempt to understand the historically concretized season in which the eternal mystery of salvation is finally revealed and offered.

The primary answer to the question of *where* to find our place in the *kairos* is: in Christ. That the true *kairos* is radically manifested in and conditioned by Christ, who has entered and shaped human time through Jesus, is the axiom that makes itself everywhere apparent in earliest Christian literature. The attempt to discern the conditioning *archê* without reference to Jesus is the theological temptation against which the movement took its main self-definitional stand. The *kairos* is Christ's, *belongs* to him. It can neither be perceived nor participated in except by reference to Jesus. One must not only know about him: one must belong to him.

To live in reality is to live in Christ; not to live in Christ is to be bound over to illusion and doom. In its weakest and most primitive form, this sharing in the true *kairos* may be thought to be secured by being sealed in the name of Christ: thus the Corinthian practice of registering in Christ those who can no longer accept him for themselves. But with the exception of baptism for the dead, the weakest form of entry into Christ is nowhere attested. One must *live* in Christ: only the dead can be exempted. And that implies that wherever human understanding is alive, it must conform itself to the basic shape of the *kairos* before it can be sealed into belonging; and this means at the minimum the acknowledgement—not with the lips only, but with the heart as well—that Jesus is the One: Christ, the Lord.

This at the minimum. In some cases, it may have sufficed as a legitimation of one's entry into the season of salvation. But there was more to be understood; and even if this more was not necessarily exacted from everyone who belonged, or made a condition of belonging, it was the truth. Those who wished to belong thoroughly were automatically invited to become mature in understanding; and maturity is seeing as God sees, knowing as God knows. Although this must wait until we are made perfect in his kingdom, it can be approximated now. Indeed, it must be approximated now: for the *kairos* of salvation is shaped by God's design and requires us to live as he has willed us to live, and we must learn what belongs to the way of life. Neither is he indifferent to what we hold to be true. We must discern what belongs to the truth— or, more simply, what belongs to Christ: for the season of salvation consists in what belongs to Jesus Christ. God has offered us in Christ the *kairos* for which we were created. It is our task to accept it, to perceive what it is and what it means, and to live in conformity with it until we are gathered definitively into his kingdom. In the meantime, we are under trial as well as under grace. God will watch and wait, to see whether we follow faithfully along the paths that he has sketched for our behavior and our thought, obedient to the life-giving Word which he has invested in us like seed to grow and flourish.

The *kairos* belongs to Christ, but does so because it has been given to him by the Father. It is a function of his will and work that "Christ" has meaning at all, and therefore the very conception of a Christ-defined *kairos* takes us inevitably to its beginning and end, to the *archê* of the creative plan and the *eschaton* of its completion, both of which belong to the Father. Paul is careful to insist to the Corinthians that the *eschaton* is ultimately specifically the Father's rather than specifically Christ's. Christ is where we encounter all this, but he is not in fact the only way in which the *archê* is expressed. Thus while early Christian kairology assumes that Christ is the source of the fundamental conditioning of this moment and of this season in which it stands, it did not assume that this is the only way in which these are conditioned or the only source of kairological understanding.

Kairology was not, after all, a Christian invention. The followers of Jesus inherited the kairological framework of the Expectation, further specified by the teaching of John the Baptist. With this, they also inherited the dialectical principle for discernment of kairology that is implicit in the structure of the *kairos*. As the season of salvation is the special providential form by which the benevolent original creation is to be perfectly completed, so its comprehension is a function not only of understanding and submitting to the News by which its character is particularized, but also of understanding and submitting to the *archê* that is not News—the long-standing revelation of the nature and will of God who made man in his image and invites him in the act of creation itself to know and live accordingly. Like the Prophets in whose tradition he stood, John the Baptist summoned his hearers to repentance and obedience. Obedience to what? Not to an alien arbitrariness, but to the law of righteousness that is imprinted on creation itself: bring forth good fruits. As a defining *verbum sapienti* it was enough to add another phrase attributed to the Baptist: fruits worthy of repentance. If one turns to God altogether, the rest will be added. If you love the Lord your God with all your heart and soul and strength and mind, it will follow that you will obey him. Obeying him is imitating him. It is by imitating him that one comes more fully to know him and oneself as his image, as a son of God. In this knowledge appear the implications that define the creational *kairos* in general, including the commandment, experienced as an analogue to the first, to love one's neighbor as oneself.

There is therefore a connaturality between human understanding and the discernment of the *kairos* as generally founded in creation, although the growth of this discernment is given through deepening obedience rather than instinctively or all at once. The special character of the particular *kairos* by which the intention of creation is finally fulfilled is not readily discernible by direct appeal to the *archê* by which we are constituted. It requires special disclosure. But just as it is the completion of creation rather than a counterstatement, so the recognition of authentic News of its character is a function of our disposition of obedience within the more general frame. Those who know God and are not yet too hardened to be vulnerable to his touch will recognize and respond to his summons to know and conform to the truth that shapes the season of salvation.

Early Christian writings vary in their sense of the means by which men will readily perceive the truth of the basic Christian Gospel but seem to be agreed both that it can be presented intelligibly to human minds, and that those who are properly disposed—that is, not too distracted by worldly lusts or too inhospitable to the possibility of genuine News—will quickly find ears to hear obediently. Obediently and with the conviction of truth: for although the modality by which confidence is achieved may vary from the general sense of plausibility which Luke appeals to in Theophilos to the illumined insight visited upon the obedient Pauline convert, it is universally supposed that Christian kairology has the resources to resolve all substantive doubts. There are indeed higher and more stable ways to certitude than through appeal to the evidences of historical event or of exegesis; but if one requires these, they can be produced. The unfolding of the *kairos* brought a surprise, but the surprise was brought by way of recognizable evidence, and its lineaments may be discerned there as well as in the joy of the obedient heart receiving the Word.

The special form of the *kairos*, that is, has been made known within the fabric of the general *kairos* of creation; and although not deducible from it, it is nevertheless fully coherent with that general frame. This is, I believe, the basic assumption governing the development of early Christian kairology. This assumption leads to the conclusion, most consistently prosecuted by Luke, that the authentic Christian understanding is conditioned by what has appeared historically and may properly be disciplined by the accurate reconstruction of the founding "fulfilled deeds." But this historical given is not the only source for this authentic conditioning. It is itself the working-out of the *archê* of God's plan, and earliest Christianity had two other means of access to this *archê*. On the one hand, God had expressed his purpose through the scriptures, and the conviction of the unity of the salvific *kairos* with the general creative intention and self-communication of God led naturally to the assumption that the former was blueprinted, however obscurely, in the documents that were expressive of the latter, in a sort of genetic code governing creation's last maturing growth-spurt. The explication of Scripture could accordingly stand either as a means of confirming the explication of history, or as a means of bypassing it conveniently. On the other hand, God's characteristic mode of self-communication in the scriptures and in history, the divine Spirit, was directly available to the Christian understanding. To be in Christ was to be in the Spirit—and thus in immediate touch with the *archê*. This experience too, because of its isomorphic congruence with the *arche*'s expression in either history or Scripture, could stand as a means of confirming either, or as a short-circuit that independently delivers the conditioning content of both. Thus arises a curious situation for early Christian reflection on the character of its kairology: while fully aware that its specific difference is a function of the historical Jesus and could be determined from a scrutiny of his career, it was also aware that it was not necessarily handicapped if there were no ready access to the details of that career, since the same interpretative norms are also available through other, and generally more conveniently accessible, manifestations.

Not that any early Christian group ever bypassed history altogether. The Gospel seems always to have rested on the grounding historical essentials, or at least what were at last taken to be the essentials. Divined and preached abroad by those who were in possession of the main details of Jesus' career, these became the core from which the particularizing side of the kairological dialectic proceeded. Both the original perception and the initial reception of this Gospel, however, took place within the context not only of the general kairology of creation but also of the more particular eschatological kairology already developed in Jewish understanding, especially that version that had been promoted in the preaching of John the Baptist. The identification of Jesus as the Christ is the most obvious example: the kairological category "Christ" was already given, and needed only to be matched with its historical fulfillment. It is plausible that the other elements of early kerygma were arrived at through a similar process of filling in prior kairological categories with historical particulars: the expected agent of judgment is identified with Jesus, the promised forgiveness of sins is correlated with his name, the season of salvation is taken to be roughly coextensive with the generation to which he preached. The logic of coherence could also be pursued in a more abstract way. A more protological reflection on the principle of coherence between the general *kairos* of creation and the special foundational conditioning in Jesus led naturally to aligning

Jesus with the *archê*, either mildly, in the form of God's having willed his work before the ages, or ambitiously, in the form of pre-existence, agency in creation itself, divinity. New events could also be accommodated by assimilation to the developed scheme: the reception of the Spirit could be taken to be at once the later baptism promised by John and the gift of the exalted Jesus from the Father. The death of Jesus, according to the principle of kairological coherence, needed to be fit in too. A variety of accommodations survive: God's allowance; the pattern of the fate of the prophets; the acting out of radical obedience; expiation by which forgiveness of sins becomes possible; the prelude to the most perfect enactment of the old theme of humiliation and exaltation. The governing procedure in early Christian kairology seems to have been to discern how the events of Jesus' career and subsequently of his followers cohere with and develop further what we already know about the will and plans of God, and about the organization of the world. And should one begin within a Hellenistic world rather than that of the Baptist, one may generate a new complementary set of insights for which kairology may be the richer, not the more confused.

The specifically Christian kairology was undoubtedly developed by such a process of assimilation of the events and understandings surrounding Jesus to the previous state of kairological understanding. On what authority were the particular forms of assimilation made? Mainly, it seems, on the authority of the axiomatic principle that Jesus is The One. Whatever helped substantiate this or enlarge its scope or concretize its implications had a claim on the Christian sense of appropriateness and could become a legitimate candidate for normative understanding. Armed with the assumption that the *kairos* is defined in Jesus Christ, early Christian thought could assimilate to him the general structure of its kairological inheritance, and appeal beyond it to further discoveries and authentications latent in its memories of Jesus or in its exegetical ingenuity.

The active presence of the Spirit offered another axis of discovery and authentication. The book of Revelation bears witness to the confidence with which this access to normative understanding could be used independently of the others (although even there the Spirit obviously relies on a great range of established norms, and works as much by reaffirmation as by peremptory authority), but what is striking in surviving early Christian literature is that despite the presence of manifold celebrations of the Spirit, there is a general absence of proffered materials based on the Spirit alone. It seems that what was discovered in the Spirit, even though it may have been accepted simply as such, was nevertheless characteristically appealed for authentication to the less volatile and more public fields of reference.

Such an appeal, however, has a double cutting-edge. If the offerings of Spirit may have been tried and interpreted by the court of Scripture or of history, there is also evidence that what earliest Christianity experienced as disclosure through the Spirit might be used as a normative point of reference by which Scripture or the teachings of Jesus should be tested and interpreted—sometimes with resulting effects on the wording of texts as well as the interpretation of meanings. And history? A similar case, I think. Similar interpretative latitudes are plainly attested, and the text was less clearly defined. The scope for inventiveness was accordingly greater than that presented by Scripture, and was undoubtedly exploited. I can see no way of accounting for various of the discrepancies in the Gospels that is as economical and plausible as the hypothesis that early Christian thought, confident in the coherence of God's plans and ways of revealing them, sometimes guessed at history to fill gaps where history was not known or was presumed misunderstood because uncongenial to received kairology. The synoptic tradition, for instance, rests within a prior kairology that derives the Messiah from Bethlehem. It identifies that Messiah as Jesus of Nazazeth. Either Luke's account of how the Nazarenes happened to be in Bethlehem or Matthew's account of how the Bethlehemites happened to move to Nazareth—or both—is evidently a fabrication of history in the image of assumptions drawn from elsewhere. I do not impute fraud; I rather presume that the inventiveness is essentially that of the good historian —the formulation, within the disciplining boundaries of the known, of a plausible hypothesis which makes illuminating and economical sense of it. The more satisfying such a hypothesis is, the more readily it becomes custom. The more investment there is in its particular satisfactions—or the more inconvenient it becomes to do without it—the more readily it turns to law.

The constituting principles for Christian kairology are thus various, mutually confirming, and (with the single exception of direct revelation through the Spirit, which is rarely appealed to without coordinate confirmation) subject to the discipline of public evidence—but they retain a certain protean quality all the same. They are capable of giving authority, but—in a way that was probably not realized by the casual and confident kairologists of early days—not so ready to yield a stable and confirmed form. Form was achieved always with reference to them, but had its primary locus elsewhere: theoretically, in the mind of Christ echoing the mind of God; practically and functionally, in the sense of coherence and appropriateness in the early Christian community as it contemplated Jesus as The One and itself in him.

Jesus as The One is the fundamental conditioning determinant of kairology, and is the common denominator of early Christian literature, as well as the essence of early Christian kerygma. But how was the kerygma itself derived? The indications are, I believe, that it was derived in the same manner as the rest of Christian kairology: by the application of the early disciples' sense of coherence and appropriateness to the conviction that Jesus is The One, within the framework of their recognitions and recollections on the one hand and the resources of pre-Christian kairology on the other. The key facts and interpretations thus discerned became the core of the Gospel and the foundation of subsequent kairological reflection, and accordingly occupy in the formation of Christian understanding a special canonical status as the *kerugmata.*

I use the plural advisedly. The *a priori* probability of varying selections and interpretations among the earliest apostles and of a gradual development and shift in the understanding from which they proclaimed the Good News is suggested by the differences between early Christian texts, and particularly substantiated in Acts. Luke, who holds no brief for an evolutionary view of the essential apostolic kerygma and has no wish to expose disunity among the earliest ministers of the Word, gives us a developmental variety of preachments by Peter and a notably different set of suppositions in the kerygma of Stephen. Surely that is the way it really was. If Paul can say that all the apostles preach the same Gospel, and if we believe—as I think the evidence suggests we should—that this is essentially true, then we must discipline our sense of history accordingly. What was held in common was of far greater moment than the differences. The differences were felt, and they sometimes smarted; but they were not supposed divisive, given their convergence on the same Gospel. In the mutuality of the early Christian community, remembering and reflecting upon what it has experienced, a common norm had been discerned.

This norm, subsequently announced in various times and various places, became then the starting point for Christian kairology. Paul's ability to shift imperceptibly between the founding events and the Gospel that reports them, essentially equating the historical realization and the Word, seems to be typical of early Christian thought. Theoretically, one might attribute an absolute and permanent priority to the historical facts and subordinate the Word to them, thus putting a premium on Luke's eyewitness as the ultimate court of appeal. And so Luke does, theoretically. But the theory he inherited and re-expressed relativizes its own historical norm by insisting upon its replication in another order—or rather, other orders: for although Luke himself witnesses mainly to Scripture as the normative point of reference outside history, he shows a firm awareness that the Word itself could manifest self-confirming power, and says enough about the role of the Spirit to permit us to see the continuity of his views with those of the Pauline

and Johannine literature. And in the fifteenth chapter of Acts, he registers a formulation that probably represents the most influential conception of the Spirit for the development of early Christian thought. Far
less spectacular than some of its manifestations, the modality of this
special communication with the *archê* that appears in the simple formula "it seemed good to the Holy Spirit and to us" touches the heart
of that process by which the truth it knew was enlarged and developed.
What seems good to the Holy Spirit is good enough for Christianity. It
appears that in Luke's view, and in the view of early Christian literature
generally, what seems good to the Holy Spirit is that which seems good
to the obedient and loving Christian community as it remembers what
it has heard from the beginning and attempts to discern in God's several
ways of revealing—including their own transformed lives—the appropriate physiognomy of the Christ-formed *kairos*.

Which of the interpretations of Jesus may be called authentically
Christian? If the search for theological validity pines after the lost data
concerning the historical Jesus, it is not without warrant from the earliest Christian sense of the constitution governing its own understanding.
But it will receive no pity from that quarter. However firmly and consistently earliest Christianity maintained that it was founded and conditioned by the historical Jesus, it manifests an equally firm and consistent
conviction that it carried in its own bosom the essential equipment for
the adequate discernment of both Jesus and the *kairos* he founded, in
the image of which Christianity itself took its form.

One of the clearest indications of what this means—instructive, I
think, for the quest for theological validity—is the phenomenon of the
early Christian *didaskalos*. Although Paul ranks this title just after apostles and prophets, and although it is one of the most frequent titles of
Jesus in the Gospels, its place in early Christendom has been little
studied. The reason is in part that the evidences are sparse. Not the
evidences for their existence, for they are attested in Thessalonica (1
Thess 5:12), Galatia (Gal 6:6), Corinth (1 Cor 12:28–29), Rome (Rom
12:7), and Antioch (Acts 13:1), mentioned in Ephesians (4:11), alluded
to in Hebrews (5:12), and discussed intermittently in the pastorals and
the Didaché. The default of evidence lies rather in our ability to define
the character of the office and the qualifications by which one entered
it. But within the framework of this study, I think that the very paucity
of evidence is itself significant. Not all are teachers, Paul reminds the
Corinthians (1 Cor 12:28–29), but to the Romans he adds that some are
given the grace of teaching and should use it for teaching (Rom 12:7;
cf. Eph 4:11). A fitness for teaching is among the qualifications for high
churchly office in the pastorals (1 Tim 3:2, Titus 1:9), although the
teaching duties were evidently distributed to elders (1 Tim 5:17) and

women (Ts 2:3) as well as bishops. It is a serious office: not only does it rate high on Paul's list, but according to the Epistle of James it entails a more severe judgment, and one should therefore not be too hasty about taking it on (Jas 3:1). Evidently, one who felt called to the office might offer oneself as a teacher. But it also appears that the office was subject to some form of discernment of fitness. The pastorals' norm of *didaktikos* as a qualification for positions of leadership, with its implication of the possibility of discerning such a quality, is echoed not only in the general Pauline principles of communal self-regulation but more vividly in the Didaché's instruction that the community should choose for itself men worthy of the Lord to minister to them the ministry of prophets and teachers (15:1). But what are the criteria to be applied to those who seek after, or are needed for, the office of teacher?

The Didaché is representative of the general drift of early Christian thought in its succinct principles for the evaluation of a teacher. "Whoever then should come and teach you all the aforementioned things, receive him; if the teacher be twisted and teach another teaching that leads to destruction, do not accept him; but if it leads to the increase of righteousness and knowledge of the Lord, receive him as the Lord" (11:1–2). That, I suspect, is the best and clearest formulation surviving for the essential governance of early Christian normative understanding, especially when taken in conjunction with another representative admonition of the Didaché: "every prophet teaching the truth, if he does not do what he teaches, is a false prophet" (11:10). By their fruits, you know that the Spirit is truly at work. If someone teaches something that leads to righteousness and knowledge of the Lord, and is himself coherent with it, he is to be received as the Lord. Naïvely but representatively, the Didaché supposes that we can recognize righteousness when we see it coming. Even more naïvely—but I think, also representatively—it assumes that we can recognize increased knowledge of the Lord when we see it. In effect, it defines knowledge of the Lord simply in accordance with that which we can recognize communally as being consonant with what we can recognize as righteousness. Or, more simply, the authentic teacher is the one with a talent for edifying; the authentic teaching is that which edifies a community already in Christ.

That appears to be typical of the earliest Christian criteria for discerning the norms of its own thought. Anything that builds on what we have received, tends to promote what we recognize as righteousness, and extends our understanding in ways that seem satisfyingly appropriate, is the real thing. No appeal to eyewitness, trained scholarship, historical documentation. No need to appeal. The presumption is that those who live faithfully within the Christian *kairos* as they have already understood it are in a position to generate and discern together further advances in kairology, through their Spirit-touched imaginations disciplined by their mere sense of coherence and appropriateness as grounded in righteousness and the Gospel. Kairology is, in the long run, a form of knowledge of the Lord, and vice versa. The Lord is known by his people, first according to the faithfulness and loving righteousness by which they are bound to him and to each other, and then according to their shared sense of what is right and appropriate, what is coherent with what they have come to know and satisfying to their capacity for pious understanding. This communal sense, historical reconstruction suggests, was the ultimate court of appeal in the constitutional law of early Christian thought. It was understood to be operative only when firmly founded on a faithful adherence to the basic outlines of God's saving plan and when exercised in a spirit of loving unity and in a context of righteous comportment; but within these conditions, it was ultimate, literally—the way in which human thought rose to its most perfect conformity with the understanding of God himself.

It is clear that a measure of such conformity was thought indispensable to avoid perdition, though it is not consistently clear where the boundary is to be placed between the essential and the optional. Was the establishment of the boundary in itself a matter to be finally determined by the communal court of appeal?

It would seem so. For early Christian thought seems to have been powerfully conditioned by Christianity's conviction that it was actively in touch with—indeed, that it was engaged in enacting—the season of salvation, the *kairos* of God's deepest purposes. So strong and basic was this supposition that it affected the address of Christian thought to the external norms whose authority it acknowledged—Scripture, history, traditional teaching. Throughout earliest Christian literature, one finds that the authoritative interpretation of these is in constant tension with proffered authoritative reinterpretation, and that careful memory competes with creative reconstruction. Given the underlying constitutional theory, it might well have been supposed that these various ways of finding the truth would finally lead to the same result, and that the process would all sort out satisfactorily and harmoniously in the end. But that does not appear to have been the consistent result. The disorder contemplated by the pastoral epistles is a natural consequence of just such a constitutional theory carelessly applied, with too much confidence in the self-sufficiency of present discernment apart from the discipline of accurate recollection, with too high a value placed on new discovery at the expense of lived unity. The pastorals try to combat this unfortunate development in a more artificial and less organic manner than Paul believed he could use with the Corinthians, who seem to have entertained such compromises in the application of their ways to right understanding. But that appears to be simply because the more organic procedure will no longer meet the situation. Things have gone too far toward falling apart. The habit of cumulative unity has been allowed to fade. There has been too little fidelity to the constitution governing Christian thought for its implicit procedures to be still readily implementable.

Had that constitution been more faithfully followed, would it have made a significant difference in the history of Christian theology? That, of course, is precisely what the quest for theological validation would now like to know. The search for the forms of understanding that are most authentically Christian should, if Christian thought is to be faithful to what it was from the beginning, be the search for the forms that emerge within the faithful application of the constitution in which Christian thought was understood to be grounded. The historical Jesus is one important constituting factor, but by no means the only one, or even the norm within the norm. There is no evading the problem or the responsibility: the ultimate practical canon is to be found within the living and cumulative consciousness of the Christian community, not outside it. Christianity took its principal self-definitional stand in its refusal to surrender the axiomatic principle that Jesus is The One through whom God's deepest truth for men is revealed, but it retained in doing so the awareness that this truth is not yet fully revealed.

The progressive character of revelation was deeply embedded in Christian history and in Christian literature. Uniformly, it is recognized that those closest to Jesus did not understand at the time of the crucifixion. Generally, it is implied that even after the resurrection, the true understanding of what had been done and revealed did not come immediately and unequivocally to hand but had to wait for something further. Some are still doubting four verses before the end of Matthew's Gospel; Luke's apostles are to wait not only for an endowment of Spirit but for further confrontation with historical experience; John's Gospel ends with the supreme moment not yet come, the disciples assured that their understanding lay still in the future and with clear hints in the final chapter that a generally accepted meaning for a saying about the Beloved Disciple was finally proved wrong by history and had to be provided with a new interpretation; Paul assures his ambitious converts that despite their arrogant confidence, they are babes in understanding with vast reaches of revelation still to come. Early Christian experience consistently suggested that results are better taken as provisional. Surprises come: what seemed sure may break down, what seemed settled may open up again, what seemed finished may turn out to be incomplete, what seemed highly unlikely may become quite convincing. Only when tested by the eschatological fire could the sturdy contributions be known from the straw definitively, and the system be known to be closed and finished. In the meantime, to the extent that God's truth is known, it is known through the communal understanding of those who live, obedient in the unity of love, in conformity with the *kairos* that is Christ's. It is there that both the progressive and the conservative forces must come to discern together what belongs to the mind of Christ.

The burden of persuasion clearly lay with the progressives. Experience showed that conservative tendencies made men slow to grasp the truth, but the theory claimed that important truths would make themselves felt eventually with those who had eyes to see and ears to hear and hearts truly obedient to the Lord. There were bound to be some awkward times in sorting out what kinds of behavior were legitimately consistent with the newly revealed righteousness in Christ, and in deciding what were the conditions of Christian belonging, and in sifting through various enthusiastic guesses about the nature and office of Jesus, especially when it was important to be faithful to the Word one had heard from the beginning. Those understandings which had been communally received and experienced as foundational had the right of way; competing ones were to be on trial until they established themselves in the life of the community. The progressive movement of Christian understanding was thus checked and braked, but not necessarily limited in scope. Even the Word presented at the beginning of one's Christian belonging could turn out to be subject to radical revision by virtue of an illumination from a more ultimate beginning; but such revision was known to be legitimated only when its appropriateness became experienced within the loving obedience of the whole body of Christian mutuality.

That, at any rate, was the theory. Earliest Christianity was not altogether successful in practicing it. Both progressives and conservatives were too impatient to wait until they could bring to gradual internal resolution disagreements that threatened them and strained their mutual respect. The historical foundation suffered from carelessness about history. The place of Scripture was weakened by inventive interpretations of doubtful responsibility. The traditional teachings were tampered with to improve their contribution by making them more explicit. The public evidence on which the constitution of right understanding was initially founded became blurred and uncertain through a carelessness about it that may have been rooted in a confidence in more direct divine guidance but did its constitutional damage all the same. By the end of the New Testament period, it was no longer easy to become assured of the certainty of the foundational "fulfilled deeds" through the examination of the public record, which had come to incorporate too many inconsistencies. That left Christianity all the more dependent on what it had cumulatively become, and on the internal communal conditions by which the truth is to be discerned from all else.

That is perhaps where the matter remains; and if so, there is a great deal to be done before the modern version of the problem of normative Christian understanding can be authentically resolved. By way of theological epilogue, I would like particularly to underscore three considerations which the study of earliest Christianity offers to the modern search for theological validity or norms of Christian thought.

One is that the truth can be discerned only with reference to its being piously lived. Paul contrasts the straw of faulty building not with brick but with gold, silver, precious stones. The edifice into which Christians are built is not a library or a museum but a temple. By earliest Christian standards, the more removed a speculation is from virtue, good works, the fruits worthy of righteousness, the less certain it is that its value may be readily discerned. Substance in understanding makes itself felt in edification, and edification is measured by love. What is, by this canon, insubstantial is perhaps impossible to validate in this world, and may be a dangerously distracting plaything.

The pastorals are the source of one of the New Testament's strongest promotions of that view, and also teach the second lesson. Despite the economy of the Spirit's operation within a given church, it is possible for a whole community to lose its head. Even if the Corinthians and the Galatians had immediate and independent access to all they needed to put things straight, they evidently needed to have Paul jar them into remembering this rightly and doing it accordingly. The self-regulation of Christian understanding really turns out to work only on the scale of the whole of Christendom. At the end of the first century, the whole Corinthian community is in trouble again; this time, it is the whole Roman community as such—not Clement, but the assembly at Rome—that writes to remind them of who they are and where they have come from, to bring them into line with what is in Christ by appealing to their memories, their knowledge, their sense of appropriateness, their capacity to love one another (and indeed all brethren), and to the fundamental principle of Christian unity.

A third point may be discouraging or not, depending upon one's disposition. Early Christianity takes a firm stand on the axiomatic point that Jesus is The One, but shows considerable variation in the way in which this principle is explicated or combined with other forms of understanding. One of the theologically significant facts about the history of Christian thought as represented in the documents is that the disciples thought before the crucifixion that they understood how Jesus conditioned the *kairos;* and thought so again just after the resurrection; and again just after Pentecost; and again when the Gentile mission became firmly established. Reinterpretation remained possible, even in the face of a fairly settled confidence of understanding. Reinterpretation became desirable when it seemed to make significantly better sense of what had or had not happened, especially if such interpretation was also practically edifying. And although understanding sufficient for salvation seems to have been available at all stages of development, there appears to have been no way of assessing at any given stage the degree of adequacy or ultimacy in the manner of understanding already achieved. The possibility of a substantive reordering of thought arising from mutual reflection on Christian experience was always there. To put it another way, there was always the possibility, and sometimes the necessity, that those who lived in Christ might discover together that they had not grasped the truth well enough and were now being invited into a more adequate understanding. What had been impressive at the level of signs might, without warning, break through to a deeper and different understanding at the level of works. What had seemed an irreformably discerned point of beginning might prove, on further contemplation, to be really a suggestive allusion to a deeper and more ultimate *arché.* An initially intolerable deviancy could, with the test of time and apparent righteousness, show itself to be definitive of the true Way.

Earliest Christianity was not altogether faithful to the lessons it had learned, or at least had tried to teach itself. The Ebionites were left to smolder in their resentful discontent; Diotrephes—perhaps in obedience to the directive of 2 John—substituted highhanded power for the graceful persuasions of contagious truth. History, in which attentive Christians had good theological reason to trust, argued the virtues (and, to a considerable extent, the safety) of a greater tolerance for diversity of provisional understanding than seems to have been practically realized. But despite its failures in application, Christianity's guiding theory shows through, standing in benevolent but candid judgment over the historical record of what was, and remains, an unfinished project in the formation of understanding.

The project continues. It may continue on essentially the same basis on which it was begun. To that end, it is worth stressing once more that, according to its best lights, early Christendom had to discover its understandings together, and that these understandings had to have something to do with the production of fruit worthy of the *kairos* of salvation. If Christian thought looks to its own earliest conditioning to recover the ground of theological validity, it should recognize that the achievement of a more substantial unity in lived Christianity may well be prerequisite to any substantive improvement in its discernment of truth; and it should also recognize that a more careful attentiveness to the behavioral and attitudinal implications of various doctrinal or theological conceptions might well produce revaluations that are unprecedented, unanticipated, even startling, but nevertheless able to claim on venerable grounds a deeper authenticity than what they offer to displace. Christendom ought accordingly to be prepared to accord at least temporary hospitality to a broader theological pluralism than it has been accustomed to accommodate.

For it is, by the standards of *ap' archês*, only under such combined conditions that it can finally be determined which interpretations of Christianity may be called authentically Christian, and only thus that we can discern in what way, and possibly even whether, Jesus is The One. But by the same standards, we must not expect definitive results too quickly. The depths of the *kairos*, says the Word from the beginning, can be known and understood only to the extent that they are well tested and enacted in the life of those who belong to it. We cannot now be confident about what we must still learn, or unlearn, before it is fulfilled. And we surely should not underestimate the difficulty of imitating well what earliest Christianity appears to have thought to be the most authentic manner of learning and unlearning as it journeyed toward the final perfection of understanding along the Way of the Word.

Notes

Introduction

[1] Let me juxtapose two passages chosen almost at random, which seem to me typical of the polarization of assumptions about what was, and what was most authentic in, the earliest Christian way of relating to its truth: ". . . the Council of Trent (sess. iv. De Canon. Script.), when it teaches that the truth of Christ is contained partly in the Bible, partly in unwritten tradition received by the Apostles from Christ or from the Holy Ghost, and entrusted by them to the Church, that Scripture and tradition . . . are to be reverenced alike, follows the express teaching of many of the earliest and greatest Fathers, the spirit of all. The advocate of private judgment, on the other hand, is committed to the conclusion that the Church was left for a generation without any true and complete rule of faith . . ." (A Catholic Dictionary, ed. William E. Addis and Thomas Arnold, revised with additions by T. B. Scannell, 9th edition, London [Kegan Paul], 1917, pp. 813–814, s.v. "Tradition.") "When did these formations begin? How and by what influence was the living faith transformed into the creed to be believed, the surrender to Christ into a philosophic Christology, the Holy Church into the corpus permixtum, the glowing hope of the Kingdom of heaven into a doctrine of immortality and deification, prophecy into a learned exegesis and theological science, the bearers of the spirit into clerics, the brethren into laity held in tutelage, miracles and healings into nothing or into priest-craft, the fervent prayers into a solemn ritual, renunciation of the world into a jealous dominion over the world, the 'spirit' into constraint and law?" (Adolph Harnack, History of Dogma [trans. Neil Buchanan from 3rd edition, 1894], 1894–; repr. in 4 vols., New York, 1961, vol. 1, pp. 45–46, s.v. "Presuppositions.")

[2] Rudolf Bultmann, Theology of the New Testament (trans. Kendrick Grobel), 2 vols., New York, 1955, vol. 2, p. 137.

[3] Under the editorship of Georg Strecker, in 1964.

[4] Orthodoxy and Heresy in Earliest Christiantiy, ed. Robert A. Kraft and Gerhard Krodel, Philadelphia, 1971.

[5] I am thinking especially of Appendix 2, giving the history of the book's reception (and reporting criticisms of it with an apologetic tentativeness), but

202

also of the remarkable team of eleven translators, with two editors, the comprehensive index prepared by a leading scholar, and the general excitement stirred up by the event.

[6]Goguel's review is quoted in Appendix 2 of *Orthodoxy and Heresy*, p. 288.

[7]*Ibid.*, p. 313.

[8]*Ibid.*, p. xxv.

[9]Helmut Koester, "Häretiker im Urchristentum," *RGG*[3], vol. 3, cols. 17–18.

[10]"Orthodoxy and Heresy in Primitive Christianity," *Interpretation* 19, (1965), p. 311.

[11]Ernst Käsemann, *New Testament Questions of Today* (from "Sackgassen im Streit um den historischen Jesus," *Exegetiche Versuche und Besinnungen*, 2nd ed., 1965), London, 1969, pp. 47–48.

[12]Helmut Koester, "*Gnōmai Diaphoroi:* The Origin and Nature of Diversification in the History of Early Christianity," *Harvard Theological Review* 58 (1965), pp. 282.

[13]G. Clarke Chapman, "Some Theological Reflections on Walter Bauer's *Rechtgläubigkeit und Ketzerei im ältesten Christentum:* A Review Article," *Journal of Ecumenical Studies*, 1970, p. 568.

[14]Rudolf Bultmann, *Theology of the New Testament* vol. 2, p. 135.

Chapter 1

[1]Elsewhere, Paul tends to represent this intervention more as an invasion and occupation by God of disorderly human impulses than as a bracing tonic to unsteady but otherwise adequate intellect and will—righteousness by overpowering rather than by correction. This portion of Romans is very likely a deliberate and circumspect corrective to those other representations, but not a falsification of their meaning. Evidently, Paul's spontaneous judgment from within gratuitous salvation was that man is importantly corrupt without it; his more measured and refined judgment seems to have acknowledged that this is not a necessary state of affairs but only a factual one.

In Romans, Paul is consciously correcting misinterpretations of his previous teaching (e.g., 3:8). It is possible that he is also consciously modifying positions taken in other extant epistles. I am reluctant, however, to develop my investigations of Paul in ways that depend on particular chronological arrangements of his epistles or particular solutions to the complex literary problems presented by them. I have accordingly attempted to find the pattern of Paul's thought within the range of variables offered by different solutions to these problems;

and having found his thinking adequately consistent and the variables not significant impediments to its reconstruction, I have developed the argument of this chapter for the most part without explicit reference to them, allowing it to move among the epistles without offering justification for particular movements.

²10:5 evidently implies this; and the same assumption, painfully tantalizing to one who simply cannot manage to be so subjected, underlies chapter 7. Paul clearly believes that being perfect in the Law is a derivative and inferior kind of righteousness by comparison with the direct righteousness of God which is accessible only through faith in Christ; but he does not deny that it is a life-giving condition all the same, or that it is at least theoretically realizable. On the other hand, Rom 3:20 echoes the hard sayings about the Law found in Galatians (2:16; 3:11–12, 21). This is Paul's characteristic abbreviated stand: there is no salvation in the Law. I find the best candidate for a link of coherence in Paul's conviction that all have sinned (Rom 3:23; cf. Gal 3:19, 22). The Law therefore must condemn—but it might have saved, were it not for sin. Galatians does not promote this emphasis, being concerned with urging the insufficiency of the Law in the most persuasive way—but even there, Paul acknowledges that the one doing the commandments of the Law will live by them (3:12) and that the Spirit, for all its rivalry with the Law, reaffirms its essence (5:13–14). But this is one issue on which I am not confident that Paul's thought is ultimately consistent.

³See Paul S. Minear, *The Obedience of Faith*, London, 1971.

⁴*Noēma*, though more ordinarily signifying *thought*, is best understood here in the more inclusive sense of mind. See Robert Jewett, *Paul's Anthropological Terms*, Leiden, 1971, pp. 381–382.

⁵Cf. the general conclusion of Günther Bornkamm in "Faith and Reason in Paul's Epistles," *NTS* 4 (1957–1958), pp. 93–100. "Prophecy is for him essentially rational speech *(lalein en noi)* in contrast to that pneumatic ecstasy *(lalein en pneumati)* . . . This is essentially Pauline . . ." (p. 98).

⁶Bultmann remarks that "It must be recognized, of course, that the apostles could become an indubitable authority only when with the disappearance of the first generation they themselves already belonged to the past, and the conflicts of the apostolic period in which Paul had been involved had died away" (*Theology of the New Testament*, vol. 2, p. 139). This seems to me an unaccountable judgment and a misleading conclusion; my next few observations will indicate why.

⁷For a most deft and illuminating discussion of this, see David L. Dungan, *The Sayings of Jesus in the Churches of Paul*, Philadelphia, 1971.

⁸See Margaret E. Thrall, "The Pauline Use of *Syneidēsis,*" *NTS* 14 (1967–1968), pp. 118–125, for the special value of the other's approving conscience in

Paul's thought, usefully correcting and augmenting C. A. Pierce, *Conscience in the New Testament*, London, 1955, which attends hardly at all to this function of conscience or to the texts that report it. I do not think, however, that Thrall is right in maintaining that the disapproving conscience is idolatrous and usurping for Paul when applied to another's actions. (It is surely not so in evaluation of one's own behavior.) 1 Cor 10:28–29 deals not with unrighteous condemnation but with the possibility of scandal given to one whose conscience is weak.

[9]This important realization was long obscured by the influence of the attractively tidy hypothesis of the Tübingen school, but is clearly there in the textual evidence. See Johannes Munck, *Paul and the Salvation of Mankind*, London, 1959, ch. 4, where the author goes so far as to dissociate the Judaizers from Jewish Christianity altogether, claiming that their movement could only be a Gentile heresy, and could arise only in Pauline churches. I do not think that Munck secures this extreme view (his argument is plausible, but wants both probability and evidence), but he firmly establishes the coherence of Paul with earliest apostolic Christianity.

[10]Bultmann, in remarking that Paul's appeal to resurrection-witness is made "inconsistently with his basic insight" (*Theology of the New Testament*, vol. 2, p. 127), is right about one basic insight, but importantly wrong about another: Paul saw that the order of the Spirit was the more perfect source of understanding and conviction, but he also saw that it corresponded in an orderly and functional way with the more ordinary human orders through which it is expressed.

[11]I do not wish to overload the significance of Paul's choice of *anoētoi* here, but it seems to me inescapable that it appeals to a normative understanding. Paul's primary appeal against the Galatians' deviance is to their reception of the Spirit (3:2), which is not only the evident seal of divine acceptance and salvation, but undoubtedly the most memorably dramatic and persuasive event of the Galatians' Christian experiences. The emphasis is on the power of the Spirit and not upon the illumination of understanding (3:5). But that, I think, is a function of Paul's rhetorical urgency. Elsewhere in the epistle, he appeals to their rescue from Gentile ignorance and the implications of their new knowledge of God (4:8–9), and to their unaccountable failure to be persuaded by and obedient to the truth (5:7–8). In short, I take Paul's views in Galatians to be essentially those of his more circumspect presentations in Romans and parts of Corinthians: viz., that the resolution to the anthropological dilemma comes when the word of truth is submitted to in faith, thus reforming the understanding and will enough to make it possible for God to accept one and transform in the Spirit one's capacity both to understand and to live out that understanding. Paul's indictment of the Galatians assumes that they have undergone this transformation enough that he can appeal to what they have grasped in order to prove to them that they have not grasped it thoroughly enough—that they can be made to understand that they have betrayed their understanding. The saving work of the Lord rests only precariously among them until they pull their new minds

together and think nothing other than the truth they know (5:10). Though not necessarily temporally prior, their right understanding holds an anthropological priority and is the arena in which their perdurance in Christian belonging must be fought out.

[12]M. J. Lagrange, *Saint Paul: Épître aux Galates*, Paris, 1942, speaks here of "l'Écriture ou plutôt celui qui l'a inspirée." But this is not quite Paul's way of putting it. His expression is cognate with a rabbinic formula (see especially Heinrich Schlier, *Der Brief an die Galater*, Göttingen, 1965) and he would probably resist the use of the term *"Spirit"* in characterizing pre-Christian events. Besides, the law was given by the angels (Gal 3:19).

[13]See D. M. Stanley, " 'Become Imitators of Me', The Pauline Conception of Apostolic Tradition . . ." *Biblica* 40 (1959), pp. 859–877. For another approach to this, see John Howard Schütz, "Apostolic Authority and the Control of Tradition: I Cor. XV," *NTS* 15 (1968–1969), pp. 439–457. This article is excellent in its scrutiny of Paul's view of his own position, but seems to me short-sighted about Paul's respect for norms operating independently of himself—e.g., Schütz is surely wrong in discrediting Paul's compliments to the Corinthians as mere sarcasm (pp. 445). Another road to virtually the same conclusion may be found well marked in Klaus Wengst, "Der Apostel und die Tradition: Zur theologischen Bedeutung urchristlicher Formeln bei Paulus," *ZTK* 69 (1972), pp. 145–162. I think that Wengst's arguments are sound and illuminating, but are similarly limited by his failure to look beyond Paul and his calling and Gospel to the other concretization present in the communities he addressed. An article on Pauline theology that does not refer to the Holy Spirit is hardly an exhaustive accounting.

[14]David L. Dungan, *op. cit.*, has shown that one must be careful about asserting where Paul is straying from Dominical tradition into creative legislation of his own authority: it appears that his style was more richly allusive than has usually been supposed.

[15]It is occasionally argued that Paul is being ironic here. It is easy enough to build a case for that claim from other parts of the Corinthian correspondence, but it seems to me highly implausible either that Paul would intend an irony here, in the midst of his solemn and affectionate salutation, or that he could suppose that his addressees would grasp an irony here if he intended one. The discussion of tone and meaning in C. K. Barrett, *A Commentary on the First Epistle to the Corinthians*, London, 1968, seems to me a much sounder and more appropriate approach to the passage.

[16]Stephen S. Smalley, "Spiritual Gifts and I Corinthians 12–16," *JBL* 87 (1968), pp. 427–433, argues that the importance of these offices in Paul's conception of the church governs even the over-all structure of this part of the epistle.

[17]The communal discernment of which Paul speaks is well set out in Luke Timothy Johnson, "Norms for True and False Prophecy in First Corinthians," *American Benedictine Review* 22 (1971), pp. 29–45.

[18]Johannes Munck, *op. cit.*, does not think that this statement points to present problems, but is rather exclusively eschatological. I do not think that a careful reading of the text will support this view (note especially the preceding verse, but also the recurring themes in the entire Corinthian correspondence), and the citation of the other texts that associate sects with the end of time does not much help it: if Paul is being allusively eschatological, it is for the purpose of reminding the Corinthian factions how urgent it is for them to mend their ways.

[19]I suggest also that this principle is the ultimate explanation for the Pauline (and also general) stand and practice as deftly isolated by David L. Dungan, *op. cit.*, p. 35: "whenever a significant conflict or dispute or problem arose in the Church over its regulations . . . the decisions made ultimately seem to have favored whatever course best promoted the further flowering of the Gospel and encouraged Christian harmony, at least as they understood these things." Dungan accounts for this by appealing to the well-established principle of *Sitz-im-Leben*, but that merely further generalizes the theoretical problem raised by the phenomenon he is specifically discussing, viz., Paul's evident willingness to take pragmatic liberties even with an express commandment of the Lord. I suggest that Paul is appealing implicitly not to mere convenience but to the conviction that the mind of Christ is most essentially expressed in the command that the Gospel be spread and best imitated in the loving harmony of the church. He sets aside one commandment of the Lord in order to observe another and greater one—a procedure frequently recommended by Jesus himself in the Gospel traditions and plausibly internalized in early Christian habit in the same operative way as the other portions of Dominical tradition examined by Dungan.

[20]The striking and solidly argued conclusions of Dungan, *op. cit.*, concerning the nature and consistency of Pauline and other early Christian uses of the teachings of Jesus lend further support to these views. Dungan confirms in a detailed way the implicit derivation of Christian self-understanding from the mind of Christ and the implicit assumption that the mind of Christ remained creatively active in the operations of Christians' reflection on their life in Christ.

Chapter 2

[1]A few words on the assumptions underlying this chapter might help situate the argument. I do not know who Luke was. I think of him as the composer of the first four verses of the third Gospel, and I assume him to have been the essentially final governing redactor of the twenty-four chapters that follow: but if there was substantive redactional work by another hand, either before or

after, it appears to be quite consonant with those first four verses. By "Luke," I therefore mean the main redactional drift, undifferentiatedly. I also suppose Luke (in one or another of his possible personal forms) to be the author of the first two verses of Acts, and the redactor of essentially all that follows, though I am willing to make similar allowance for compatible further redaction. (Even, in fact, a little incompatible further redaction, which is what I take 1:3 to be: but I do not find grounds for supposing that there is a substantive degree of such interference in the rest of Acts.) As for Luke's relationship to the traditional material with which he worked, I do not know where he got it, or in what form it came to him, or what available elements he omitted, or what he added from his own invention. I assume that some of the things he records seemed more centrally important to him than others, and I am willing to entertain the possibility that he might have regretted some of them altogether but included them out of some sense of duty or prudence. I assume only that their inclusion is in some way his affirmation of them: if not that he knew them to be true or important, at least that he thought that they were held to be right, or believed them to be appropriate. That is: the text of Luke contains a cumulative set of early Christian memories and understandings, including some of Luke's own, which may be held to be representative of some habits of mind obtaining in early Christian circles. I suppose similar things to be true of Matthew and of Mark, although I am less confident of the essential univocity of final redactional control in these cases (not a great deal less confident, however). I also suppose that the general coherence of the thinking implicit and explicit in the body of the Third Gospel, and its plausible resonance with the prologue, and the overall compatibility of both with the first two Gospels, are phenomena significant of an important consensus in early Christian thought. Just how universal, I do not know: but widespread, and without evidence of early Christian demurrer. Neither do I know at what moment in time to place this consensus: however it is important whenever it may have occurred, and it is my opinion that the evidence is most properly served by supposing that is was in fact early, traditional, and cumulative.

Some of the grounds for these suppositions will emerge in the course of this chapter's development. In part, the chapter is an induction and a defense of them. But it seemed to me good to forewarn the reader where I am headed, since the direction is somewhat unconventional. I would also like to repeat and particularize the Preface's remarks about my argument's procedure, since this chapter is especially susceptible of being misunderstood with respect to its relationship to current scholarship. Writings on the synoptic Gospels ordinarily stay close to the assumptions and preoccupations of literary (especially form and redaction) criticism. This chapter is concerned with an issue with respect to which their findings are less relevant. They have shown that it is risky to generalize on the synoptic Gospels; but if my view of the character of the first three Gospels is substantially correct (and I hope to make it ring true in the course of the discussion), then the dissociative force of these types of criticism is—at least for the purposes of the problem I pursue—relativized to the substantive consensus within the material on which these critical techniques make their discriminations. I have considered them throughout, but have allowed my own purposes and judgment to determine what is relevant and what is sound. Where others' concerns seemed to be beside the point, or where their assertions did not appear to be more firmly based than my own counter-assertions, I have not always felt obliged to redeem my views by paying the tribute of argumentative footnotes.

[2]A. J. B. Higgins, in "The Preface to Luke and the Kerygma in Acts" (Ch. 4 of *Apostolic History and the Gospel: Biblical and Historical Essays Presented to F. F. Bruce*, ed. W. Ward Gasque and Ralph P. Martin, Exeter, 1970), pp. 78–79, gives the basis for the majority's conclusion that the preface applies to both works. Although he then goes on to argue (pp. 81–82) that verses 1–2 apply only to the Gospel, and verses 3–4 to both works, his argument depends upon unnecessary assumptions. It is simply not true that the words of 1–2 cannot refer to early apostolic events along with pre-ascension events, and in fact Higgins' own subsequent observations strengthen the case for supposing the contrary.

[3]See W. C. van Unnik, "Remarks on the Purpose of Luke's Historical Writing," in *Sparsa Collecta*, Leiden, 1973, pp. 6–15.

[4]It is not clear whether John preached "the kingdom," for Luke tends to dissociate the term from him. But it is surely wrong to say that in 16:16 it "is made plain . . . as a point of principle" that "John does not proclaim the Kingdom of God" (Conzelmann, *The Theology of St. Luke*, trans. Geoffrey Buswell, London, 1960, p. 20)—the more plausible reading of the verse leads precisely to the opposite conclusion. It is also wrong to say that John's Gospel "relates not to the imminence of the kingdom but to that of the messiah" (Walter Wink, *John the Baptist in the Gospel Tradition*, Cambridge, 1968, p. 58). If "kingdom" is a doubtful item in John's theological vocabulary, "Messiah" is even more so. His emphasis falls rather, even in the tendentious Gospels, on the imminence of the destroying or saving judgment.

[5]I appreciate that Luke does not use the nominal form *(euaggelion)* in reference to John, but it hardly follows that "for Luke the verb has a quite general connotation, *viz.*, that of 'preaching' " (Willi Marxsen, *Mark the Evangelist* trans. James Boyce, *et al.*, Nashville, 1969, p. 143). (Cf. Conzelmann, *The Theology of St. Luke*, p. 23, where the same arbitrary assertion is made.) Luke saves the noun for the fullest realization of the Word, that of the fourth stage; but the verb is used only in conjunction with the still revelational earlier stages, not for preaching generally. A comparison with Acts will readily suggest that the verb may have great weight even alone—e.g., 8:25, 39, where it deserves in translation nothing short of "evangelized." What John and Jesus preach may thus legitimately be called gospels, though not *the* Gospel par excellence.

[6]By "offers," I mean primarily that he makes it available to critical discernment. He himself organizes his narrative in accordance with this scheme, but

it is more significant that it can also be induced from the materials he preserves. For the correspondence of the other synoptists to this model, cf. *infra.*, pp. 128–133.

[7]This extension of Luke's use of *euaggelizomai*, like that of 2:10, is justified by its being part of the divine disclosure that the Promise was drawing nearer in concrete identifiable stages. That is, it is not a casual usage, but one that draws a technical authority from its connectedness to the ultimate Word: an aspect of gospel en route to the Gospel.

[8]John's question within the Lucan (and Matthean) frame is of course not about Jesus' authenticity but about his specific identity with John's own proclaimed *ho erchomenos*. In effect, John poses a question from within the second level of the Word on the occasion of the third level, that seeks to penetrate the fourth level; Jesus returns an answer that stays within the boundaries of the third level.

[9]This is true, I think, quite independently of the historical facts of the matter. If things happened, say, in the purely psychological way in which Johannes Weiss reconstructs them (*Earliest Christianity* [*Das Urchristentum,* 1937], trans. & ed. Frederick C. Grant, 2 vols., New York, 1959, vol. 1), there would clearly be strong motivation to validate precisely this mode of realization and avoid the fabrication of literal-material correlatives. On the other hand, even if we suppose the most literal resurrection-events, Paul reminds us how attractive and convincing is the argument that spiritual appropriation of a spiritual reality is a higher form of experience anyway, leaving the last as privileged as the first. The vulgar literalism of the synoptic tradition is thus a significant phenomenon, even quite apart from its historical value: it defines what counts, and thus shows something about the criteriological habits of mind that obtained in its creators and custodians.

[10]Conzelmann is seriously wrong in saying that "Luke xxiv assumes that one can only understand it [Scripture] in the light of the Resurrection" (*The Theology of St. Luke,* p. 162). On the contrary, Luke 24 firmly implies that a true reading can be arrived at quite independently of the occurrence of the resurrection (though a true reading will of course point to its necessity). Note that Cleopas and his companion are enlightened about the true reading *before* they come to a belief in the resurrection: the former in fact is what makes the latter possible for them, not vice versa. This point is of considerable importance theologically.

[11]Here, of course, I once more part company with Conzelmann, who maintains that "The significance of xxiv, 11 is that it expresses the truth that the Resurrection cannot be deduced from an idea (of Messiahship) or from the historical life of Jesus, but that it is announced as something new" (*The Theology of St. Luke,* p. 93). This verse is rather only a bald registration of the fact that the disciples did not in fact make this deduction, not that they could not have

done so. Indeed, the balance of evidence seems to me to make it incontroverti-
bly true that Luke sides with the general tradition in acknowledging that they
had no adequate excuse for failing to perceive that both the idea of messiahship
contained in Scripture and the life (especially the communications, both public
and private) of Jesus pointed to the necessity of the messianic death and resurrection. Their failure to see this is not, in the tradition, because it was intrinsically unintelligible before the resurrection occurred, but because they were
dull-minded and slow to believe.

[12]For the general applicability of these Luke-based conclusions to the other
synoptists, cf. *infra.*, pp. 66–72.

[13]The object of belief is evidently the kingdom itself, or possibly the Gospel
of the kingdom. Obviously, a certain confusion arises when believers in the
fourth-stage Gospel reflect on such urgings concerning the Gospel of the third
stage: but I think it makes most sense to understand this and the next few
citations in precisely the way Luke is presenting them. The Gospel in question
does not proclaim Jesus, but the kingdom, and a "Son of Man" who is distinguishable from Jesus. The reason it is important not to reject Jesus is simply
because he does in fact bear the authentic word of God: he is the kingdom's
special prophet, and is to be received according to his sender's dignity. Superficially, it may appear as if we are into full Gospel territory in these quotations,
but in fact they claim no more for Jesus than Jesus is ready to claim elsewhere
for John: rejection of John's baptism is rejection of the purposes of God (7:30);
failure to believe in John is an ominous fault (20:5). The balance of evidence
seems to indicate that even the third stage of the Word is crucial to accept, to
believe—just as some aspects of the second stage had been, and on similar
grounds.

[14]The wording of this sentence is, I confess, deliberately elusive. It is not clear
whether the Good Thief is confessing the firmest version of the third-stage
Gospel (asking the innocent prophet not to be ashamed of him when entering
the kingdom he has proclaimed) or a weak version of the fourth stage (asking
the Lord of the kingdom for mercy). It does not matter much for the present
business which it is.

[15]I do not, however, find that there is conclusive evidence to support the
contention that the Gospels were composed for liturgical use, as has been
argued for Matthew by G. D. Kilpatrick (*The Origins of the Gospel According
to St. Matthew*, Oxford, 1946) and for Mark by Philip Carrington (*The Primitive
Christian Calendar*, Cambridge, 1952).

[16]The idea of "witness" is accordingly not clearly differentiated. The most
privileged are "witnesses" in all four senses, as well as in another to be discussed
shortly. It is neither necessary nor possible to figure out precisely what historical
dynamics were at work in isolating one or another sense of "witness" in various

texts, and there is no good reason to suppose that the unified multiple-sense notion was not earliest and basic.

[17]Here and in the next observation, I use "Mark" in reference to the usual ending of the Second Gospel, which of course did not necessarily come under the same redactional auspices as the rest of the text (but see William R. Farmer, *The Last Twelve Verses of Mark*, Cambridge, 1974 for an argument that these verses *are* Marcan). Although its date of composition is uncertain, I suggest that it at least witnesses independently to assumptions present in the tradition to which a Lucan Theophilos might appeal. In that respect, it has a significance it would not have if it had merely been, for instance, copied from the ending of Matthew. Despite various attempts to argue that Mark originally ended at 16:8, I believe that it is far more plausible that an original Marcan ending has been lost; the alternative seems to be to propose the most unnecessarily anticlimactic ending in the history of world literature. If its original ending has in fact been lost, I know of no indications in the rest of the text to suggest that it would have deviated in any significant way from the adduced pattern.

[18]The closest we come to a partial exception is when Luke witnesses to the conviction that a proper reading of Scripture can demonstrate the necessity that the messiah pass through crucifixion and resurrection into glory. Matthew is not quite so explicit, but nevertheless clearly manifests essentially the same assumption. Jesus pleads just such a scripturally demonstrated necessity when he explains why it is inappropriate to resist his arrest through the intervention of either men or angels: for "how then should the scriptures be fulfilled, that this is the way it must happen?" (Mt 26:54). The various Matthean recollections of scriptural hints in conjunction with the final stages of Jesus' career are similarly a way of illustrating the general assurance of Matthew's Jesus that "you should not suppose that I came to abolish the Law and the Prophets: I came not to abolish but to fulfill. For I tell you solemnly, until heaven and earth come to an end, not the least letter or mark will be lost from the law until all things have taken place" (5:17–18). That is, I think, the Law and the Prophets are especially about the career on which he is embarked, and it is therefore his work that will validate them above all. Mark does not confirm this part of the general theory quite so clearly. From his citations of Scripture to show fulfillments in Jesus, and from the succinct remark of Jesus in his account of the arrest, "that the scriptures may be fulfilled" (14:49), it is evident that he is no stranger to some such assumption; but he does not articulate it overtly. His only partial neglect, however, can hardly stand as a refutation of Luke's and Matthew's—not to mention Paul's—witness to this conviction as an axiom of the earliest Christian understanding.

[19]As part of the restored ending, this is not editorially of a piece with the rest of Mark, but clearly in the same spirit as well as the same tradition.

[20]This *is*, after all, what it says: and against Marxsen ("Redaktionsgeschichtliche Erklärung der songenannten Parabeltheorie des Markus," *Zeitschrift für*

Theologie und Kirche 52 [1955], p. 269) and Jeremias (*op. cit.*, p. 17), I side with Matthew Black (*An Aramaic Approach to the Gospels and Acts,* third edition, Oxford, 1967) in his insistence that whatever Jesus himself may have said, no benevolent exegesis can legitimately rescue Mark's grim words from such a meaning—not even the subtle ingenuity displayed more recently by C. F. D. Moule (Mark 4:1–20 Yet Once More," in *Neotestamentica et Semitica: Studies in Honour of Matthew Black,* Edinburgh, 1969, pp. 95–113).

[21]Commentators frequently struggle to avoid this conclusion: e.g., Willoughby C. Allen (*op. cit.*), Alan Hugh M'Neile (*The Gospel According to St. Matthew,* London, 1915), Pierre Bonnard (*L'Evangile selon Saint Mattieu,* Neuchatel. 1963), Julius Schniewind (*Das Evangelium nach Mattäus,* Göttingen, 1964), Vincent Taylor (*The Gospel According to St. Mark,* 2nd ed., New York, 1966), Norval Geldenhuys (*Commentary on the Gospel of Luke,* Grand Rapids, 1952), Lonsdale Ragg (*St. Luke,* London, 1922). (But cf. Floyd V. Filson [*A Commentary on the Gospel According to St. Matthew,* London, 1960], Ernst Lohmeyer [*Die Briefe an die Philipper, an die Kolosser und an Philemon,* ((KEK)), Göttingen, 1964].) Analogies in rabbinic texts show it to be at least possible that this passage might be legitimately decoded to mean "how can the Messiah be [only!] David's son?" But I take John 7:41–42 to be good supportive grounds for an early tradition of a non-Davidic origin for Jesus, and I find slim grounds for supposing that either Jesus or John the Baptist really thought in terms of a Davidic-messianic scenario.

[22]Despite the presence of such inconsistencies and contradictions, some consistent patterns emerge: and in case it may have occurred to the reader to wonder whether I have just invalidated the conclusions I have drawn from my siftings of the synoptic texts, I would like to reaffirm them. They are not affected by these variables. Theophilos may have trouble fixing the *content* of the saving truth, but he will not find confusing inconsistencies about the modes of its authentic and normative disclosure. The constitution is willing even if the due process is procedurally weak.

[23]Cf. 18:19–20, on which a few more remarks presently.

[24]Again, not the original Marcan ending—but see note 17. In view of Marcan hints such as 11:22–24, 13:11, ect., it appears that he has *at least* a notion of a functional equivalent to Luke's theory.

[25]I shall pick up this point again in dealing with Acts: but here I am concerned with what can be induced from the Gospels alone. I am not pretending that these Dominical provisions are historically reliable—what Jesus says in this reconstructed setting is likely to be as much conditioned by the author's sense of later times as is much of the material in Acts—but I do consider it of some importance to keep the ways in which the tradition itself represents things distinguished from critical reconstruction of how they probably really were.

The influential and formative facts are the ones supposed by those who are influenced and formed, not those of the subsequent historian.

[26]The Gospel of Matthew has itself been particularly associated with the phenomenon of the Christian scribe: see Kilpatrick *(op. cit.)* and Krister Stendahl *(The School of St. Matthew and its Use of the Old Testament,* Uppsala, 1954).

[27]This is the weighting of the term even if the historical fact may be that opinions attributed to the "sages" were merely those of a majority or those of Judah ha-Nasi himself. Curiously, Strack-Billerbeck has no entry on the first part of 23:34, where these terms occur.

[28]If the rabbinic analogy holds, the categories *sophos* and *grammateus* are probably not mutually exclusive, and could be identical. The absence of corroboration for these as technical or official terms in early Christian communities further suggests that Matthew is pointing by metaphorical analogy to functions rather than positions, reminding his readers that the Christians have their own equivalents of the most authoritative roles in Judaism—cf. the Didaché's references to the Christian "high priests." Presumably, the functions did not require official titles to be effectual, any more than the early stages of the Pharisaic movement required priestly titles to absorb priestly interpretative functions effectively.

[29]The synagogue-persecution alluded to in Mt 23:34 (cf. Mk 13:9 and Lk 11:49) undoubtedly has at least in part to do with rejections for doctrinal offenses (for potential grounds for excommunication, see Strack and Billerbeck, *op. cit.,* vol. 4, pt. 2, pp. 305ff.). Those who made themselves offensive by asserting the Gospel, and suffered pain and rejection as a result, and took this suffering to be a mark of honor, would not be likely to have unlimited tolerance for doctrinal waffling within the Christian fold. Nor, of course, would a community on guard against *pseudoprophētai.* Again, what is important here is not to divine what their limits were, but only to note the indications that they held some limits to be important as a condition of Christian belonging, and to see how they would have been determined in both theory and practice.

[30]This principle is obviously in close continuity with Paul's theory, and corrects Bultmann's supposition that the authority present in the apostles could be available to the later church only through certain "authorized bearers of the tradition . . . the bishops" (Bultmann, *New Testament Theology,* vol. 2, p. 139).

Chapter 4

[1]M.-E. Boismard, "Saint Luc et la rédaction du quatrième évangile," *Revue Biblique,* 69 (1962), pp. 185–211.

²The most important reconstructions of the pre-Johannine "signs-source" are those of Rudolf Bultmann, *Das Evangelium des Johannes*, (KEK), Göttingen, 1968 (see also D. M. Smith Jr., *The Composition and Order of the Fourth Gospel*, [New Haven, 1965] and Robert Tomson Fortna, *The Gospel of Signs*, Cambridge, 1970. The former has been found only partially persuasive—see the sketch of its critical reception in D. M. Smith, "The Sources of the Gospel of John: An Assessment of the Present State of the Problem," *New Testament Studies*, 10 (1963–1964), pp. 336–351—but the latter fared better in critical reception, despite many misgivings about Fortna's extension of this putative document to include the passion-resurrection narrative. For my part, I cannot see that one can seriously question the existence of an originally independent set of signs-material, though it matters little to my argument whether it was written or oral, whether it was a collection of miracle stories only or a rudimentary Gospel.

On the other hand, Bultmann's argument for the existence of a Gnostic *Offenbarungsreden* source, despite support from Hans Becker's more widely comparative *Die Reden des Johannesevangeliums und der Stil der gnostischen Offenbarugsreden*, Göttingen, 1956, has not generally been found persuasive. The fatal flaws are the absence of extant *antecedent* examples of Gnostic revelation-discourses, and the possibility that these discourses are precisely the original and characteristic work of the evangelist himself. (See D. M. Smith, "The Sources of the Gospel of John: An Assessment of the Present State of the Problem," *New Testament Studies*, 10 [1963–1964]. pp. 336–351.)

³These assertions cannot stand without qualification: in another sense, Jesus does judge (8:16; 5:30), and there will be a Last Day and a literal resurrection (6:39, 40, 44; cf. 11:24). But even aside from the possibility of arguing that the more conventional touches of eschatology are the work of corrective redaction and alien to the main thrust of the Gospel (see especially Rudolf Bultmann, *Das Evangelium des Johannes*) one may readily see that the eschatological views of the synoptists appear in the Fourth Gospel only in thin, sketchy, and much enfeebled forms. Dodd's general conclusion that the eschatological motifs of earliest Christianity are presented in the Fourth Gospel as partially *realized* rather than exclusively awaited in a historical future is now apparently received, quite properly, as one of the permanently established achievements of New Testament critical scholarship, even if one may wish to make some radical readjustments in Dodd's way of formulating this insight (see especially Ernst Käsemann, *The Testament of Jesus*, London, 1968). One need not alienate John from Mark as thoroughly as Bultmann's conjectures do in order to recognize that they are, at the very least, estranged.

⁴See F.-M. Braun, *Jean le Théologien*, vol. 1, Paris, 1959, pp. 147–149.

⁵R. E. Brown, *The Gospel According to John* (The Anchor Bible), vol. 1, New York, 1966, p. 271, suggests a polemic here against the synagogue (with reference to Moses, Enoch, Elijah, etc.?)—cf. p. 37 and p. 225, re 1:17–18 and 5:37.

This is plausible enough; but I should think it equally plausible that the polemical thrust is directed rather against more contemporary visionaries who claimed to have seen God or to have been taken up into heaven (cf. 2 Cor 12:2).

[6]That is, the portions which, in the present form of the Gospel, deal with Jesus' public ministry. I do not mean to suggest that these are also necessarily earlier in composition. My procedure, as I stated earlier, is to deal first with the Fourth Gospel as such; and within it, to begin with its representation of what was available in the public ministry. Later, I shall also consider the discourses represented to be more private and privileged and the passion-resurrection narrative. This gives us one version of the unfolding of earliest Christian understanding and the criteria for its norms. Another version may be constructed, with varying degrees of plausibility, from a reconstruction of the history of the Fourth Gospel's own development. I will attend to that later; here I will remark only that I think it very probable that the two levels of belief now under discussion correspond to two levels of redaction—i.e., that the belief correlative with the signs-source was later judged deficient by the redactor who incorporated that source, under critical judgment, into his more ambitious treatment of Jesus' ministry.

[7]The just evaluation proposed by Nicodemus (7:51) stands adequately for the sort of provisional agnosticism that is appropriate for a time—though in view of Nicodemus' already registered secret belief (3:2, 7:50), it is uncertain how far one may legitimately go in comparing his stand with that of Gamaliel in Acts. On the whole, the Fourth Gospel presses for decision and seems to disallow much hesitation. The two tendencies undoubtedly have some correlation with the difference between the Fourth Gospel's intermittent interest in reconstructing a plausible version of Jesus' historical ministry (promoting a more patient attitude toward hesitant belief) and its more dominant interest in galvanizing a faith-decision on the part of its later audience (promoting a more urgent view). The most persuasive and illuminating reconstruction of the context in which the Fourth Gospel worked out these tendencies is that of J. L. Martyn, *History and Theology in the Fourth Gospel*, New York, 1968.

[8]This rendition is not necessarily correct. R. E. Brown, *The Gospel According to John*, vol. 1, p. 126, has "He needed no one to testify about human nature" (thus similarly in Hermann Strathmann, *Das Evangelium nach Johannes*, Göttingen, 1963; Alfred Wikenhauser, *Das Evangelium nach Johannes*, Regensburg, 1961; E. C. Hoskyns, *The Fourth Gospel*, ed. F. N. Davey, 2nd ed., London, 1948; etc.). The passage is puzzling, but I think it makes best sense if understood as a comment on the inadequacy of a belief arising merely at the level of human impressionability: that is not enough to rely on, and given the instability and fickleness of benighted humanity, as well as its great capacity for misunderstanding, Jesus knows better than to be either gratified or satisfied that such a result has come about.

[9]Or "the Son of God." The other reading is more strongly attested, but this one is perhaps more theologically characteristic. I agree with E. D. Freed, "The Son of Man in the Fourth Gospel," *Journal of Biblical Literature*, 86 (1967), pp. 402–409, that there is no very important functional or theological difference in the Fourth Gospel's uses of Son, Son of Man, Son of God, but there is a tendency to associate "Son of Man" with contexts involving the humanity or the exaltation/glorification of Jesus or involving his role in judgment. "Son of God" is more common is contexts involving belief. The reason for this distinction is doubtless that the Fourth Gospel's over-all uses of these terms derive from the synoptic tradition (see R. Schnackenburg, "Der Menschensohn im Johannesevangelium," *New Testament Studies*, 11 [1964–1965], pp. 123–137) and in antecedent Jewish apocalyptic traditions (see S. S. Smalley, "The Johannine Son of Man Sayings," *New Testament Studies*, 15 [1968–1969], pp. 278–301). Freed blurs this tendency by reading more implications into the relevant passages than they really invite.

[10]Cf. the similar use of this verb at 17:24. In other places—e.g., 2:23, 4:19, 6:2—it does not signify so deep a perception: to that extent, G. L. Phillips, "Faith and Vision in the Fourth Gospel," in F. L. Cross, ed., *Studies in the Fourth Gospel*, London, 1957, pp. 83–96; and E. A. Abbott, *Johannine Vocabulary*, London, 1905, are right in placing it low on their graduated scale of Johannine seeing.

[11]G. L. Phillips, "Faith and Vision in the Fourth Gospel," following E. A. Abbott, *Johannine Vocabulary*, claims that this verb signifies a deeper perception. One may, I think, argue that what the Jews here *may* "see," leading to belief, is exactly the deeper grasp of Jesus that it is the episode's main business to point to; to that extent, the verb has overtones of depth. But the dialogue is characteristically ambiguous. *We* know that there are ways for them to see and believe at such a level; but what they are asking is more modest: they want evidence which they can observe, leading to a basic confidence in his authenticity. It does not occur to them to mean by the verb as much as the context reminds us they might mean.

[12]The main tendency in the Fourth Gospel's use of *doxa* is to reserve the term for the ultimate post-crucifixion state of Jesus' life—cf. 7:39, 12:16, 13:31–32, 17:5. There are instances, however, of a lesser manifestation of glory: 2:11 and 11:4. But in the light of the deeper motif of glory, these lesser instances need be no more misleading than the difference between the inadequate *belief* of 2:23 and the fuller *belief* to which the Gospel constantly invites—for there too it is fairly clear (as I shall argue below) that the deepest belief, like the deepest glory, is not achieved before the crucifixion.

[13]The wording of this verse does not compel this reading, but it is the most likely one in the light of the occasional Jewish advertence to the fact that God

does not observe the Sabbath proscription of work—see Philo, *Legum Allegoria*, I, 7, and Strack-Billerbeck, vol. 2, pp. 461–462.

[14]There is some inconsistency on the question of self-witness in the Fourth Gospel, but it occasionally invokes the principle against the sufficiency of self-witness—see Strack-Billerbeck on 8:16. Behind this, I would hazard, lies the early community's struggle to interpret the teaching of Jesus in the light of both Christian belief and the remembered disinclination of Jesus to anticipate the kerygma explicitly—a problem faced in other ways by the doctrine of post-passion glory, the interpretation of parables, etc. 8:17–18 takes care of the cavil about self-witness by arguing from a scriptural text. Given the Gospel's interest in scriptural confirmation, it is curious that it provides no counter-argument to the claim that Jesus does not fulfill the required Davidic qualifications for messianic status, especially when the synoptic tradition universally attests to a piece of Dominical exegesis that would readily do the trick (Mt 22:41–46, Mk 12:35–37, Lk 20:40–47)—and which not only suits the Fourth Gospel's style of argumentation, but is far more congenial to its ideas than to those of the synoptists. The claim occasionally made that a counter-argument to 7:41–42 is implicit in the community's knowledge of Jesus' Davidic descent and Bethlehem birth (e.g., C. K. Barrett, *The Gospel According to St. John*, London, 1955; M.-J. Lagrange, *Evangile selon Saint Jean*, Paris, 1936; Leon Morris, *The Gospel According to John*, Grand Rapids, 1971, and, although with considerable misgiving, J. N. Sanders and B. A. Mastin, *A Commentary on the Gospel According to John*, London, 1968) begs the question of what the Fourth Gospel's community believed to be his place and line of origin, and is probably wrong. My best guess, feeble as it is, is that the response which Jesus might plausibly have given in an earlier form of the text was edited out of the Fourth Gospel when the David-Bethlehem convictions gained a sufficient hold in its circles to make offensive what I take to be its earlier position, namely, that the expectation that the true redeemer will be of David and Bethlehem is a misunderstanding based on a superficial and misguided reading of Scripture. The argument against Jesus from the principle of messianic abiding (12:34) is not answered directly, but may obviously be countered by the Fourth Gospel's representation that he *does* abide (14:23, etc.).

[15]Bauer's dictionary makes no such distinction, defining the cited instances of *ergon*, along with others, as referring specifically to miracles. Bertram's article on *ergon* in *TWNT* sees more in the word than miracle alone, but takes it to mean miracle at base.

[16]This is, as I shall illustrate presently, the implication of the Fourth Gospel's management of these motifs in the present form of the text. I consider this editorially deliberate. I have no doubt, however, that the elements of this complex came from different redactional strata: the objection of 4:45 is not from the same interpretative level as the acquiescence (cf. Fortna, *The Gospel of Signs*, p. 227: "The few points at which Jesus goes through the motions of

refusing to work a sign [2:4, 4:48, 7:6–8] are John's additions"—that is, not from the postulated "Gospel of Signs" itself). The unrebuked requests for signs may be still another wave. But despite their historical diversity, and the theological diversity of their original implications, their relative relationship results in a pattern that serves the later redactor's purposes with respect to his theology of *works*.

[17]There is substantial coincidence between the division I am proposing here and that worked out by other means by Fortna in *The Gospel of Signs:* the "works" texts cited in this paragraph, for instance, do not appear in Fortna's reconstructed signs-source, but only in what he takes to be the later Johannine redactional stratum.

[18]The basic root is likely to be one of pre-Christian Jewish liberalism rather than of specifically Christian revisionism. A controversy between a conservative position on the circumcision of proselytes and a more latitudinarian one is likely to have focussed on an interpretation of Abraham. *Pirqe Aboth* 3:11, identifying circumcision as the covenant of Abraham our father, represents the conservative polemic; Philo reports (and partly repudiates) the extreme liberal view in *De Migratione Abrahami* 92, and also in *Quaestiones et Solutiones in Genesis* 48: "They [viz, the liberals he criticizes] say that the circumcision of the skin is a symbol, as if (to show that) it is proper to cut off superfluous and excessive desires by exercising continence and endurance in matters of the Law." Of course, the controversy over circumcision was not exclusively a matter for proselytes: as the reports from the Seleucid period show, circumcision was not universally practiced among the native sons of Abraham. The Maccabean chronicles represent this as a sheer thoughtless infidelity, but it must certainly have been accompanied by a theological reinterpretation. Whether such an interpretation had several generations' continuous history before Paul or was recreated in his time is doubtful, but its arguments are relatively predictable in either case.

[19]The stratification between the level of *signs* and the level of *works* is doubtless partially a function of the Fourth Gospel's literary history. Fortna remarks concerning the absence from his reconstructed signs-Gospel of that pointed transcendence of the Law that is so important at the level of works: "it is noteworthy that when John wishes, even in his unhistorical way, to take up the Sabbath question, he cannot find it in his source but must quite artificially introduce it at points where the source breaks off" (*The Gospel of Signs*, p. 223). Similarly, the "Gospel of signs" as reconstructed by Fortna shows a "seeming ignorance of the (probably dominical) polemic against those who seek signs" (p. 227), a polemic obviously congenial to the works-stratum.

[20]E.g., "messianic" is not so emphatic in the Fourth Gospel—though "Word of God" is of course more resonant there than in the synoptic accounts—and *submission* is not so much the mode of reception as *understanding acceptance.*

The shift of emphasis away from the passion and toward the pre-crucifixion comportment of Jesus, especially vis-à-vis the Sabbath, is itself a noteworthy difference.

[21]Admittedly, it comes close enough to allow the contrary argument to be plausibly made. I suppose that the evangelist never completely decided between his hope for an ignorant world (and his concomitant exhortations to the invited) and his indignation at the unredeemable enemies of the light (and his concomitant denunciations of those who have not seen). Both motifs are present. Interpreters accordingly may choose—or, if they are more circumspect, waver. The irresolution about this matter in the Fourth Gospel is affected by its incorporation of "primitive" sources, but is more ultimately attributable to the failure of its major redactor to take adequate theological responsibility for the darkness he sketches. I do not suppose this to be due to an imperfect assimilation of Gnostic sources, but merely a carelessness analogous to, and quite possibly related to, Paul's failure to work through the theological implications of his negative evaluation of *sarx*. What I present as the main stand of the Fourth Gospel is not its only stand, but it is the most theologically adequate of its attempts to confront the problem—and therefore, I take it to be its most advanced and determinative view.

[22]The lack of association between this level of discourse and the title *Christos* is striking. The exceptional instances, 1:17 and 17:3, are perhaps no more than a reflex employment of what had become even by Paul's time almost a formal surname for Jesus. At any rate, the term as a title or office is associated in the Fourth Gospel with the level of signs: the deeper truth of the level of works transcends the normal implications of Messianism, and the title tends to be conspicuously absent. I suspect that this has something to do with the polemical insistence upon it in 1 John. There is further supporting reflection to be found in M. De Jonge, "Jewish Expectations about the 'Messiah' According to the Fourth Gospel," *New Testament Studies* 19 (1972–1973), pp. 246–270.

[23]W. J. P. Boyd, "The Ascension according to St. John," *Theology*, 70, (May 1967), pp. 207–211, argues in detail for the post-resurrection character of 17, and asserts that 14:1–29, 15, and 16:1–16 also belonged originally to a post-resurrection instruction. That seems to me a more satisfactory way of understanding some particular elements in the text (e.g., the final words of 16:4, the use of the perfect tense in 16:33) and to give a striking verisimilitude to the whole, which reads (to my mind, at any rate) rather better thus than at present, both in what it says and in what it omits. It would also better account for the uncharacteristically private nature of the teaching, and in part, for the disappointing character of what now remains in the Gospel's representation of Jesus' post-resurrection communications. I have other arguments, but you cannot bear them now; I shall point only to the uncharacteristic limpness of Brown's apologia for this reversal of the Gospel's tendency to give explanatory discourses only *after* the events they bear on: "The reason for the change in

pattern is easy to see: . . . it would be anticlimactic to place so long a discourse after the resurrection. Moreover, in the psychology guiding the evangelist's presentation, since the disciples would be affected by Jesus' passion and death, they had to be prepared for this by Jesus' explanation and consolation" (vol. 2, p. 581). The psychological argument is circular (this is not Jesus' procedure for earlier startling and shocking events) and Brown's sense of anticlimax is not mine, nor, I think, that of Johannine theology.

[24]Brown insists that the shift of preposition between 28 *(ek)* and 30 *(apo)* is not significant. Perhaps: but he is more clearly right in asserting that "they are accepting what Jesus said of himself to the extent that they can understand it" (vol. 2, p. 276). That, however, is a limited extent. Their confession of belief that he comes *apo theou* does not mean all that Jesus means, and I do not see grounds for insisting that the change of words is meaningless. It is at the very least a curious coincidence that while Jesus uses *ek theou* or *ek patros* to describe himself elsewhere in the Fourth Gospel, he never says *apo theou* or *apo patros*, although that formula is used for the obviously less profound confession of Nicodemus (3:2). Perhaps more than coincidence?

[25]Luke points to the coming gift of the Spirit, eventually to be reported in Acts; but he gives no indication that there will be any advance on the disclosures already made. It is with *power* rather than understanding that they are to be invested (Lk 24:49). The initial verses of Acts come closer to the Johannine schema by showing the deficiency of the disciples' understanding (Acts 1:6), but this motif is very subdued even there. The increment of understanding later in Acts does not point emphatically to earlier misunderstandings, but to unanticipatable increments in those portions of revelation that only complement (and do not change) the achieved understanding of the essential Gospel.

[26]R. E. Brown, "The Paraclete in the Fourth Gospel," *New Testament Studies*, 13 (1966–1967), pp. 113–132, emphasizes the polysemous character of the untranslatable *paraklētos*. G. Johnston, *The Spirit-Paraclete in the Gospel of John*, Cambridge, 1970, likewise recognizes the variety of senses, but hazards the translation "representative." A deft choice, but not rich enough. To the already current catalogue of overtones, Harald Riesenfeld has proposed another, pointing out the uses of *parakalein* in the LXX Wisdom literature, in I. de la Potterie, "L'Esprit Saint dans l'Evangile de Jean," *New Testament Studies*, 18 (1971–1972), pp. 448–451. For my own suggestions, see *infra*, footnote 27.

[27]I suggest that the sense of this term, in the usage of the ambiguity-cherishing Fourth Gospel, might best be understood in this way. The Advocate is, forensically, the one who attempts to vindicate one's righteousness under pressure of opposition—the liberties of Jesus with the Law are obviously taken by the Fourth Gospel as a paradigmatic justification of liberties taken by the Gospel's community, and he is in that sense their advocate. As the assurance of their righteousness, and as the abiding presence of their Way and Truth and Life, he

is also their Comforter. But when their assurance is firmly internalized, it may be ambiguously experienced either as a more perfect mode of appropriating Jesus or as another, more intimately internal, source of divine justification and comfort.

[28]For surely there was no more need to retain miracle-stories than to report exorcisms, or to record Jesus' baptism by John, or to treat the institution of the Eucharist. The contemporary reaction represented by, e.g., J. Becker, ("Wunder und Christologie," *New Testament Studies,* 16 (1969–1970), pp. 130–148), seems to forget that the putative "Gospel of Signs" is not, as it has come to us, a document which is rejected by the Fourth Gospel but pre-eminently one which is *accepted* by it—not uncritically, and not without qualifications, but nevertheless *accepted.* J. Becker, "Wunder und Christologie," correctly emphasizes the Fourth Gospel's disclosure of the inadequacy of signs-level understanding. But he misses the continuum in overemphasizing this aspect: "Der Evangelist polemisiert durchweg gegen die Christologie (und damit verbundun: gegen den Offenbargunsbegriff) der Semeiaquelle. Diese Polemik geht so weit, da der Evangelist in Joh, XI den Sinn des Wunders theologisch in Frage stellt" (147). The polemic is muted: it argues that this level is inadequate, but allows that it is not seriously misleading, does bring disciples to the first plateau of recognition, and cannot yet be fully supplanted until the Spirit is received. More editing would be required before the Gospel would take as firm a stand as Becker would have it; and the raising of Lazarus can hardly be said to be "fur den Glaubenden auch sinnleer" (146), but merely relatively trivial. J. L. Martyn, *History and Theology in the Fourth Gospel,* strikes a happier balance between the evangelist's thematic employment of signs and his acceptance of their implications precisely as miracles, but seems to me to exaggerate the Gospel's suspicions of miracles nevertheless.

[29]*Theology of the New Testament,* vol. 2, p. 66. Bultmann's neat formula needs some important elaboration. One cannot derive from it other points of revelation urged by Jesus in the Fourth Gospel, such as Jesus' unity with the Father, the scriptures' revelation of himself, the coming of the Paraclete, the requirements for belonging to him, etc.

[30]The verb here is the same as that used in the synoptic logion about those who exalt themselves (Mt 23:12; Lk 14:11, 18:14). The Fourth Gospel otherwise uses it mainly in the literal spatial sense, but since the glory implicit in Jesus' exaltation to heaven is apprehended by a correlative non-spatial exaltation of him by our understanding and our reverence, it seems to me plausible that the evangelist who is so devoted to double-senses would readily take advantage of a theologically convenient ambiguity. Such an exaltation is, after all, what the Fourth Gospel enjoins throughout as its main preoccupation, even if not otherwise unambiguously employing that verb. I see no other way of accounting adequately for the wording of this text, and this way seems to me throughly characteristic of the Gospel theologically.

[31]"If they kept my word, they will keep yours too" (15:20). Raymond Brown, *The Gospel According to John*, vol. 2, p. 687, properly resists a common tendency to read this negatively (if they have not kept my word, they will not keep yours), but introduces his own version of a negative frame: "they will keep your word to the extent that they have kept mine (and they have not kept mine)." But I see no compelling grounds for avoiding the explicit positive statement: "be assured that those who are really faithful will recognize the authority of that which is spoken in my name because they abide in me and I in them." The unity of the community's understanding is due to the abiding presence of Jesus-Spirit-Paraclete, but manifests itself through the recognition of truth. It is notable that the disciples are here not constituted authoritative leaders *ex officio* or *ex ordinatione*, for the Gospel insists that they are to be servants of one another. Rather they are assured that they will be successful in attracting and keeping those who respond to Jesus believingly because they will be perceived to be, as the collective foliage of the true vine, the locus of the words of eternal life.

Chapter 5

[1]In grouping these two epistles together as a coherent manifestation of one phase of the post-Pauline development, I am not presuming common authorship, but simply acknowledging that the relationship between them "is doubtless considerably greater than the relationship of any other Pauline epistle to the remainder of the Pauline epistles" (Werner George Kümmel, ed., *Introduction to the New Testament*, founded by Paul Feine and Johannes Behm, 14th ed. trans. A. J. Mattill, Jr., New York, 1966, p. 253, which work may also be profitably consulted on the other questions of authorship). Not all the points I shall make can be equally well documented from both epistles, but in my judgment they can be argued from the evidence of either one soundly enough that one may justly treat them together. The implicit harmonizing inevitably entails a degree of distortion, but it is not, in this case, a significant degree.

[2]The authorship of the pastoral epistles is still a much unsettled question. For the purposes of this study, it is not of great consequence, since the pastoral epistles in any event bear witness to at least someone's understanding of early Christianity. My own opinion is that if they are by Paul, it is a significantly changed Paul (although I find 2 Timothy in closer consonance with the thought of the major Pauline epistles than the other two pastorals); and if they are not by Paul, they are clearly in the Pauline tradition. The basic terms of the authorship debate are adequately represented in Werner George Kümmel, ed., *Introduction to the New Testament*, pp. 259–272; the more recent discussions do not seem to me to have added significantly to what had already been said on the question.

Chapter 6

[1]I have nothing to add to the ongoing discussion concerning the relationship between 1 John and the Fourth Gospel. The important differences between them seem to me aptly summarized in Werner George Kümmel, ed., *Introduction to the New Testament*, pp. 310–312. I think 1 John and 2 John are closely linked in tradition, and possibly even identical in authorship. My views on the authorship of 3 John will be presented within.

[2]I omit the qualifying phrase *en sarke eleluthota*, partly because I suspect it to be an editorial addition but mainly because it is something of a red herring. The place of the Incarnation in traditional Christian theology tends to keep commentators from seeing how uncharacteristic of 1 John this emphatic phrase is. P. S. Minear, "The Idea of Incarnation in First John," *Interpretation*, 24 (1970), pp. 291–302, rightly perceives its contextual oddity, and attempts ingeniously to resolve the problem by reading the phrase as a reference to the flesh of the believers; that would restore it to thematic consistency, but does not resolve the uncharacteristic (and with respect to that meaning, improbable) turn of phrase. I think it more economical to appeal to editorial interference (see J. C. Meagher, "John 1:4 and the New Temple," *Journal of Biblical Literature*, 88 [1969], pp. 66–67). At any rate, the flesh of Jesus is not the locus of I John's over-all dogmatic emphasis, and it is to that characteristic emphasis that my discussion here appeals.

[3]H. Conzelmann, " 'Was von Anfang war,' " in W. Eltester, ed., *Neutestamentliche Studien für Rudolf Bultmann*, Berlin, 1957, pp. 194–201, understands it basically thus, deriving the phrase from John 6:64, 15:27, and 16:4. In this view, 1 John may be characterized as a "johanneischer Pastoralbrief" (p. 201).

[4]Thus the usual view of commentaries: e.g., R. Bultmann, *Die Drei Johannesbriefe*, (KEK), Göttingen, 1967; J. Schneider, *Die Briefe des Jakobus, Petrus, Judas und Johannes* (NTD), Göttingen, 1967; C. H. Dodd, *The Johannine Epistles*, London, 1946; A. E. Brooke, *A Critical and Exegetical Commentary on the Johannine Epistles* (ICC), Edinburg, 1964. The latter also allows the possibility of a reference to the scriptures, appealing to the addressees' pre-Christian experience in the synagogue, but nothing in the epistle supports this.

[5]Thus also R. Bultmann, *Die drei Johannesbriefe* and C. H. Dodd, *The Johannine Epistles* against J. Schneider, *Die Briefe des Jakobus, Petrus, Judas und Johannes* and A. E. Brooke, *A Critical and Exegetical Commentary on the Johannine Epistles.* If the latter are right, it would possibly indicate a greater appreciation of the historical Jesus as a factor constitutive of Christian understanding than I find otherwise in the Johannine epistles, just as the usual interpretation of *ap' arches* in 1 John 2:24 argues for a greater appreciation of the apostolic kerygma. But neither would be decisive: the teaching of Christ might still be conceived to be essentially the commandment of love and belief in

himself as the Son, and the kerygma originally preached to these Christians may have been this alone. If more, it would draw the theological ambience of 1–2 John closer to the more usual early Christian pattern than I have supposed it to be.

[6]I suspect the concluding phrase to be in this case too an editorial addition with anti-Docetic motives. My subsequent interpretative suggestions therefore entertain meanings that would be possible in the hypothesized ur-text, though less likely (if not altogether excluded) if we retain the received reading.

[7]3 John met resistance into the third century: see T. W. Manson, note to "Entry into Membership of the Early Church," *Journal of Theological Studies*, 48 (1947), pp. 32–33. This division of historical fate is, I think, suggestive. Among other things it lends weight to the hypothesis that 3 John is an imitation of 2 John rather than an authentic product by the same hand. (Their similarities scarcely leave room for a third alternative.) A hypothesis arguing that the author of 3 John was a Johannine presbyter excommunicated by a conservative-orthodox Diotrephes was proposed by E. Käsemann, "Ketzer und Zeuge," *Zeitschrift für katholiche Theologie*, 48 (1951), pp. 292–311, but generally rejected (as *"phantastisch"* by Bultmann, *Die drei Johannesbriefe*, pp. 95, 100). J. Edgar Bruns has pointed out to me that the characterization of the churches of Ephesus and Sardis in Rev 2:2–6 and 3:1–5 correspond interestingly to what I suggest concerning 2 John and 3 John respectively.

Index of Biblical References